The Catholic Biblical Quarterly
Monograph Series

45

The Story within a Story in Biblical Hebrew Narrative

BY

David A. Bosworth

The Catholic Biblical Quarterly
Monograph Series

45

© 2008 The Catholic Biblical Association of America,
Washington, DC 20064

Produced in the United States of America

Library of Congress Cataloging-in-Publication Data

Bosworth, David Alan, 1972-
    The story within a story in biblical Hebrew narrative / by David A.
Bosworth. — 1st ed.
        p. cm. — (The Catholic Biblical quarterly monograph series ; 45)
    Includes bibliographical references and index.
    ISBN 0-915170-44-2 (alk. paper)
    1. Narration in the Bible. 2. Mise en abyme (Narration) 3. Bible.
O.T. Genesis XXXVIII—Criticism, interpretation, etc. 4. Bible. O.T.
    Samuel, 1st, XXV—Criticism, interpretation, etc. 5. Bible. O.T. Kings, 1st,
XIII—Criticism, interpretation, etc. I. Title. II. Series.

    BS521.7.B67 2008
    221.6'6—dc22

Contents

Preface

Biblical narrative frequently employs various kinds of repetition and narrative analogy. The present work concerns a specific kind of narrative analogy or repetition involving a story within a story called the *mise-en-abyme*. The *mise-en-abyme* is a device in which a part reduplicates the whole. The most famous example is the play within the play in Shakespeare's *Hamlet*. The embedded play duplicates the main aspects of the drama in which it occurs (regicide, the murderer seduces the queen, the regicide will be avenged).

Certain biblical passages also duplicate the larger narratives in which they occur. I will discuss Genesis 38, 1 Samuel 25, and 1 Kings 13 as stories within stories, more specifically as *mises-en-abyme*. All three chapters have presented commentators with the difficulty that they appear to be interruptions of the larger narratives that envelope them. The first chapter will discuss the *mise-en-abyme* (what it is, how to recognize it). The next three chapters will show how each of the three biblical passages noted above are *mises-en-abyme* within their contexts and indicate some consequences for this interpretation. The conclusion will relate the biblical examples of the device to the wider discussion of the theory of the *mise-en-abyme*.

This work is a dramatic revision and rewriting of my doctoral dissertation originally completed under the direction of Michael O'Connor at The Catholic University of America. Several people made my years of study at CUA possible and profitable. Michael is first among these. Sadly, he died unexpectedly in the summer of 2007 and did not live to see this revision of the first thesis he directed at CUA. Those who knew him know what the world has lost. He excelled in the various dimensions of his work. He was a patient pedagogue to students, a fruitful researcher to the academy, a tireless editor to writers, an amicable colleague to fellow faculty, and an excellent mentor and advisor to those of us fortunate enough to have studied with him. More precious than his professional qualities were his personal virtues. His sincere care and concern for others informed the whole of his life. It made him a good teacher and a good friend. One of my last emails to him asked his advice on a range of issues. I concluded my exhaustive requests with the remark, "I guess you can stop being my mentor when you are dead." I had no idea that day was so near. He lived to answer every one of my questions. He spent his last days as he spent every day: concerned for other people, especially his students. This work is dedicated to his memory: ויספדו עליו הוי אחי (1 Kgs 13:30).

Others also contributed to my studies at Catholic University. I would especially like to acknowledge Alexander A. Di Lella, Francis Gignac, Joseph Fitzmyer, Christopher Begg, Joseph Jensen, Francis Maloney, Sydney Griffith, and Monica Blanchard. The two reviewers for the CBQ Monograph Series provided helpful feedback on an earlier draft. I also thank Mark Smith for his editorial work on the manuscript. I can think of no higher praise than to say that his editorship of this series is "O'Connoresque." I also wish to thank my parents, Barry and Nancy Bosworth and especially my wife, Britt Silkey, a woman טובת־שׂכל ויפת תאר (1 Sam 25:3).

CHAPTER ONE

The Mise-en-Abyme

A *mise-en-abyme* is a device in which a part reduplicates the whole. The term has become current in literary studies since it was introduced by the French novelist and critic André Gide.[1] The play within the play in Shakespeare's *Hamlet* represents the classic example of the device. Hamlet stages a play that parallels the action of *Hamlet*. Although the term occasionally surfaces in the discipline, "no full length treatment of the *mise en abyme* has been conducted within biblical studies."[2]

The present work seeks to fill this gap. I will argue that biblical Hebrew narrative includes three *mises-en-abyme*, specifically Genesis 38, 1 Samuel 25, and 1 Kings 13. I am not convinced that there are any additional examples. All three of these stories duplicate the larger contexts in which they occur. In each case, scholars have had difficulty fitting the stories into their contexts and have not fully appreciated how the stories reflect their surrounding narratives.

The story of Judah and Tamar encapsulates the larger narrative of Joseph and his brothers. Joseph and Tamar are parallel characters. Each is the victim of a crime perpetrated by family members. Each suffers alienation from the family and resorts to deception as a means of restoring their circumstances. Genesis 38 therefore emerges as a micro-

---

[1] The phrase literally means "placement in abyss." The term is normally spelled as given above, but some writers omit the hyphens, and others write *abîme* for *abyme*. The first spelling is the more common French spelling of "abyss," but the second spelling, used by Gide, is also permissible. The French term is related to other *mise-en-x* terms in French, such as *mise-en-scène* (in the theatrical arts, staging), *mise-en-page* (in typography, page-setting), and *mise-en-place* (in the culinary arts, the collection and preparation of ingredients).

[2] Joshua A. Berman, *Narrative Analogy in the Hebrew Bible: Battle Stories and Their Equivalent Non-battle Narratives* (VTSup 103; Leiden: Brill, 2004) 25.

1

cosm of the larger story of Genesis 37–50 rather than an unrelated interruption in the narrative.

The story of David and Nabal in 1 Samuel 25 similarly duplicates its larger context in 1 Sam 13:1–2 Sam 5:3. In this case, Nabal and Saul are parallel characters. David performs favors for both men, but both repay his kindness by doing him harm. In both cases, God is seen to vindicate the justice of David's cause. The story in 1 Samuel 25, then, serves as a narrative reflection on the larger narrative of David's conflict with the house of Saul, not just the two incidents in which David spares Saul's life (1 Samuel 24 and 26).

The story of the two prophetic figures in 1 Kgs 13:11-32 with its conclusion in 2 Kings 23:15-20 seems strange because the old prophet who lies is not punished for his deception, but the man of God who believes the lie is punished for his naiveté. The peculiarities of the story can be explained by appeal to its context within the history of the divided kingdom. The two prophetic figures represent the two kingdoms from which they come and the relationship that unfolds between them parallels the relationship between their respective nations. In both cases, the relationship begins with mutual hostility, followed by friendship or alliance that terminates in a role-reversal. The relationship then returns to hostility, but the southern representative saves his northern counterpart just as Josiah seeks to save the north by reforming Bethel. Ultimately, both share a common grave, just as the two nations both suffer exile in Mesopotamia.

Chapters Two through Four will discuss these biblical examples of the *mise-en-abyme* in detail. This first chapter is devoted to the theory of the *mise-en-abyme* (what it is, how to recognize it, what it means). The chapters on the biblical examples largely stand on their own, and make minimal reference to theoretical issues. The concluding chapter will connect the details of the biblical exegesis with the theory of the *mise-en-abyme* from the first chapter.

The greatest problem with the *mise-en-abyme* has been defining the term in such a way that it is neither too broad nor too narrow. The discussion in this chapter will be devoted to the theory of the device and will articulate a conception of the *mise-en-abyme* that steers a middle course between these extremes and may be useful for subsequent discussion. First, I will review the definition of the device and discussion of the types of *mises-en-abyme* and criteria by which it may be recognized. Second, I will note how the *mise-en-abyme* may be distinguished from other similar literary devices. Third and finally, I will discuss four non-biblical examples of the device: two from modern literature, and two from ancient literature. These examples help to clarify the topic under discussion and prepare for the more detailed treatment of the biblical examples.

Definition, Types, and Criteria

André Gide borrowed the term *mise-en-abyme* from heraldry. Heraldry includes the study of familial coats-of-arms, which is an illustration within a shield-shaped space called a field that may include various traditional designs with symbolic meanings. There are various national and ecclesiastical traditions of heraldry. Gide thought the term *mise-en-abyme* was used in French heraldry to describe "the device . . . that involves putting a second representation of the original shield 'en abyme' within it."[3] Gide apparently imagined the device as a representation of a shield shape placed in the center of the larger shield-shaped field. Gide became fascinated with this visual device, which occurs in painting and graphic art. Gide sought to apply this visual device to literary narrative.

Since Gide introduced the term *mise-en-abyme* and employed the device in his own novels, it has become prominent in literary-critical circles. The term became especially common in discussions of *avant-garde* novels, both those known as the *nouveau roman* (in the 1950s) and the *nouveau nouveau roman* (in the 1970s).[4] Since the literary critic Lucien Dällenbach published *Le récit spéculaire: essai sur la mise en abyme* in 1977, this has become the classic treatment of the device and the basis for subsequent discussion. Dällenbach defines the *mise-en-abyme* as *"any internal mirror that reflects the whole of the narrative by simple, repeated, or 'specious' (paradoxical) duplication."*[5] Several aspects of this definition require further clarification. I will treat first the image of the mirror and then discuss the three types of *mise-en-*

---

[3] Gide, *Journals 1889-1949* (trans. J. O'Brien; London: Penguin, 1984) 31.

[4] Dällenbach, *Le récit spéculaire: essai sur la mise-en-abyme* (Paris: Seuil, 1977) 151-208; in English as *The Mirror in the Text* (trans. Jeremy Whiteley with Emma Hughes; Chicago: University of Chicago Press, 1989) 117-63. Dällenbach's italics.

[5] Dällenbach, *Le récit*, 52; *Mirror*, 36 (emphasis his).

abyme that emerge from the threefold definition (simple, repeated, paradoxical).

By "internal mirror," Dällenbach means the duplication of the whole within one of its parts. He argues that the *mise-en-abyme* is interchangeable with the analogy of the mirror. Dällenbach borrows the idea of the mirror from visual art. Mirrors are sometimes employed in paintings to show the viewer something that would not be visible if the mirror were not there. Similarly, a *mise-en-abyme* in a work of literature may shed light on other parts or aspects of the text that might be invisible or less obvious without the device. Below, I will suggest that the mirror is a helpful analogue, but that the kind of equivalence posited by Dällenbach is misleading.

As the name suggests, "simple" duplication is the simplest type of *mise-en-abyme*. In simple duplication, a part of the narrative reproduces the whole. Shakespeare's *Hamlet* provides a classic example. Within the play *Hamlet*, the character Hamlet stages a play for his uncle and mother, who are the king and queen. The play is *The Murder of Gonzago* (3.2.129-130). Hamlet expects to confirm that his uncle Claudius murdered King Hamlet by representing a similar crime on stage and observing Claudius's reactions. Although the murder of King Hamlet is not represented on the stage, it is revealed in the first act and forms the basis for the plot of the whole play. *Gonzago* duplicates the action that sets *Hamlet* in motion and draws attention to the motifs of regicide and second marriage that are central to Shakespeare's tragedy. I will discuss this famous example in more detail below. All of the biblical examples are simple *mises-en-abyme*.

The second type of *mise-en-abyme* involves infinite duplication and is the type that most interested Gide. In infinite duplication, a part is similar to the work that encloses it and itself encloses a part that is similar to it, etc. The Quaker Oats box is the most recognizable example of this type. Scholars agree that the device is well represented visually by the illustration for the Quaker Oats package that represents a Quaker holding a box of Quaker Oats, on which is represented a Quaker holding a box of Quaker Oats.[6] The idea of this device involves a suggestion of infinite regression. A similar illustrative device may be found

---

[6] The Quaker Oats packaging has been modified in such a way that the visual example is no longer evident. The older illustration was in use for so long and so well-known that it has informed discussion of the *mise-en-abyme*.

on packages of Land O'Lakes butter. The classic literary example is André Gide's *Les faux-monnayeurs*. Gide's novel includes a character named Éduard who is writing a novel called *Les faux-monnayeurs*. From what we learn about Éduard's novel, it will be similar (maybe identical) to the novel of Gide, which we are reading. Éduard is interested in putting himself into his novel as a writer. Gide's technique of placing the novelist into the novel suggests the *mise-en-abyme* as infinite regression.[7] Aldous Huxley also employs a character-novelist in his novel, *Point Counter Point*. Like Éduard, Huxley's protagonist Philip Quarles keeps a journal about the novel he expects to write using the people and events around him as inspiration. In one entry, he writes:

> Put a novelist into the novel. He justifies asthetic generalizations . . . [and] experiment . . . . And if you have him telling parts of the same story as you are, you can make a variation on the theme. But why draw the line at one novelist inside your novel? Why not a second inside his? And a third inside the novel of the second? And so on to infinity, like those advertisements of Quaker Oats where there's a Quaker holding a box of Quaker Oats, on which there is a picture of another Quaker holding another box of oats, on which etc., etc.[8]

Jean Louis Ska suggests that Hebrew narrative has two examples of this type of *mise-en-abyme*.[9] According to Exod 24:1-11, Moses wrote "the Book of the Covenant," which seems to be identical to Exodus 20–23. Similarly, Moses writes most of Deuteronomy according to Deut 31:9-13. As Ska notes, the purpose of these passages is to claim the authority of Moses for the legal texts in question. The biblical writer is not engaging in the kind of playful infinite regression of Gide's *Les faux-monnayeurs* in order to represent the problem of representation, and the passages do not duplicate their broader contexts. These bibli-

---

[7] André Gide, *Les faux-monnayeurs* (Paris: Gallimard 1994), originally published in 1925; it appeared in English as *The Counterfeiters* (trans. Dorothy Bussy; New York: Vintage, 1973).

[8] Huxley, *Point Counter Point* (Normal, IL: Dalkey Archive Press, 1996) 294. Originally published in 1928. See Dällenbach, *Le récit*, 33-35; *Mirror*, 21-22.

[9] Ska, *"Our Fathers Have Told Us:" Introduction to the Analysis of Hebrew Narrative* (Subsidia Biblica 13; Rome: Pontifical Biblical Institute, 1990) 47-53.

cal passages, therefore, seem not to be *mises-en-abyme*. The passages attributed to Moses are not embedded in the narrative; they are not separated from it in the way that the journal entries of Éduard and Philip Quarles are.

The third type of *mise-en-abyme* arises from paradoxical duplication. Paradoxical duplication involves a part that is supposed to enclose the work that encloses it. This phenomenon may occur when the narrative frame is broken. Miguel de Cervantes Saavreda's *Don Quixote* offers a well-known example.[10] Cervantes wrote the novel in two parts. After the first part was published (1605), another author, Alonso Fernández de Avellaneda borrowed the characters for his own novel, now known as the *False Quixote* (1614).[11] The second part of Cervantes' novel was published after Avellaneda's work (1615). In this second part, the characters periodically discuss the first part of Cervantes' *Don Quixote* and condemn Avellaneda's *False Quixote*. The characters thereby step out of the fictional world. They even discuss the author's plans for a forthcoming second volume, yet we are reading this supposedly unwritten second part. These discussions among the characters are enclosed within Cervantes' second part, yet they critique that novel as if it did not enclose them.[12]

Simple, infinite, and paradoxical duplication represent three types of *mises-en-abyme* noted in Dällenbach's definition. The *mise-en-abyme* may be further described and classified by observing two of its aspects, namely its method of incorporation and placement.

The *mise-en-abyme* may be incorporated in one of three ways. It may be presented all at once, divided up so that it alternates with the embedding narrative, or repeated so that it occurs several times in the narrative. The first method of incorporation is the most common. In *Hamlet*, *Gonzago* appears all at once, although the performance is punctuated with commentary by the spectators. Two of the biblical

---

[10] Cervantes, *Don Quixote of La Mancha* (trans. Walter Starkie; Signet Classic; New York: Penguin, 1979). See Dällenbach, *Le récit*, 115-18; *Mirror*, 87-89.

[11] Fernandez de Avellaneda, *Don Quixote de la Mancha (part II): Being the Spurious Continuation of Miguel de Cervantes' Part I* (trans. Alberta Wilson Server and John Esten Keller; Juan de la Cuesta Hispanic Monographs; Newark, DE: Cuesta, 1980).

[12] Similarly, in Luigi Pirandello's play *Six Characters in Search of an Author* (trans. Mark Musa; London: Penguin, 1995), the characters insist that they are more real than the actors who play them. The play was first performed in 1921.

examples (Genesis 38 and 1 Samuel 25) are incorporated similarly en bloc. Gide uses the alternating method of incorporation in *Les faux-monnayeurs*. The *mise-en-abyme* occurs in the form of Éduard's journal, selections of which occur throughout the novel. Similarly, 1 Kgs 13:11-32 and 2 Kgs 23:15-20 are incorporated by the alternating method. The repeated presentation of a simple *mise-en-abyme* several times in the narrative is unusual. Something close to it occurs in Alain Robbe-Grillet's *La jalousie*.[13] The characters A. and Frank are reading a novel together and their discussions concerning the story are described periodically. From these passages, we learn that the novel that the characters are reading bears certain similarities to the novel we are reading.

A *mise-en-abyme* may have one of three possible temporal relations with its surrounding narrative, depending on its placement. It is prospective if it occurs near the beginning of the story, retrospective if near the end, and "retro-prospective" if in the middle.[14]

A prospective *mise-en-abyme* foreshadows the subsequent story by duplicating its major elements near the beginning of the narrative. For example, in Agatha Christie's *And Then There Were None*, ten murders are committed reflecting the ten deaths in the nursery rhyme, "Ten Little Indians." The poem is presented early in the novel, and the method of each murder is recognizably similar to the means by which each Indian in the verse dies. The characters in the novel remark on the similarity and they (and the reader) can see how the story will continue to reflect the rhyme. I will discuss this example in detail below.

A retrospective *mise-en-abyme* occurs near the end of a narrative and recapitulates certain features of the previous story. Dällenbach notes that examples of this placement are not found. The reason, he suggests, is that such a *mise-en-abyme* would add nothing to the story. Dällenbach classifies most *mises-en-abyme* as retro-prospective because "the middle" of a narrative is much greater than the very beginning or end. Although *mises-en-abyme* seem not to occur after the narrative is complete, they may appear close to the end of the middle. For example, the parable "Before the Law" is located in the second to last chapter

---

[13] Robbe-Grillet, *La jalousie* (Paris: Minuit, 1957); in English as *Jealousy*, in *Two Novels* (trans. Richard Howard; New York: Grove, 1965) 33-138. See Dällenbach, *Le récit*, 163-71; *Mirror*, 127-33.

[14] Dällenbach, *Le récit*, 82; *Mirror*, 60.

of Franz Kafka's *Der Process* (*The Trial*).[15] In the parable, the man from the country stands in a similarly equivocal relationship to the doorkeeper as Joseph K. does to his trial. The parable and its discussion by the priest and Joseph K. recapitulate the problem of Joseph K.'s attitude toward the Law. In this sense, it duplicates the prior narrative. However, it also duplicates material included after its placement so is still retro-prospective.

Most *mises-en-abyme*, including all the biblical examples, are retro-prospective. They both summarize the preceding narrative and foreshadow the subsequent development. For example, in *Hamlet*, the *Gonzago* play recapitulates the murder of King Hamlet and foreshadows Hamlet's own murder of Claudius.

Dällenbach identifies three main types of *mise-en-abyme* (simple, repeated, paradoxical), three possible methods of their incorporation into a work (en bloc, periodic, repeated), and three possible placements (beginning, middle, end). He observes that the vast majority of *mises-en-abyme* are simple, en bloc, and located in the middle of the work. Two of the biblical examples (Genesis 38 and 1 Samuel 25) fit this most common pattern, but the third is alternating (1 Kgs 13:11-32 and 2 Kgs 23:15-20). By the "middle" of the work, Dällenbach means that most examples are retro-prospective. I noted that he even treats the example of Kafka's *Der Process* as retro-prospective even though the *mise-en-abyme* occurs near the end of the novel. In Dällenbach's terms, therefore, the middle is the bulk of the narrative. All the biblical examples are retro-prospective, although two of the three appear near the beginning of the section of narrative that they reflect. Specifically, Genesis 38 occurs near the start of the Joseph Story (Genesis 37–50). The story in 1 Kgs 13:11-32 and its conclusion in 2 Kgs 23:15-20 occur near the beginning and end of the divided monarchy (1 King 11–2 Kings

[15] Kafka, *Der Process* (Berlin: Fischer, 1999), originally published in 1925; in English as *The Trial* (trans. Willa and Edwin Muir; New York: Schocken, 1992). Dällenbach (*Le récit*, 111-13; *Mirror*, 85-86) evidently considers this a retro-prospective *mise-en-abyme*, most likely because the parable anticipates the death of Joseph K. before it happens. Similarly, the description of the musical work *Fausti Wehe-klage* in Thomas Mann's *Doctor Faustus: The Life of the German Composer Adrian Leverkühn* (trans. H. T. Lowe-Porter; Vintage Books; New York: Random House, 1971) comes near the end of the novel and is almost entirely retrospective, except that it anticipates the death of Adrian.

23). The example of 1 Samuel 25 is located near the center of its context (1 Sam 13:1–2 Sam 5:3).

In addition to discerning the possible varieties of *mise-en-abyme*, Dällenbach is also concerned about observing textual features that may indicate the presence of the device. These features may help critics recognize it when it occurs. Dällenbach identifies five textual elements that sometimes occur with *mises-en-abyme* and indicate the presence of a duplication of the narrative in one of its parts.[16] Dällenbach does not claim that these criteria are necessary elements in a *mise-en-abyme*, but only notes that one or more of them occur in many examples of the device. They therefore offer helpful guidlines for judging whether a given passage is a *mise-en-abyme*.

1. A doubling of the whole story in one of its parts may be indicated by words that posit an analogy between the whole and the part. For example, *The Murder of Gonzago* is specifically related to the story of *Hamlet* by Hamlet's remark that the play will "catch the conscience of the king" (2.2.605). Hamlet explicitly makes the analogy between the two by describing *Gonzago* in these words: "I'll have these players / play something like the murther of my father / before mine uncle" (2.2.594-96). The similarity between a part of a text and the whole that contains it is most obvious when the text itself states the similarity.

2. A *mise-en-abyme* may be signaled by character identity, or by a similarity of the name of a character in the enclosing narrative and a character in the enclosed narrative. For example, Thomas Mann's "Wälsungenblut" concerns twins named Sigmund and Sieglinde who go to see Wagner's opera *Walküre*, which also involves twins named Sigmund and Sieglinde.[17] In both stories, the twins consummate an incestuous union. Two of the biblical examples (Genesis 38; 1 Samuel 25) involve a character common to the larger narrative and the *mise-en-abyme* (Judah and David, respectively).

3. An inserted narrative may be a *mise-en-abyme* if it has the same title as the narrative in which it is embedded. For example, the novel that the character Éduard is writing in Gide's *Les faux-monnayeurs* is also called *Les faux-monnayeurs*. Similarly, in A. S. Byatt's *Babble*

---

[16] Dällenbach, *Le récit*, 65; *Mirror*, 46-47.

[17] In English as "The Blood of the Walsungs," in *Death in Venice and Seven Other Stories* (trans. H. T. Lowe-Porter; Vintage International; New York: Random House, 1989) 289-316.

Tower, a character named Jude writes a story called *Babbletower* that other characters read and discuss.[18] Selections of Jude's novel are presented at various points in Byatt's book. Ultimately, the divorce trial of the main character in *Babble Tower*, Frederica, coincides with the pornography trial of Jude's *Babbletower* in the England of the 1960's. Jude's story serves as a commentary on the major motifs of Byatt's novel. These issues are clarified in the embedded story because Jude's narrative is written in a simple prose style and has allegorical references discussed by Frederica and her friends. Like Éduard's journal in *Les faux-monnayeurs*, Jude's novel is an alternating *mise-en-abyme*, with parts of it scattered through Byatt's novel.

4. The repetition of setting and character combination may indicate the presence of a *mise-en-abyme*. In Boccaccio's *Decameron* (Day 1, Story 7), Filostrato introduces his story as one in which the hero Bergamino "censured a great prince . . . by telling a charming tale in which he represented, through others, what he wanted to say about himself and Can Grande."[19] Bergamino suffers inhospitality from the normally hospitable Can Grande, so he finds an opportunity to tell Can Grande "a story relevant to his own case" about how Primas suffered inhospitality from a normally hospitable abbot. The abbot realizes his error and repairs his miserliness with an outburst of generosity. Can Grande sees the point of Bergamino's story and says, "Bergamino, you have given an apt demonstration of the wrongs you have suffered. You have shown us your worth, my meanness, and what it is that you want from me."[20] Can Grande and the reader of *Decameron* discern the reflexive quality of the story on the basis of the similar narrative situation. In two of the biblical examples (Genesis 38 and 1 Samuel 25), a character in the *mise-en-abyme* also appears in a similar role in the larger narrative. Judah wrongs both Joseph and Tamar and realizes his error by means of the deceptions of his victims. David does favors for Nabal and Saul, and both men return his kindness by seeking to harm him. Thus, in two biblical examples, character identity (see number 2 above) is supplemented by similarity of the character's role and relationship to others.

---

[18] Byatt, *Babble Tower* (Vintage International; New York: Random House, 1997).

[19] Giovanni Boccaccio, *The Decameron* (trans. G. H. McWilliam; London: Penguin, 1972) 99. See Dällenbach, *Le récit*, 109-110; *The Mirror*, 82-83.

[20] Boccaccio, *Decameron*, 103.

5. Repetition of other textual elements in the *mise-en-abyme* may occur in the larger narrative. Such repetitions clarify the relationship between the whole story and the part that duplicates it. For example, Flem Snopes in William Faulkner's *The Hamlet* carries a straw suitcase and habitually chews tobacco. The novel includes a short narrative about a mysterious visitor who arrives in hell to check on the status of his soul. This visitor also carries a straw suitcase and chews tobacco. These habits connect Flem to the visitor and establish that the fable is a *mise-en-abyme* within the novel. Certain words and motifs also connect the biblical *mises-en-abyme* to their contexts. For example, recognition is important to Genesis 38 and to the larger narrative. The theme of returning good with evil connects 1 Samuel 25 to David's conflict with Saul. The altar at Bethel is central to the story of the two prophetic figures in 1 Kgs 13:11-32 and 2 Kgs 23:15-20 and to the story of the divided kingdom. These and other textual elements will be discussed in further detail in the chapters relevant to each example.

Since Dällenbach's work, scholars have continued to identify *mises-en-abyme* in literature. This identification is frequently problematic because the definition of the *mise-en-abyme* as a duplication or reflection of the whole story in one of its parts does not provide clear boundaries concerning what qualifies as duplication of the whole. One possible extreme is that scholars might discover the *mise-en-abyme* everywhere. Parts necessarily have some reflexive relationship with the whole; otherwise the text becomes incoherent. At the other extreme, critics might deny all suggested examples of the device because parts rarely if ever duplicate the whole perfectly. Although judgment always enters into the identification of *mises-en-abyme*, Moshe Ron discusses nine aspects of the device that provide helpful direction for critical judgment.[21]

1. *Totality.* "The requirement that what is reflected in the *mise-en-abyme* should in some sense be 'the work as a whole' is surely essential to the definition of this figure."[22] However, as Ron also notes, this kind of duplication seems neither possible nor desirable. The duplication

---

[21] Ron, "The Restricted Abyss: Nine Problems in the Theory of the *Mise en Abyme*," *Poetics Today* 8 (1987) 417-38.

[22] Ron, "Restricted Abyss," 422.

of the whole must be confined to pertinent aspects.[23] If *The Murther of Gonzago* literally duplicated the whole of *Hamlet* in detail, then it would have to begin with the dialogue of the guards in the opening scene of *Hamlet* and reproduce every word of the play up to *Gonzago*, at which point it would have to return to the beginning again. Such literal duplication could never end. Rather, *Gonzago* isolates pertinent aspects of *Hamlet* for doubling. The definition of the *mise-en-abyme* should stipulate that the figure duplicates pertinent aspects of the whole. "But how to determine pertinence is something that a theory of the *mise en abyme* cannot and should not claim to teach you."[24] The pertinent aspects should relate to a central theme or main plot of the whole.

2. *Reflection.* As noted above, Dällenbach sees the analogy of the mirror as adequate to discussion of the *mise-en-abyme*. This similarity may be misleading, however. The image of the mirror and the relationship of reflection are much more extensive than the *mise-en-abyme* usually is. Parts must have some relationship to the whole, if "whole" is to mean anything at all. In other words, "anything can be said to resemble [or reflect] anything else in some respect."[25] Every *mise-en-abyme* reflects the whole, but not everything that reflects the whole is *mise-en-abyme*. Therefore, the *mise-en-abyme* should not be considered identical or co-extensive with reflection.

3. *Explicitness.* Dällenbach wonders if the *mise-en-abyme* must be accompanied by some kind of textual marker that identifies the presence of the figure. He tries to steer between the extremes of explicit authorial intention and deconstruction. He does not require evidence of the author's intention to employ the device in his or her work, but Dällenbach and Ron reject "the deconstructionist view that all literary texts are emblematic of themselves, . . . which would automatically make them nothing but *mise[s] en abyme*."[26] The textual markers enumerated above should be understood as helpful guides to identifying *mises-en-abyme*, not part of the definition of the *mise-en-abyme*.

---

[23] Ron, "Restricted Abyss," 422-24. Ron here relies on Mieke Bal, "Mise en abyme et iconicité," *Littérature* 29 (1978) 116-28.

[24] Ron, "Restricted Abyss," 425.

[25] Ron, "Restricted Abyss," 426.

[26] Ron, "Restricted Abyss," 427. Cf. Dällenbach, *Le récit,* 65; *Mirror,* 46.

4. *Isolatability*. Most of the examples of the *mise-en-abyme* discussed so far are separated from the narrative in which they are embedded. Each example is isolated from or subordinated to the rest of the narrative by being identified as a separate story or part of a story with a separate narrator. For example, *Gonzago* in *Hamlet* is a play ostensibly written by someone other than Shakespeare or Hamlet, although Hamlet adds some lines to it. Similarly the omniscient narrator of Gide's *Les faux-monnayeurs* is absent from Éduard's journal, in which Éduard speaks in his own voice. The question therefore arises whether all *mises-en-abyme* must be similarly isolated from the main narrative and subordinated to it. Dällenbach thinks not. He suggests that a *mise-en-abyme* may be articulated in the speech of a character or in the narrator's description of an object, or as an episode within the main narrative. Since the device is not always clearly separated from the remainder of the narrative, isolatability is a subjective criterion for the identification of a *mise-en-abyme*. The device should be isolated from its context, but the issue is how much. In my view, Dällenbach's discussion is too broad. Below, I will explain why apparent instances of the *mise-en-abyme* that lack isolatability more likely exemplify other literary devices (like the emblum). In other words, isolatability is an important criterion for a *mise-en-abyme*.

5. *Orientation*. If one uses the metaphor of reflection, one might wonder whether the part reflects the whole or vice-versa. Ron suggests that a *mise-en-abyme* must be located at a lower narrative level than the whole that it reflects.[27] For example, *Gonzago* reflects *Hamlet*, but *Hamlet* cannot be said to reflect *Gonzago*. Since *Gonzago* is embedded within *Hamlet* and subordinated to its plot, it must be the *mise-en-abyme*. Subordinate narratives serve to illuminate the main story, not the other way around. However, Ron's restriction is better expressed negatively: a *mise-en-abyme* may not be located at a higher narrative level than the whole it reflects. This expression recognizes that a *mise-en-abyme* may occur on the same level as the narrative that it duplicates. All the biblical examples occur on the same narrative level as the larger stories that they duplicate.

---

[27] Ron, "Restricted Abyss," 429.

6. *Extent.*[28] Apart from the question of subordinate narratives discussed above, the critic is also faced with the issue of *mises-en-abyme* on the same narrative level as the duplicated whole. A lengthy *mise-en-abyme* may be difficult to distinguish from a short subplot. Ron notes the utility of the heraldric metaphor for this problem. In heraldry, a shield represented in the center of the shield-shaped field is said to be "en-abyme." If the shield is large, however, and its edges approach the edges of the coat-of-arms, it creates a "bordure." Whereas the shield "en-abyme" can have no further images on it, images may be placed within a bordure. A literary equivalent to a bordure may be small frame narratives, such as those that hold together the stories in Chaucer's *Canterbury Tales*, Boccaccio's *Decameron*, and the *Arabian Nights*.[29] By contrast, one can hardly claim that *Hamlet* is a similar frame narrative for *Gonzago*, which is short enough to constitute a *mise-en-abyme*. George Eliot's *Middlemarch* provides an example of how extent can affect the recognition of the figure.[30] *Middlemarch* is a multiplot novel. All the various plots illuminate one another and involve sometimes striking parallel plots and motifs. As a multiplot novel, however, *Middlemarch* does not allow the critic to isolate one story as the whole and then identify other plots as subplots or *mises-en-abyme*.

7. *Distribution.* Ron's discussion of the distribution of the *mise-en-abyme* largely reproduces Dällenbach's observations on this aspect of the device. Distribution refers to how the *mise-en-abyme* is placed within the narrative: all at once in one place, scattered throughout the narrative, or repeated in its entirety periodically.

---

[28] Ron ("Restricted Abyss," 429) calls this "quantity," which seems a strange term to apply to texts.

[29] Chaucer, *Canterbury Tales* (ed. A. C. Cawley; New York: E. P. Dutton, 1958); *Arabian Nights* (trans. Husain Haddawy; New York: Norton, 1995).

[30] Eliot, *Middlemarch: A Study of Provincial Life* (ed. David Carroll; Oxford World's Classics; Oxford: Oxford University Press, 1996), originally published in 1871-72. Similarly, the Gloucester subplot in Shakespeare's *King Lear* (in *The Oxford Shakespeare* [2nd ed.; ed. Stanley Wells and Gary Taylor; Oxford: Oxford University Press, 2004] 909-41 [Quarto text]1153-84 [Folio text]) duplicates the main plot so closely that it may be a *mise-en-abyme*, although one might argue that it is too extensive to be an example of the device. See Bidget Gellert Lyons, "The Subplot as Simplification in King Lear," in *Some Facets of King Lear: Essays in Prismatic Criticism* (ed. Rosalie Colie and T. F. Flahif; Toronto: University of Toronto Press, 1974) 23-38; John Reibetanz, "The Gloucester Plot and Its Function," in *Critical Essays on Shakespeare's King Lear* (ed. John Halio; New York: G. K. Hall, 1996).

8. *General function.* Ron attempts to discuss the function of the *mise-en-abyme* in general. The device frequently works against the grain of the narrative in which it is embedded. When it occurs in a realistic representational story, the device draws attention to the fact that the narrative is an artificial construction. The *Gonzago* play in *Hamlet* reminds the audience that *Hamlet* is a play, thereby disrupting an otherwise realistic representation.[31] When a *mise-en-abyme* occurs in a fragmentary text that disrupts conventional representation, the device tends to integrate the narrative in which it is placed. For example, Robbe-Grillet's *La jalousie* includes discussion of a book similar to *La jalousie* as well as descriptions of a musical tune that mimics the nature of the narrative. Both these features work to integrate the fragmentary narrative.

The device does not seem to function this way in the Bible. The biblical *mises-en-abyme* occur as episodes within the larger narratives rather than as separate representation such as *Gonzago*. Therefore, they do not disrupt the manner of narrative representation. Rather, the biblical examples highlight certain aspect of the narrative by duplicating some parts rather than others. In the process of duplication, the *mise-en-abyme* creates an analogy with the whole by which both stories mutually illuminate one another. The analogy thus created functions similarly to a metaphor without a specific point of comparison (or *tertium quid*) "in order to allow an analogy to open up, inducing the reader to engage the analogy and find not one but many contacts between the things compared."[32] Within the analogous structure, most of the mutual illumination shines in one direction. As the shorter and simpler narrative, the *mise-en-abyme* serves to elucidate pertinent aspects of the whole. The *mise-en-abyme* exists for the sake of the larger story in which it occurs. The larger story does not exist for the sake of the *mise-en-abyme*.

9. *Motivation.* The motive behind the *mise-en-abyme* may be of two kinds. One may speak of the author's or narrator's motive for introducing the device, or of a character's motive. For example, Ham-

---

[31] Ross Chambers (*La comédie au château: contribution à la poétique du théâtre* [Paris: José Corti, 1971] 29-37) explores the play scene (and drama generally) as a mirror of nature. After the *Gonzago* play shows Claudius his crime, Hamlet later makes his mother see her own folly.

[32] Bruce K. Waltke and M. O'Connor, *An Introduction to Hebrew Syntax* (Winona Lake, IN: Eisenbrauns, 1990) 203.

let stages the *Gonzago* play because he wants to determine the truth of the ghost's accusation that Claudius is guilty of murder. Within the play *Hamlet*, however, *Gonzago* appears to have a different motive. It encapsulates the main theme and plot of the larger play and emphasizes the most important elements by repetition. It also permits an opportunity to reflect on dramatic art and how it mirrors nature. The biblical examples are not created by characters, but by the narrator. The biblical *mises-en-abyme* provide a narrative analogy to the primary story. The function of this parallel is largely specific to each case. In general, the analogy between the *mise-en-abyme* and its context provides mutual illumination and reinforces themes and motifs through repetition.

Ron's discussion of the *mise-en-abyme* offers significant critiques of Dällenbach's discussion and identifies specific issues not treated by Dällenbach. Mieke Bal has also criticized Dällenbach's work, but from a different perspective. While Ron seeks to limit the possible scope of the device, Mieke Bal seeks to expand it. For example, Ron correctly notes that reflection is far too broad to be a synonym for the *mise-en-abyme* as Dällenbach proposes. Bal, by contrast, embraces reflection and expands it. Bal suggests that the term *mise-en-abyme* be replaced by "mirror text."[33] She continues to expand on the notion of the mirror until the *mise-en-abyme* becomes pervasive. She argues that the stories of Ruth, Rachel and Leah, and Tamar form a "*mise-en-abyme* of the history of Israel."[34] Her identification of these stories as a single *mise-en-abyme* is not convincing because she does not demonstrate the literary parallels between these stories and the larger historical narrative. It is not even clear that by her expression "l'Histoire d'Israël" she is referring to a specific literary text. Ruth, for example, is not even part of the narrative complex that tells the history of Israel. I prefer Ron's effort to specify and restrict Dällenbach's understanding of the *mise-en-abyme* rather than Bal's expansion of it.

In conclusion, this discussion articulates a description of the *mise-en-abyme* that is neither too broad nor too narrow. The above definition and criteria can separate the *mise-en-abyme* from other devices

---

[33] Bal, *Narratology: Introduction to the Theory of Narrative* (2d ed.; Toronto: University of Toronto Press, 1997) 57-60.

[34] Bal, *Femmes imaginaries: L'ancien testament au risqué d'une narratologie critique* (Utrecht: Hes, 1986) 198.

with which it is often confused. The following section discusses some of these other devices and why they do not fit the definition and criteria outlined above.

Non-examples: What is not a *Mise-en-abyme*

A further way to clarify the notion of the *mise-en-abyme* is to examine literary devices that resemble, but are not necessarily the same as, the *mise-en-abyme*. Some of these devices are not *mises-en-abyme* because they serve an explanatory function within their contexts (e.g., allegory, exemplum, fable, parable). This explanatory function implicates these devices in their contexts so deeply that they lack the isolatability expected of the *mise-en-abyme*. Other textual units reflect the context in which they occur, but lack isolatability for a different reason: they are summaries of the contexts in which they occur and not separate stories or episodes.[35] Finally, since many *mises-en-abyme* are embedded narratives, various embedded stories that reflect their contexts may appear to be *mises-en-abyme*, but are not when they lack totality.

Explanatory devices that are not the same as *mises-an-abyme* include allegory, exemplum, fable, and parable. A story that maintains a systematic symbolic reference in all its parts is an allegory. An allegory "involves a continuous parallel between two (or more) levels of meaning in a story, so that its persons and events correspond to their equivalents in a system of ideas or chain of events external to the tale."[36] John Bunyan's *Pilgrim's Progress* is an allegorical narrative that illustrates Puritan notions of salvation.[37]

An exemplum is a very short narrative that provides a particular illustration of a general moral lesson or principle. Since the focus of the story is moral, the term exemplum has generally been reserved for

[35] Consequently, Ska's suggestion (*"Our Fathers"*, 47-53) that certain biblical passages like Gen 24:34-49 (Abraham's servant's introduction of his mission) and Gen 28:12-15 (Jacob's dream) are *mises-en-abyme* is mistaken.

[36] Baldick, *Concise Oxford Dictionary of Literary Critical Terms* (Oxford: Oxford University Press, 1990) 5. The theory of allegory is more complex than a dictionary definition can suggest. See Angus Fletcher, *Allegory: The Theory of a Symbolic Mode* (Ithaca, NY: Cornell University Press, 1964).

[37] Bunyan, *The Pilgrim's Progress* (Grand Rapids, MI.: Zondervan, 1967), originally published in 1678-84.

anecdotes in religious homilies. The device was especially popular in medieval literature. In Chaucer's "The Pardoner's Tale," the Pardoner relates the story of three drunks who kill each other over some gold to illustrate his theme that greed is the root of all evil. Outside homiletic contexts, the Chanticleer in "The Nun's Priest's Tale" employs ten exempla to show that bad dreams do not predict disaster.

The fable is not easily distinguished from the exemplum, because it also illustrates a general moral thesis. Fables commonly involve animal characters that behave like their human types. Aesop's *Fables* have been frequently translated and retold, most famously by Jean de La Fontaine.[38] Fables may occur in a larger literary context. In such cases, the fable has some relation to the surrounding text, but is not that of a *mise-en-abyme*. For example, Jotham's fable (Judg 9:7-15) indicates to his audience the folly of accepting Abimelech as king, as Jotham clarifies. It is not a *mise-en-abyme*, however, because it lacks isolatability. Jotham applies the fable to the folly of the Shechemites and this application implicates the fable in its context so that it is not isolated.

A parable is a brief story that "stresses the tacit analogy, or parallel, with a general thesis or lesson."[39] Unlike the fable and exemplum, the lesson of the parable is not necessarily a moral thesis. For example, Jesus' parable of the sower (Matt 13:1-9) provides insight into the way the word is received among various people, but the demand that one be fertile soil is only implicit. Parables are generally not *mises-en-abyme* because they do not duplicate pertinent aspects of the whole narrative in which they occur. Jesus' parables provide insight into the kingdom of God, but do not recapitulate the Gospels in which they occur.[40] A parable that does have totality may lack isolatability. For example, Nathan's parable (2 Sam 12:1-6) does reflect the whole story of David's involvement with Bathsheba. Like Jotham's fable, it can be isolated from

---

[38] Aesop, *Fables* (ed. Émile Chambry; 3d ed.; Paris: Société d'Édition, 1967); La Fontaine, *Fables choisies mises en vers* (ed. Georges Couton; Paris: Garnier Fréres, 1962), originally published in 1668-94.

[39] M. H. Abrams, *A Glossary of Literary Terms* (7th ed.; Fort Worth, TX: Harcourt Brace, 1999) 7.

[40] However, Robert Brawley (*Text to Text Pours Forth Speech: Voices of Scripture in Luke-Acts* [Bloomington: University of Indiana Press, 1995] 27-41) argues that the parable of the wicked tenets (Luke 20:9-19 is a *mise-en-abyme*. The prophets and John the Baptist are the servants whom the tenants beat and the murdered son is Jesus. He understands the new tenants as the apostles who will provide a new and faithful leadership for Israel (cf. Luke 22:30).

its context in the sense that the speech is easily discernible. However, it lacks isolatability because it cannot be separated from its context and understood as an independent narrative. It is deeply implicated in its context by Nathan's use of the parable to accuse David. By contrast, the three biblical *mises-en-abyme* that I will discuss have frequently been read as independent narratives because they are isolatable.

Allegory, exemplum, fable, and parable are literary devices that may be distinguished from the *mise-en-abyme* because they are typically not sufficiently isolatable from their contexts due to the explanatory function they serve. Other literary devices, such as retrospective and prospective plot summaries, are not isolatable for a different reason: they are not separate and distinct stories or episodes.

Long narratives frequently include reflective retrospective plot summaries that may appear to be *mises-en-abyme* because they recapitulate the whole narrative or a major portion of it. As straightforward summaries, these passages do not offer a story analogous to the one in which they are embedded. Sometimes these summaries remind the reader of past events, but their functions may be more sophisticated. For example, the trial near the end of Theodore Dreiser's *An American Tragedy* recapitulates the prior story of the novel from a different perspective.[41] The trial scene shows certain significant differences between events as they were presented by the omniscient narrator and as they are set out at the trial by the prosecution and the defense.

Plot summaries may also be prospective, foreshadowing subsequent events. One form of prospective plot summary is prophecy (understood broadly). Anne Jefferson argues that prophecies are *mises-en-abyme*.[42] Specifically, she identifies the oracular predictions made to Laius about Oedipus and to Oedipus himself in Sophocles' *Oedipus Rex*.[43] Like retrospective plot summaries, however, they do not offer a separate and analogous narrative. Instead, prophecies foreshadow subsequent events much as plot summaries review prior events. Prophetic dreams, divine promises, and miscellaneous predictions are other forms of pro-

---

[41] Dreiser, *An American Tragedy* (Signet Classic; New York: Penguin, 1981). The novel was originally published in 1925.

[42] Jefferson, "Mise en abyme and the Prophetic in Narrative," *Style* 17 (1983) 196-208.

[43] Sophocles, *Oedipus Rex*, in *Fabulae* (ed. H. Lloyd-Jones and N. G. Wilson; OCT; Oxford: Oxford University Press, 1992) 121-80.

spective plot summary. Like prophecy, they should not be confused with the *mise-en-abyme*.

A *mise-en-abyme* is typically a short narrative embedded within a longer narrative, but not all embedded narratives are *mises-en-abyme*. Such stories as "The Grand Inquisitor" in Fyodor Dostoevsky's *Brothers Karamazov* and "The Impertinent Curiosity" in Cervantes' *Don Quixote* have some thematic relationship to their contexts, but do not parallel the novels in which they occur.[44] They lack the totality required of a *mise-en-abyme*. The staging of "Pyramus and Thisbe" in Shakespeare's *A Midsummer Night's Dream* provides an interesting example. Like *Gonzago* in *Hamlet*, the Pyramus story is a dramatic representation within a drama. Unlike *Gonzago*, however, "Pyramus" lacks totality. For example, it is a tragic story of two lovers rather than a comic story of several couples. (The Pyramus play would be a *mise-en-abyme* if it were staged within *Romeo and Juliet*.[45]) Within *Dream*, the Pyramus play adds to the thematic treatment of imagination and extends this theme from love to dramatic art.

In order for the term *mise-en-abyme* to have value as a literary critical term, it needs to be distinguished from a variety of devices that resemble it. The idea of the *mise-en-abyme* is notoriously slippery, and it may be expanded to include some or all of the poetic, explanatory, and reflective devices enumerated above. Such an expansion, however, is not desirable if the term *mise-en-abyme* is to remain useful. The term needs to be carefully delimited by applying criteria such as totality and isolatability.

The *Mise-en-abyme* at Work: Examples in Detail

Thus far, I have discussed the *mise-en-abyme* in general with relatively minimal discussion of the noted examples. In this section, I will attempt to further clarify what a *mise-en-abyme* entails and how it functions by treating several examples in detail. Previous theoretical discussions of the device have suffered somewhat from a lack of

---

[44] Dostoevsky, *The Brothers Karamazov* (trans. Richard Pevear and Larissa Volokhonsky; Vintage Classics; New York: Random House, 1991).

[45] Shakespeare, *A Midsummer Night's Dream* and *Romeo and Juliet*, both in *The Oxford Shakespeare*, 401-423 and 369-400, respectively.

detailed examination of proposed examples. As a result, theoretical generalizations sometimes lack the benefit of close textual analysis that can provide a reasonably firm basis for discussion. This lack of detailed analysis partly explains the confusion that prevails about what the *mise-en-abyme* is, how it works, and what qualifies as an example of the device. The following discussion of selected examples will bring some concreteness to the discussion and illustrate how the definition and criteria outlined above are helpful, but still require interpretive judgment for discerning a *mise-en-abyme*.

I have selected the following examples for various reasons. First, I will treat Agatha Christie's *Ten Little Indians* (1939) because it is a particularly clear example that fulfills many of the criteria outlined above. I will then discuss Shakespeare's *Hamlet* (ca. 1600) because it is the classic example of the simple *mise-en-abyme*, which is the most common type. The biblical *mises-en-abyme* are all simple. Finally, I will discuss examples in Homer's *Iliad* (ca. 7th century BCE) and in Apuleius' *The Golden Ass* (2nd century CE), to show that although the term *mise-en-abyme* is of recent coinage, the device itself is not confined to modern literature.

Agatha Christie's Ten Little Indians

A clear example of the *mise-en-abyme* occurs in Agatha Christie's mystery novel *Ten Little Indians*, also published as *And then There Were None*.[46] In this classic mystery scenario, foul weather strands ten strangers in a large house on a small island. The ten are invited to Indian Island by an unknown host who never materializes. One by one, each of the ten guests is murdered. The method of each murder bears some relation to the nursery rhyme, "The Ten Little Indians," which one character finds framed in her bedroom. Furthermore, as

---

[46] Christie, *And Then There Were None* (New York: St. Martin's, 2001), originally published in Great Britain as *Ten Little Niggers* in 1939. The American edition of 1940 was published as *And Then There Were None* and every occurrence of "nigger(s)" in the text was changed to "Indian(s)." The British edition title was changed to *Ten Little Indians* in 1965, but now all English language editions use the title *And Then There Were None*. However, note the current French title *Dis petite nègres*, or German *Zehn Kleine Negerlien*. See Dällenbach, *Le récit*, 84; *Mirror*, 62. Baruch Halpern alludes to this Agatha Christie novel in his *David's Secret Demons: Messiah, Murderer, Traitor, King* (Grand Rapids, MI: Eerdmans, 2001) 77.

each guest is murdered, one of the ten Indian figurines in the dining room disappears. The nursery rhyme is a *mise-en-abyme* of the novel. The characters in the novel soon realize that the poem is related to the murders:

Dr. Armstrong recited:

"Ten little Indian boys going out to dine;
One went and choked himself and then there were nine.

Nine little Indian boys sat up very late;
One overslept himself and then there were eight."

The two men looked at each other. Philip Lombard grinned and flung away his cigarette.

"Fits too damned well to be a coincidence! Anthony Marston dies of asphyxiation or choking last night after dinner, and Mother Rogers oversleeps herself with a vengeance."[47]

The guests thereafter continue to discern the connection between each murder and the poem. The eighth couplet of the poem refers to a zoo, but one character points out that there is no zoo on the island. Another character, however, says, "Don't you see? *We're the Zoo* . . . . Last Night, we were hardly human any more. *We're the Zoo* . . . ."[48]

The entire nursery rhyme is printed in full near the beginning of the novel and parts of it are recalled in reference to each murder. The characters themselves do the interpretive work of noting the similarities between the murders and the poem. The commentary of the characters makes the relationship between the poem and the events of the novel explicit. The poem is short in relation to the novel and embedded within it. Since each couplet of the poem corresponds to a murder in the novel, the poem encapsulates pertinent aspects of the whole novel. As noted above, identity between the title of the poem and the title of

---

[47] Christie, *And Then There Were None*, 107.
[48] Christie, *And Then There Were None*, 226.

the novel also indicates a *mise-en-abyme*.[49] The disappearing Indian figures and the location on Indian Island also connect the poem to the novel by indicating similarity of character and setting. Of Dällenbach's three types, the poem is a simple *mise-en-abyme*, given en bloc near the beginning of the novel. Parts of the poem are repeated later in order to make the *mise-en-abyme* explicit. These considerations show that the poem meets many of the criteria for the device outlined by Dällenbach and Ron. Christie's novel provides an example of the *mise-en-abyme* that is clearer and more explicit than other literary cases. Christie's *mise-en-abyme* is a pre-existing text around which she (like her murdering character) constructs a plot. In other instances, the author of the larger work is also the author of the *mise-en-abyme*. Such is the case with the next example I will discuss from William Shakespeare.

William Shakespeare's Hamlet

Almost every discussion or even short mention of the *mise-en-abyme* refers to the play within *Hamlet* as an example of the device. Since it is a universally accepted and classic instance of the *mise-en-abyme*, it merits more discussion than it typically receives.

Hamlet commissions the players to perform *The Murther of Gonzago* in order to discover whether the ghost's claim that Claudius murdered King Hamlet is true. Hamlet refers to this play as "The Mouse-trap" (3.2.226) because with it he expects to "catch the conscience of the king" (2.2.607).[50] Scholars use both titles to refer to the play within the play. The *Gonzago* play is prefaced by a dumb

---

[49] Christie's title for the novel, *Ten Little Indians*, is the same as the title and opening words of the nursery rhyme. The alternative title, *And Then There Were None*, is identical to the last line of the poem.

[50] The present discussion uses the text of *Hamlet* in *The Oxford Shakespeare*, 681-718. The scholarship on Hamlet is extensive. See A. C. Bradley, *Shakespearean Tragedy: Lectures on Hamlet, Othello, King Lear, MacBeth* (3d ed.; New York: St. Martin's Press, 1992), originally published in 1902; Paul S. Conklin, *A History of Hamlet Criticism: 1601-1821* (New York: King's Crown, 1947); *Readings on the Character of Hamlet, 1661-1947: Compiled from Over Three Hundred Sources* (ed. Claude C. H. Williamson; London: George Allen, 1950); *Twentieth Century Interpretations of Hamlet: A Collection of Critical Essays* (ed. David Bevington; Englewood Cliffs, NJ: Prentice-Hall, 1968). See also Dällenbach, *Le récit*, 22; *Mirror*, 12-13.

show which pantomimes the whole plot of the play before part of it is performed. The stage directions as given in the *Oxford Shakespeare* (3.2.129-130) describe this pantomime:

> Enter a King and Queen very lovingly, the Queen embracing him. She kneels and makes show of protestation unto him. He takes her up and declines his head upon her neck. He lays him down upon a bank of flowers. She, seeing him asleep, leaves him. Anon come in a fellow, takes off his crown, kisses it, and pours poison in the King's ears, and leaves him. The Queen returns, finds the King dead, makes passionate action. The poisoner, with some two or three mutes, comes in again, seeming to lament with her. The dead body is carried away. The poisoner woos the Queen with gifts. She seems loathe and unwilling a while, but in the end accepts his love.

The dumb show has been the source of several problems, apart from text-critical issues. The pantomime is frequently omitted in performance. Several scholars have argued for its inclusion by pointing out that the show supplies the plot of the upcoming play. This fact is important, because the play will be interrupted before all the similarities between *Gonzago* and *Hamlet* can be observed. The audiences of both *Hamlet* and *Gonzago* therefore need to know the plot of the whole so that the fragment makes sense.[51] One of the most common objections to the dumb show is that Claudius does not react to it. The most popular method of dealing with this problem is to have Claudius not see the show because he is whispering with Gertrude.[52] This objection, however, is a pseudo-problem.[53] Without the dumb-show, Claudius would not realize how similar the crime depicted in the subsequent dialogue is to his own. Without the pantomime, he reacts merely to the unusual

---

[51] J. Dover Wilson (*What Happens in Hamlet* [3d ed.; Cambridge: Cambridge University Press, 1951] 148) recalls a performance in which "I myself, sitting in the gallery, . . . overheard a discussion between two spectators who were mystified by the Gonzago-play simply because the story of *Hamlet* was new to them and the producer had deprived them of the assistance which Shakespeare provided [in the dumb show]."

[52] See Wilson, *What Happens*, 160; Harold Jenkins, *Hamlet* (The Arden Shakespeare; London: Methuen, 1982) 502.

[53] See Jenkins (*Hamlet*, 501-5) for a review of scholarly discussion which also concludes that the problem is "strictly speaking, no problem" (p. 505).

method of murder; with the pantomime, he reacts also to the murderer's wooing of the widow. The dumb show is as necessary for Claudius and the other spectators as it is for the audience of *Hamlet*.

Scholars have noted that among extant Elizabethan dumb shows, the present case is unique. Other pantomimes either "presented things that could not be conveniently given in dialogue," or foreshadowed subsequent dialogue in an emblematic or allegorical way.[54] The dumb show in *Hamlet*, however, presents the whole plot of the play in advance. As Ophelia remarks, "this show imports the argument of the play" (3.2.133). It therefore contextualizes the ensuing dialogue, which would otherwise appear to be a dull and pointless disquisition on second marriages. This discussion becomes far more interesting since we (and the court of Claudius) know that there will be a murder and second marriage.

The play proper begins with dialogue between the Player King and the Player Queen, who are celebrating their thirtieth wedding anniversary. The Queen hopes for thirty more years of wedded bliss, but the King expects to leave her a widow before that time. She consistently resists his repeated suggestion that she will remarry and Gertrude famously remarks that "The lady doth protest too much, methinks" (219). Following the plot of the dumb show, the Queen exits and the King goes to sleep.

When the murderer enters the scene, Hamlet remarks, "This one is Lucianus, nephew to the king" (244). By making Lucianus nephew (rather than brother) to the king, Hamlet collapses Claudius's murder of King Hamlet with his own threatened murder of Claudius. Here, the murderer and the revenger are represented in the same person so that the dumb show duplicates both the preceding murder and subsequent revenge. After Lucianus pours poison in the King's ears, Hamlet remarks that the murderer seeks his estate and adds, "You shall see anon how the murderer gets the love of Gonzago's wife" (251-52). At these words, Claudius interrupts the play and everyone leaves except Hamlet and Horatio. Hamlet's remark, together with the dumb show, indicate the fullness of the parallel between the murder of Gonzago and the murder of King Hamlet. By the time Claudius ends the play,

---

[54] Jenkins, *Hamlet*, 501. See also Wilson, *What Happens*, 147; Lee Sheridan Cox, *Figurative Design in Hamlet: The Significance of the Dumb Show* (Columbus: Ohio University Press, 1973) 17-32.

he knows both that Hamlet has learned of his crime, and that Hamlet intends to avenge the crime. Similarly, Hamlet knows that Claudius is guilty, and that Claudius knows that Hamlet knows of his guilt and his intention to avenge his father.

Although *Gonzago* resembles events that take place before *Hamlet* begins, it also duplicates the salient features of the play within which it is embedded. The murder of King Hamlet is revealed by his ghost in the first act. The murder presented in the dumb show and the play reflects the story told by the ghost in detail. The ghost relates first how Claudius won the affections of Gertrude (1.5.43-46):

> With witchcraft of his wits, with traitorous gifts—
> O wicked wit and gifts that have the power
> So to seduce!—won to his shameful lust
> The will of my most seeming virtuous queen.

He later reveals the method of the murderer (59-64, 74-75):

> Sleeping within my orchard,
> My custom always of the afternoon,
> Upon my secure hour thy uncle stole,
> With juice of cursèd hebona in a vial,
> And in the porches of my ears did pour
> The leprous distilment . . .
>
> Thus was I, sleeping, by a brother's hand
> Of life, of crown, of queen, at once dispatched.

The details of the murder as related by the ghost closely resemble the *Gonzago* play. Both Hamlet and Gonzago are murdered by family members who pour poison in their ears while they sleep in an Edenic paradise. Both victims appear to have happy marriages, but the murderer seduces the widow with gifts and wit. The murderer's motive in both cases is the victim's power (estate/crown).

In addition to the murder, the discussion of second marriages in *Gonzago* mirrors a major motif in *Hamlet*. Near the beginning of the play, Claudius alludes both to the recent death of King Hamlet and the quasi-incestuous nature of his marriage with Gertrude ("our sometime sister, now our queen," 1.2.8). Hamlet takes up the topic with a vengeance (e.g., 1.2.153-59, 180-81; 3.4.64-70, 140-43). In addition to the details of the murder, both *Hamlet* and *Gonzago* deal extensively with the marriage of the murderer and his victim's widow.

The *Gonzago* play is a *mise-en-abyme* in *Hamlet*. It duplicates in microcosm the motifs of murder and second marriage. It also duplicates Hamlet's ultimate revenge by making the murderer a nephew of the king. Hamlet specifically indicates the parallel between *Gonzago* and *Hamlet* and understands Claudius' reaction as a confession of guilt.

The *mise-en-abyme* is isolated from its contexts. It is a fragment of another play embedded in *Hamlet*. The passage employs a style of verse strikingly different from the surrounding poetry. The consistently rhyming couplets of the *Gonzago* play set it apart from the speeches of the characters in *Hamlet*.

The fragment of the *Gonzago* play within *Hamlet* draws our attention to murder, revenge, and the marriage of Claudius and Gertrude. The murderer and avenger are the same person. This fact suggests that the justice of vengeance is a significant issue in *Hamlet*. The *mise-en-abyme* places emphasis on motifs other than Hamlet's delay. The combined role of avenger and murderer suggest that, contrary to much of the critical tradition, Hamlet's moral obligation to revenge *can* be questioned. Therefore, the play does concern the relationship of vengeance to justice. This example from Shakespeare illustrates the complexity of the *mise-en-abyme*. It is not as simple and straightforward as the example from Agatha Christie's *Ten Little Indians*.

I have articulated examples of *mises-en-abyme* in Agatha Christie's *Ten Little Indians* and Shakespeare's *Hamlet*. These examples illustrate the basic concept of *mise-en-abyme*, some of its possible varieties, and the issues involved in identifying literary examples of the device. The example from Agatha Christie's novel is significant for its unusual clarity and the large number of criteria that it satisfies. The *Hamlet* example meets several criteria, but is complicated by such factors as Lucianus duplicating both Hamlet and Claudius. The complexity of *Hamlet* lead to intricate interrelationships among its parts that complicate the one-to-one correspondence between part and whole that emerges in simpler texts like Christie's. Before I discuss the biblical examples, I will describe two more examples of the device to demonstrate that it occurs in ancient as well as modern literature.

Deliberations concerning the *mise-en-abyme* generally draw primarily or entirely on modern literature and all the examples I have mentioned above are modern.[55] I will next discuss in detail two examples from ancient literature; one from Homer's *Iliad* and one from Apuleius' *The Golden Ass*. The existence of these ancient examples demonstrates that the device is not unique to modern Western literature.

Homer's Iliad

Homer's *Iliad* is the story of the anger of Achilles and includes a *mise-en-abyme*.[56] The first book narrates how Achilles becomes angry with Agamemnon. Agamemnon refuses to accept the ransom offered by Chryses the priest of Apollo for his daughter. Apollo sends a plague on the Achaean army until Agamemnon finally returns the girl to her father with additional gifts. As compensation for his loss, Agamemnon takes the captive Briseïs away from Achilles. Achilles becomes angry and refuses to participate in the war against Troy. Without Achilles, their best warrior, the Achaeans suffer at the hands of the Trojans. Finally, Achilles allows his close friend Patroclus to assist the Achaeans. Hector kills Patroclus in battle, which so enrages Achilles that he rejoins the battle in order to exact revenge on Hector.

Within the *Iliad*, the story of Meleager (9.524-605) is similar to the story of Achilles.[57] The story is told by Phoenix, an old friend and father figure to Achilles. Nestor advises Agamemnon to send an embassy to Achilles "to persuade him with kindly gifts and gentle words" (9.112-13). At Nestor's suggestion, Agamemnon sends Phoenix, Ajax, and Odysseus to offer to return to Achilles the captive Briseïs along with substantial gifts. Achilles declines these gifts and refuses

---

[55] Dällenbach (*Le récit*, 79-80; *Mirror*, 57-58) discusses the Apuleius example, but not the one from Homer.

[56] Homer, *Iliad* (2 vols.; LCL; trans. A. T. Murray and rev. by William F. Wyatt; Cambridge, MA: Harvard University Press, 1999). Translations modified from Loeb.

[57] Homeric scholars have long noticed the similarity and attempted to derive diachronic conclusions from it. Some have suggested that "the wrath of Meleager was the model on which Homer formulated the wrath of Achilles" (Johannes Th. Kakridis, *Homeric Researches* [New York: Garland, 1987] 19), originally published in 1947. Others have proposed that Homer reshaped the Meleager story to support the parallel with Achilles. Kakridis reviews the variety of opinions concerning the composition of the *Iliad* and the Meleager story.

to join the battle. Achilles claims to love Briseïs as a "wife fitted to the heart" (ἄλοχον θυμαρέα, 9.336). He notes that the Trojan War is fought for Helen and asks if the sons of Atreus are the only men who love their wives (αλόχους, 9.340-41). He thereby establishes the similarity between Agamemnon's crime against him and Alexander's crime against Menelaus. Briseïs is likened to Helen. Phoenix then tells the story of Meleager to persuade Achilles to accept the gifts and return to the fight. The story involves some interpretive problems, but it is similar to the plot of the *Iliad*.[58]

Meleager's father Oeneus is king of the Aetolians. Oeneus neglects to offer the first fruits of his orchard to the goddess Artemis alone among the Olympians. Consequently, Artemis sends a wild boar to uproot trees in the orchard. Meleager leads a small army of Calydonians and Curetes against this large boar and finally kills it. Artemis then causes strife between the Calydonians and the Curetes concerning the spoils of the boar. This strife leads to war between the neighboring peoples. Meleager the Calydonian becomes angry with the Curetes because they object to his desire to award the spoils to the Amazon Atalanta, who had helped kill the boar. He kills his mother's brother when he tries to take the spoils from Atalanta. After the beginning of the war between the Calydonians and Curetes, Meleager's mother Althaea curses her son because of his murder of her brother. Meleager refuses to fight in defense of his city because he is angry with his mother.[59]

As long as Meleager fights in defense of his city, "so long it went badly for the Curetes, nor could they remain outside the wall, though they were many" (9.551-52). Earlier and later in the story, the Calydonians are clearly defending their city from the Curetes' attack. Possibly, the wall behind which the Curetes are constrained to defend

---

[58] The present discussion relies primarily on Kakridis, *Homeric Researches*, 11-42; Gregory Nagy, *The Best of the Achaeans: Concepts of the Hero in Archaic Greek Poetry* (rev. ed.; Baltimore: Johns Hopkins University Press, 1998) 103-11; Bryan Hainsworth, *The Iliad: A Commentary* (6 vols.; Cambridge: Cambridge University Press, 1993) 6. 130-40. See Hainsworth (*Iliad*, 130) for further bibliography.

[59] One of the major obscurities in Homer's text is that it does not describe Meleager's killing of his uncle which leads to his mother's curse. I have clarified the story on the basis of details provided by Ovid, *Metamorphoses*, 8.260-525. Homer does not clarify that, like the anger of Achilles in the beginning of the *Iliad*, the anger of Meleager originates in a religious offense and its punishment that lead to a dispute over spoils. Homer makes no mention of Atalanta and does not clarify exactly when or why Meleager kills his uncle, although it may be in the course of battle.

themselves is similar to the wall that the Achaeans build around their ships to defend their camp (7.334-343, 435-41).[60] Meleager is able to force the Curetes behind their defensive walls as Achilles is able to constrain the Trojans behind their city walls. Then both Meleager and Achilles refrain from combat as a result of their anger. Their absence from battle leads to a reversal in the fortunes of war. The Calydonians, like the Achaeans, hide behind defensive walls because they cannot face their enemy without their best warrior.

The anger of Meleager and that of Achilles are described in identical terms. Meleager lies by his wife's side

. . . χόλον θυμαλγέα πέσσον ("nursing his grievous anger," 9.565)

just as Achilles is among the ships

. . . χόλον θυμαλγέα πέσσον ("nursing his grievous anger," 4.513).

Also, during the same embassy in which Phoenix tells the story of Meleager, Odysseus urges Achilles to abandon his χόλον θυμαλγέα ("grievous anger," 9.260).

Many people beg Meleager to return to the fight. The list of those who intercede is significant. By poetic convention, such lists in Homer occur in ascending order of affection.[61] The order suggests that Meleager loves his wife most of all, then his companions, his mother, his brothers, his father, the priests, and the elders least of all. As Phoenix tells the tale, he identifies himself, Ajax, and Odysseus as Achilles' closest companions (φίλατοι, 9.522), who should succeed in persuading him. The similarity between the names of Meleager's wife Cleopatra and Achilles' friend Patroclus, however, point to a different correspondence.[62] Patroclus is closest to Achilles and will finally be able to persuade him to fight. Cleopatra persuades Meleager to fight by her pleading, and Patroclus persuades Achilles to fight by his own death in

---

[60] Hainsworth, *Iliad*, 134.

[61] Kakridis, *Homeric Researches*, 20; followed by Hainsworth, *Iliad*, 138.

[62] Both names mean "the glory of the ancestors." Scholars have observed the similarity of the names Cleo-patra and Patro-clus, and speculated that Homer calls her Cleopatra in order to strengthen her connection to Patroclus. Homer reports that her parents called her Halcyone (cf. 9.561-64), yet he refers to her as Cleopatra. See Hainsworth, *Iliad*, 136.

battle. There are further connections between the embassies to Achilles and to Meleager. Meleager refuses his father, "the old horseman" Oeneus (γέρων ἱππηλάτα, 9.581), as Achilles refuses "the old horseman" Phoenix (γέρων ἱππηλάτα, 9.432), who is like a father to him (9.485-95). Furthermore, the person who causes the hero's wrath in each story also intercedes to end it. Meleager's mother caused her son's wrath, but is among those who ask her son to return to the battle.[63] Similarly, Agamemnon offends Achilles, but sends the embassy to offer gifts to persuade him to fight. In the embassy scene, however, Achilles, like Meleager, refuses the gifts and advice of his companions.

Meleager finally relents when the enemy sets fire to the city and his wife Cleopatra begs him to defend it and describes to him the fate of a defeated city: "they kill the men, burn the city with fire, and lead away the children and low-belted women" (9.593-94). Similarly, Achilles finally allows his friend Patroclus to fight with the Achaeans after the Trojans set fire to some Achaean ships (16.122-29). The death of Patroclus finally stirs Achilles to fight. Both Cleopatra and Patroclus are close companions of the warriors and keep them company while they refuse to fight. Both characters motivate the hero to fight by conjuring grief: Cleopatra describes the fate of a fallen city and Patroclus occasions Achilles' sorrow by his death. The grief that each creates in the hero leads to the hero's glory (κλέος).

Phoenix tells the story of Meleager to Achilles to persuade him to accept the gifts that are now offered with the pleading of his closest companions and return to the battle. Meleager declined a similar opportunity under similar circumstances, but delayed in returning to the fight so long that the proffered gifts were withdrawn. Phoenix suggests that Achilles not make the same mistake. The Meleager story has a different meaning in the *Iliad* from what Phoenix intends. Phoenix does not realize that Achilles' closest companion is Patroclus, who has not yet interceded.

This *mise-en-abyme* within the *Iliad* meets several of the criteria outlined by Dällenbach and Ron. The story is short and easily isolated from the epic by Phoenix's introduction and concluding remarks. Phoenix makes explicit the analogy between Meleager and Achilles.

---

[63] Hainsworth (*Iliad*, 139) reports that a scholiast "noted that as an offending party Althaea is analogous to Agamemnon." Homer does not clarify why Althaea shifts from cursing her son to begging him to fight.

Although Phoenix urges Achilles not to behave like Meleager, Achilles does so by rejecting the gifts and persisting in his angry refusal to fight. Thus, the analogy between the two stories becomes more extensive than Phoenix would like. The similarity between narrative circumstances and characters is reinforced by a similarity of the personal names Cleopatra and Patroclus and the same epithet "old horseman" applied to Meleager's father and Phoenix. The story of Meleager encompasses the whole plot of the *Iliad* from the source of the hero's wrath to his final and successful return to battle. In Cleopatra's words, the Meleager story also duplicates descriptions in the *Iliad* of the fate of a fallen city (Priam's words in 22.62-71, Andromache's in 24.725-45).

Classicists have long noted the duplication of the *Iliad* in the Meleager story, but have not identified it as a *mise-en-abyme*. They have generally used this story to develop hypotheses about the composition of the *Iliad* rather than examining its function in the poem. Biblical scholars show a similarly diachronic interest in the biblical examples of the device that I will discuss below.

Apuleius' Golden Ass

Classicists have also observed the similarity between the story of Cupid and Psyche and *The Golden Ass* within which it occurs. However, they have not characterized it as a case of *mise-en-abyme*. *The Golden Ass* was written in Latin by Apuleius in the second century of the common era.[64] Lucius, the protagonist and narrator of this ancient story, pursues pleasure and has a fascination with magic, by which he is accidentally transformed into a donkey. As he is about to be returned to his human shape, robbers break into the house where he is staying, and kidnap him to carry their loot. He then embarks on a series of misadventures in the course of which he hears many stories from various characters. Ultimately, he returns to his human form with the assistance of the goddess Isis, into whose mysteries he is initiated. The priest of Isis explains to Lucius that his interest in

---

[64] Apuleius, *The Golden Ass, or Metamorphoses* (trans. E. J. Kennedy; New York: Penguin, 1998). The first title is preferred in order to avoid confusion with Ovid's *Metamorphoses*. Also, the manuscripts use this title, which was known to Augustine (*De civitate dei*, 18.18). See Dällenbach, *Le récit*, 79-80; *Mirror*, 57-58.

magic and sensual pleasure distracted him from the right path. The religious conclusion suggests that the whole story has an allegorical force. Lucius' transformation into a donkey is a metaphor for his failure to live up to his philosophic ancestry by his interest in magic and lust. The priest's speech at the end draws attention to the significance of episodes earlier in the work. For example, Lucius is warned against impertinent curiosity when he sees the statue of Actaeon spying on Diana, and his kinswoman Byrrhena reinforces the warning. Even the slave girl Photis warns Lucius that he may get more than he bargained for by involving himself with her. Photis appears to be a kind of antitype to Isis. The hair of both female figures are described in similar terms (2.9.7 and 11.3.4). Also, Lucius asks of Photis "a boon I can never repay" (*inremunerabile beneficium*, 3.22.5) in the form of an ointment that will transform him into a bird. Much later, his final salvation by Isis is also called *inremunerabile beneficium* (11.24.5). This connection is particularly significant since the term *inremunerabile* is otherwise unattested in Latin.[65] Although *The Golden Ass* may appear at first to be mere entertainment, the religious conclusion casts a different light on the prior events.

The story of Cupid and Psyche contributes to the religious themes of the work. The story occurs in the middle of *The Golden Ass*. The story is told by an old woman to Charite, who is a captive of the robbers who are also holding Lucius the donkey. In the story, the mortal Psyche is so beautiful that she is mistaken for Venus. As punishment, she is married to an unknown, non-human husband, who comes to her only at night and cautions her never to attempt to see him. Her envious sisters lead her to believe that her husband is a monster and persuade her to examine him by the light of a lamp while he sleeps. She does so and discovers that her husband is the god Cupid. Cupid had been ordered by Venus to make Psyche fall in love with a contemptible man. Instead, he had made Psyche his wife without the knowledge or consent of his mother Venus, who now discovers the union and torments Psyche. Venus assigns impossible tasks to Psyche who completes them with the help of Cupid's agents. Cupid ultimately reconciles Venus to the marriage, and Psyche becomes immortal. The personal names in the story indicate its allegorical force. The union of love (Cupid) and the human

[65] Kennedy in Apuleius, *Cupid & Psyche* (ed. E. J. Kennedy; Cambridge Greek and Latin Classics; Cambridge: Cambridge University Press, 1990) 12 n. 51.

soul (Psyche) results in the birth of the child Pleasure (*Voluptas*). This plot parallels the story of Lucius finding pleasure in union with Isis.

Kennedy says most critics accept "that this longest and most elaborate of all the inserted stories . . . has a special significance for the allegorical interpretation of the novel as a whole."[66] Kennedy summarizes the reasons that have led scholars to this conclusion. Although he does not use the term *mise-en-abyme*, his observations support the recognition that the Cupid and Psyche story recapitulates pertinent aspects of the whole of *The Golden Ass*. The way the old woman introduces her story "clearly echoes the prologue of the novel itself and can only be meant to suggest an analogy."[67] Both prologues characterize the subsequent narratives as charming (*lepidus*) stories (*fabula*). Lucius does not see the connection between himself and Psyche as he listens to the story and the reader of *The Golden Ass* can hardly be aware of it until the end of the novel is known. Both Lucius and Psyche come from distinguished families, but suffer misfortune in an uncaring world. Also, both are finally saved "by the *undeserved* intervention of divine grace."[68] Kennedy emphasizes that Psyche, like Lucius, seems to learn nothing from her experience and is saved not by her performance of tasks, but Cupid's desire to be with her.

Both stories involve the theme of impertinent curiosity, which motivates the novel as a whole and links the stories together. Both Lucius and Psyche "obstinately persist in the path to ruin, blind and deaf to repeated warnings."[69] Lucius is as stubborn as the donkey he becomes. Psyche's similar crime is disobedience. Both characters submit to a goddess and undergo various trials before coming to a state of union with love (Cupid/Isis). Psyche's descent into the underworld is similar to Lucius' more symbolic death. Both finally experience pleasure (*voluptas*).

The goddesses in each story are parallel. At the end of the novel, Venus is noted as one of the guises of Isis. Both goddesses are identified with fortune and providence. Also, the beginning of Venus' description of herself (4.30.1) is echoed by Isis in her epiphany (11.5.1).

---

[66] Kennedy, *Cupid*, 12.
[67] Kennedy, *Cupid*, 13,
[68] Kennedy, *Cupid*, 14. Emphasis his.
[69] Kennedy, *Cupid*, 15.

The several connections between the story of Cupid and Psyche and the larger narrative in which it is embedded suggest that the former is a *mise-en-abyme* within the latter. Dällenbach argues that without the story of Cupid and Psyche, *The Golden Ass* reads like an adventurous romance that seems to have nothing to do with religion. The embedded story prepares for the epiphany of Isis at the end of the novel and suggests a deeper reading of Lucius' adventures. "Without the *mise en abyme*, the novel would not be able to convert its narrative events into a redemptive code."[70]

The *mises-en-abyme* in Homer's *Iliad* and Apuleius' *The Golden Ass* demonstrate that the device is not unique to modern literature. Classics scholars do not discuss these stories as *mises-en-abyme* in part because the term is current in literary studies that focus on modern literature. As the methods and theories developed by literary critics are applied to ancient literature, more examples of the *mise-en-abyme* may be discovered in ancient literature.

Conclusion

The present chapter has reviewed the critical discussion of the *mise-en-abyme* in order to provide an understanding of this device. In literary studies, a *mise-en-abyme* is a part of a literary work that duplicates pertinent aspects of the whole within which it is placed. The precise definition of the *mise-en-abyme* admits of considerable variety. In the above discussion, I have attempted with the assistance of Dällenbach and Ron to chart a middle course between a rigid definition that would make the device extremely rare and a loose definition that would find the device almost everywhere. The various criteria discussed above help the critic find this middle course. Theoretical discussions of the device allude to a variety of examples without pursuing any one in significant detail. As a consequence, these treatments do not achieve sufficient clarity concerning this device. Above, I have tried to overcome this deficiency by examining several examples in detail.

These examples show the complex of issues involved in identifying a *mise-en-abyme*. As described in the introduction, the following chapters will articulate three biblical examples of the *mise-en-abyme*.

---

[70] Dällenbach, *Le récit*, 79; *Mirror*, 58.

Each of the following chapters on the three biblical examples of the *mise-en-abyme* will summarize relevant prior scholarship and then delineate the device. A further section will describe how each biblical *mise-en-abyme* fits into a larger pattern of repetition within its surrounding narrative. Each chapter will conclude with some remarks on the consequences of understanding the biblical passages as *mises-en-abyme*. The last chapter will integrate the biblical examples into the general theory of the *mise-en-abyme*.

CHAPTER TWO

Genesis 38

What is the story of Judah and Tamar doing in the Joseph Story? Interpreters have long puzzled over this question. This chapter will argue that Genesis 38 is a *mise-en-abyme* in the Joseph Story. Specifically, Genesis 38 reduplicates the larger story in which it occurs. Tamar and Joseph are parallel characters. Both suffer alienation from the family as a result of crimes committed against them by their relatives. Both resort to deception as a means of restoring their circumstances. Both of their deceptions lead to restoration to their circumstances before the crime. Judah plays a similar role in both these stories. He wrongs Tamar and he cooperates with his brothers in wronging Joseph. He is also instrumental in ending both deceptions and bringing both narratives to their conclusions.

Understanding Genesis 38 as a *mise-en-abyme* explains both why scholars have seen its presence as a problem and why it is part of Genesis 37–50. As a *mise-en-abyme*, Genesis 38 is isolatable from its context. Commentators have long responded to the independence of the chapter and attempted to account for its presence. As a *mise-en-abyme*, Genesis 38 also recapitulates the most salient aspects of its embedding narrative (Genesis 37–50), and establishes analogies with it so that the stories become mutually illuminating. Thus, despite its isolatabilty, Genesis 38 is an important element within the Joseph Story. The present chapter will explain how the placement of Genesis 38 has been seen as a problem and how scholars have tried to resolve it. The discussion will then show how Genesis 38 reduplicates the Joseph Story. The consequences of understanding Genesis 38 as a *mise-en-abyme* will finally be noted.

The Problem

Bryan Smith notes that scholars "begin by praising Genesis 37–50 for its high literary quality, but then contradict that praise by denying that the narrative possesses one of the most basic characteristics of high quality narrative, namely unity."[1] Smith's own approach "highly values observations that support a unified reading, operating on the assumption that an analysis that demonstrates unity is superior to one that denies it."[2] Smith's concern for unity is grounded in part in his commitment to the Mosaic authorship of Genesis. Although I disagree with much of Smith's article (including his insistence on Mosaic authorship), he does have a point. Scholarly praise for the quality of Genesis 37–50 generally depends on ignoring chapter 38.[3] Commentators have characterized the "Joseph Story" as Genesis 37 and 39-50.[4]

There are two major features that have led many critical scholars to conclude that Genesis 38 is not an integral part of the Joseph Story. The first and most obvious problem is topic. A story maintains unity through such means as a consistent set of characters, a common setting, and a logical connection between consecutive events. The apparent intrusion of Genesis 38 after Joseph's brothers sell him into slavery violates all of these expectations. The topic shifts away from Joseph and the divisions within Jacob's family. Among the characters, Judah is the only thread that connects Genesis 38 to the Story of Jacob's Line

[1] Bryan Smith, "The Central Role of Judah in Genesis 37–50," *BSac* 162 (2005) 159.

[2] Smith, "Central Role of Judah," 160.

[3] Friedemann W. Golka notes a comment from a lecture by Rolf Rendtorff at Heidelberg: "a text you make for yourself is always easier to interpret than the one that is actually there" (Golka, "Genesis 37–50: Joseph Story or Israel-Joseph Story?" *Currents in Biblical Research* 2 [2004] 153-77).

[4] For example, Lothar Ruppert, *Die Josephserzählung der Genesis: Ein Beitrag zur Theologie der Pentateuchquellen* (SANT 11; Munich: Kösel, 1965); Donald B. Redford, *A Study of the Biblical Story of Joseph (Genesis 37–50)* (VTSup 20; Leiden: Brill, 1970) 16; George W. Coats, *From Canaan to Egypt: Structural and Theological Context for the Joseph Story* (CBQMS 4; Washington, DC: The Catholic Biblical Association of America, 1976); R. E. Longacre, *Joseph: A Story of Divine Providence* (Winona Lake, IN: Eisenbrauns, 1989); Claus Westermann, *Genesis 37–50: A Commentary* (trans. John Scullion; Minneapolis: Augsburg, 1986) 24. Since the advent of literary criticism, some scholars have attempted to understand Genesis 38 as part of its context (see below), though none has described the chapter as a *mise-en-abyme*.

(Genesis 37:2–50:26).[5] This thread seems weak. The setting of Genesis 38 shifts to the region around Adullam rather than remaining focused on Jacob's family near Hebron (Gen 37:14) or following Joseph to Egypt. The storyline is similarly interrupted. The events of Genesis 39–50 follow as a consequence of Genesis 37, but do not depend on Genesis 38.

Modern commentators generally do not elaborate on the reasons for treating the story of Judah and Tamar as separate from the Story of Jacob's Line. The lack of cohesion is generally mentioned as something obvious.[6] The less obvious problem of chronology, however, has attracted much more attention. Benedict Spinoza discussed this issue in 1670 and set the exegetical pattern for over three hundred years. Spinoza uses Genesis 38 as his leading example of chronological inco-

---

[5] I prefer to speak of the Story of Jacob's Line rather than the Joseph Story. By "the Story of Jacob's Line," I mean Genesis 37:2–50:26, although I will refer to Genesis 37–50 for the sake of simplicity. I regard the *toledoth* notices in Genesis as indicating the boundaries between major sections of text. Other scholars who understand the *toledoth* notices this way include Frank Moore Cross, *Canaanite Myth and Hebrew Epic: Essays in the History of the Religion of Israel* (Cambridge: Harvard University Press, 1973) 302; Brevard S. Childs, *Introduction to the Old Testament as Scripture* (OTL; Philadelphia: Fortress, 1979) 145; Richard Elliot Friedman, *The Exile and Biblical Narrative: The Formation of the Deuteronomistic and Priestly Works* (HSM 22; Chico, CA: Scholars, 1981) 81; Sven Tengström, *Die Toledotformel und die literarische Struktur der priesterlichen Erweiterungsschicht im Pentateuch* (ConBOT 17; Lund: Leerup, 1981); Gordon J. Wenham, *Genesis 1–15* (WBC 1; Waco, TX: Word Books, 1987) 49; Allen P. Ross, *Creation and Blessing: A Guide to the Study and Exposition of the Book of Genesis* (Grand Rapids, MI: Baker Books, 1988) 69-88; Victor P. Hamilton, *The Book of Genesis Chapters 1–17* (NICOT; Grand Rapids, MI: Eerdmans, 1990) 2-10; David M. Carr, *Reading the Fractures of Genesis: Historical and Literary Approaches* (Louisville, KY: Westminster: John Knox, 1996) 74-75; Bruce K. Waltke with Cathi J. Fredericks, *Genesis: A Commentary* (Grand Rapids, MI: Zondervan, 2001) 17-19. Others disregard the *toledoth* notices when outlining Genesis because they are thought to be later additions. These scholars include Herman Gunkel, *Genesis* (3d ed.; Göttingen: Vandenhoeck & Ruprecht, 1964 [originally published 1910] 100; the English translation (*Genesis* [trans. Mark E. Biddle; Macon: Mercer University Press, 1997]) indicates the German pagination; Gerhardt von Rad, *Genesis: A Commentary* (rev. ed.; trans. John Marks; OTL; Philadelphia: Westminster, 1972) 63 and 70; Claus Westermann, *Genesis 1–11: A Commentary* (trans. John J. Scullion; Minneapolis: Fortress, 1994) 16, 26, and 81; Bruce Vawter, *On Genesis: A New Reading* (Garden City, NY: Doubleday, 1977) 63; Walter Brueggemann, *Genesis* (IBC; Atlanta: John Knox, 1982) 35; Thomas Brodie, *Genesis as Dialogue: A Literary, Historical & Theological Commentary* (Oxford: Oxford University Press, 2001) 132.

[6] For example, von Rad (*Genesis*, 356) states, "Every attentive reader can see that the story of Judah and Tamar has no connection at all with the strictly organized Joseph story at whose beginning it is now inserted."

herence in the Bible. He notes that "Joseph was seventeen years old when he was sold by his brothers [Gen 37:2], and he was thirty years old when he was summoned by Pharaoh from prison [Gen 41:46]," so thirteen years elapse.[7] Including the seven years of plenty (41:47-49) and two of famine (45:6), he calculates that Jacob's family moved to Egypt twenty-two years after Joseph was sold.[8] Since Tamar's children are among the members of Jacob's family who move to Egypt, all the events of Genesis 38 must unfold within these twenty-two years. He does not think that twenty-two years is sufficient time for all the events in the narrative.[9]

Most critical scholars since Spinoza have arrived at similar conclusions for the same reasons.[10] Other scholars tried to defend the twenty-two years as sufficient time for the events of Genesis 38.[11] If one assumes (1) that Judah married soon after the sale of Joseph, and (2) that the marriageable age for men assumed by the story is about eighteen,[12] and (3) that Er and Onan died soon after marrying Tamar, then Tamar could have had her twins before the famine and the first trip to Egypt. This solution to the chronological problem suggests that Judah's statement to Tamar, "She is righteous, not I" (צדקה ממני, Gen

---

[7] Spinoza, *Theological-Political Treatise* (2d ed.; trans. Samuel Shirley; Indianapolis: Hackett, 2001) 1170. Originally published in 1670.

[8] Spinoza almost certainly derives these calculations from Rashi (commentary on Genesis 37:34).

[9] Spinoza (*Theological-Political Treatise*, 118) therefore concludes that the various passages in Genesis–2 Kings "were collected indiscriminately and stored together with a view to examining them and arranging them more conveniently at a later time."

[10] U. Cassuto ("The Story of Judah and Tamar," [originally published 1927] in *Biblical and Oriental Studies*, vol. 1 [trans. Israel Abrahams; Jerusalem: Magnes, 1973] 29-40) notes "since the days of Spinoza and onwards [biblical expositors] have regarded [the chronological problem] as providing one of the strongest arguments against the unity of the book of Genesis." Such expositors include: Gunkel, *Genesis*, 410; von Rad, *Genesis*, 357; John Skinner, *A Critical and Exegetical Commentary on Genesis* (2d ed.; ICC; Edinburgh: T & T Clark, 1930) 450; E. A. Speiser, *Genesis* (AB 1; New York: Doubleday, 1964) 299; Redford, *A Study*, 16; Westermann, *Genesis 37–50*, 49; George W. Coats, *Genesis, with an Introduction to Narrative Literature* (FOTL 1; Grand Rapids, MI: Eerdmans, 1983) 260.

[11] Cassuto, "The Story of Judah," 29-40; Steven D. Matthewson, "An Exegetical Study of Genesis 38," *BSac* 146 (1989) 381-84.

[12] So Cassuto, "The Story of Judah," 39; Matthewson ("Exegetical Study," 382) suggests sixteen.

38:26)[13] and his speech offering to be a slave in place of Benjamin (Gen 44:18-34) are chronologically close.[14]

A further chronological irregularity cannot be resolved in this way. Included in the list of the members of Jacob's family who went down to Egypt are not only Tamar's twins, Perez and Zerah, but also the two children of Perez, Hezron and Hamul (Gen 46:12). Even if one accepts that Tamar could have had her twins before the descent into Egypt, the chronology of the story cannot allow for her to be a grandmother. This problem has sometimes been grounds for concluding that the list of Jacob's family (like Genesis 38) is a later insertion.[15] A possible solution allows that the narrator tolerates chronological irregularities for the sake of more important narrative and thematic considerations.[16] The list in Gen 46:8-27 numbers the family of Jacob at seventy persons, and the sons of Perez are needed for that sum. This consideration may be more important than chronology.

Since the rise of (new) literary criticism in biblical studies in the past few decades, scholars have searched for connections between the story of Judah and Tamar and the Story of Jacob's Line that might

---

[13] This translation assumes that the Hebrew is a comparison of exclusion (Bruce Waltke and M. O'Connor, *Introduction to Biblical Hebrew Syntax* [Winona Lake, IN: Eisenbrauns, 1990] 265-66). See also Waltke, *Genesis*, 513-14. On the ancient interpretation of Judah's statement, see C. E. Hayes, "The Midrashic Career of the Confession of Judah (Genesis XXXVIII 26), Part I: The Extra-Canonical Texts, Targums, and Other Versions," *VT* 45 (1995) 62-81; Hayes, "Part II: The Rabbinic Midrashim," *VT* 45 (1995) 174-87. On the ancient interpretation of the story in general, see Pieter W. van der Horst, "Tamar in Pseudo-Philo's *Biblical History*," in *A Feminist Companion to Genesis* (ed. Athalya Brenner; Sheffield: Sheffield Academic Press, 1993) 300-4; Cecilia Wassén, "The Story of Judah and Tamar in the Eyes of the Earliest Interpreters," *Literature & Theology* 8 (1994) 354-66; Esther Marie Menn, *Judah and Tamar (Genesis 38) in Ancient Jewish Exegesis: Studies in Literary Form and Hermeneutics* (JSJSup 51; Leiden: Brill, 1997).

[14] Waltke, *Genesis*, 507-8.

[15] Gunkel, *Genesis*, 493; Skinner, *Genesis*, 492-95; Speiser, *Genesis*, 344-45; von Rad, *Genesis*, 357, 402-3; Ruppert, *Josephserzählung*, 130-31, 136-39; Westermann, *Genesis 37-50*, 158; W. Lee Humphreys, *Joseph and his Family: A Literary Study* (Columbia, SC: University of South Carolina Press, 1988) 207.

[16] André Wénin, "Le temps dans l'histoire de Joseph (Gn 37–50): Repères temporels pour une analysis narrative," *Bib* 83 (2002) 32: "Mais si le narrateur se permet ces entorses chronologiques, c'est que le fait d'insérer ces digressions est narrativement plus significatif qu'une parfaite cohérence temporelle." There are far more serious irregularities than this one in Scripture, so it seems likely that "regularity" was not the highest priority for biblical writers (or at least the final editors).

explain the placement of Genesis 38.[17] Richard Clifford speaks of "the emerging consensus that chap. 38 belongs within chaps. 37–50."[18] However, this consensus does not offer a convincing account. Two of these explanations have merit, but others do not.

First, some have tried to make sense of the placement of Genesis 38 by noting that "The Joseph Story" is a title applied by modern scholars to Genesis 37–50, while the text identifies its topic as "The Story of Jacob's Line" (Gen 37:2).[19] While Genesis 38 may have nothing to do with a "Joseph Story," it is clearly related to the "Story of Jacob's Line," since Judah is a son of Jacob. While Joseph is the focus of Genesis 37–50, the narrative is unified around a larger topic. This observation does not claim that Genesis 38 is closely related to its context, but it does seek to overcome the scholarly habit of thinking of Genesis 37–50 as the "Joseph Story."[20]

Second, many scholars have noted the role of the chapter in generating suspense.[21] Suspense refers to the reader's lack of certainty concerning future plot developments, especially as they affect characters with whom the reader sympathizes. The interest that the text has shown in Joseph is suspended in chap. 38 and his subsequent fate is not narrated until chap. 39. Commentators have also recognized, however, that this function does not fully explain the presence of the story. Any

---

[17] Many of the observations below were made by Robert Alter (*The Art of Biblical Narrative* [New York: Harper Collins, 1981] 1-12) and frequently repeated by others. Just as Spinoza uses Genesis 38 as his leading example of chronological irregularity in the Bible (and therefore the need for source criticism), so Alter uses the chapter as his leading example of how biblical texts may be read as artful narrative without appeal to source criticism. However, Alter never refers to Spinoza.

[18] Richard J. Clifford, "Genesis 38: Its Contribution to the Jacob Story," *CBQ* 66 (2004) 519-32.

[19] Ross, *Creation*, 611; Humphreys, *Joseph*, 37; Matthewson, "Exegetical Study," 384-85; Gordon J. Wenham, *Genesis 16–50* (WBC 2; Waco, TX: Word Books, 1994) 345; Waltke, *Genesis*, 49. Smith ("Central Role of Judah," 169) argues for seeing the text as "the Joseph-Judah Story," which moves in the right direction, but not far enough considering the non-trivial roles of Jacob, Reuben, and Benjamin. Golka's suggested "Israel-Joseph Story" ("Genesis 37–50," 172) overlooks the roles of Jacob's other sons.

[20] Similarly, Lindsay Wilson, *Joseph Wise and Otherwise: The Intersection of Wisdom and Covenant in Genesis 37–50* (Waynesboro, GA: Paternoster, 2004) 86-87.

[21] George W. Coats, "Redactional Unity in Genesis 37–50," *JBL* 93 (1974) 15-21; Alter, *Art*, 3-4; Humphreys, *Joseph*, 37; Nahum M. Sarna, *The JPS Torah Commentary: Genesis* (Philadelphia: Jewish Publication Society, 1989) 263; Wenham, *Genesis 16–50*, 363; Wilson, *Joseph*, 86. See also Speiser, *Genesis*, 299-300.

interruption would create suspense; suspense does not explain Genesis 38 in particular.

There are parallels among various characters in Genesis 38 and the Story of Jacob's Line (as we shall see). However, in order to provide an adequate explanation for the presence of Genesis 38, several scholars have drawn on contrasting characterizations that have no foundation in the text. They note character contrasts in the sequence of Genesis 37–38 or Genesis 38–39. Some commentators, for example, claim that Judah does not mourn the death of his sons the way that Jacob mourns the loss of Joseph. When he believes that Joseph is dead, Jacob rends his clothes, puts on sackcloth, mourns, and "refused to be comforted" (וימאן להתנחם, Gen 37:34-35). When Judah's sons die, there is no mention of his mourning. Also when Judah's wife dies, he "was comforted" (וינחם יהודה, Gen 38:12).[22] Some scholars would conclude from this contrast both that Jacob's mourning is "excessive" and that "there is a real lack of responsiveness in Judah" concerning his sons' death.[23] However, this comparison is illegitimate. The narrative does not describe Jacob mourning for Rachel (Gen 35:19-21), even though he loved her (Gen 29:18, 30). This omission can hardly mean that he did not mourn or that he was not sad. Indeed, most narrated deaths in Genesis–2 Kings include little or no description of the survivors' mourning.[24] Furthermore, Judah does not marry his third son to Tamar precisely because he is afraid that his last remaining son will die (Gen 38:11). The alleged contrast between Jacob and Judah thereby breaks down. The lack of descriptive detail concerning mourning requires no explanation; its presence does. The elaborate description of Jacob's mourning for Joseph is related to Jacob's favoritism as the moving force of the plot,

---

[22] Most translations understand this to mean that the customary period of mourning has passed.

[23] Alter, *Art*, 7; followed by Humphreys, *Joseph*, 37; Wenham, *Genesis 16–50*, 345, 364-65; Hamilton, *The Book of Genesis: Chapters 18–50* (NICOT; Grand Rapids, MI: Eerdmans, 1995) 432; David M. Gunn and Danna Nolan Fewell, *Narrative in the Hebrew Bible* (Oxford: Oxford University Press, 1993) 37-38; Brodie, *Genesis*, 363; Waltke, *Genesis*, 491.

[24] Jacob's mourning for Joseph is the most detailed description of mourning in Genesis–2 Kings, with the arguable exception of the Egyptians' mourning for Jacob. Compare Deut 34:8; 1 Sam 6:19; 2 Sam 13:37; 19:2-3. Also, several passages in which a loved one dies include a minimal or even no description of mourning (Gen 23:2; 25:8-9; 35:28-29; Num 20:28-29; Deut 34:5-8; Josh 24:29-30, 33; Judg 8:32; 16:31; 1 Sam 25:1). Jacob's mourning is exceptional; Judah's is not.

which the text reinforces be recalling Jacob's grief (Gen 42:4, 36, 38). His profound grief illustrates for Judah and his co-conspirators that the problem of Jacob's preferential love cannot be solved through murder or kidnapping. Jacob still loves Joseph most even when he thinks him dead. Indeed, without the unusually elaborate description of Jacob's mourning, Judah's climactic speech (Gen 44:18-34) would lack motivation.

A similarly misguided contrast is sometimes drawn between Judah's sexual incontinence with respect to Tamar and Joseph's continence with respect to Potiphar's wife.[25] This contrast is also not fair to Judah. According to the Old Testament, sex with one taken for a prostitute is not wrong (Prov 6:26); sex with another man's wife is (Deut 22:22).[26]

Genesis 38 in Context: Toward the *Mise-en-abyme*

The observations that the Story of Jacob's Line concerns a broader topic than Joseph, and that Genesis 38 creates suspense are correct, but not adequate to explain the presence of the story of Judah and Tamar. Some commentators have therefore appealed to character contrasts that do not stand up to scrutiny. Two further observations come closer to articulating the relationship between Genesis 38 and the Story of Jacob's Line. These two most important observations concern the role of Judah and the motifs of deception and recognition. The full significance of these connections has not yet been appreciated.

The role of Judah in Genesis 38 is generally treated as preparatory to his prominence in the remainder of the Story of Jacob's Line.[27] This observation is correct but does not go far enough. Not only is Judah a major character in both narratives, but his role in Genesis 38 as the wrongdoer deceived by his victim is similar to his role in the Story

[25] Alter, *Art*, 7. Followed by Thomas W. Mann, *The Book of the Torah: The Narrative Integrity of the Pentateuch* (Atlanta: John Knox, 1988) 68; Hamilton, *Genesis 18–50*, 432; Waltke, *Genesis*, 507-8; Smith, "Central Role of Judah," 162; Wilson, *Joseph*, 91.
[26] Clifford ("Genesis 38," 526) acknowledges that the text does not judge his intercourse with a prostitute, but thinks Judah appears a fool for leaving his cord, seal, and staff in the hands of a prostitute.
[27] Clifford, "Genesis 38," 527; Mann, *Book*, 67; Carr, *Reading the Fractures of Genesis*, 247. See also Smith, "Central Role of Judah," 165.

of Jacob's Line. Clifford sees the importance of Judah's role in both narratives. He recognizes that Judah's statement in Genesis 38:26 prepares for his speech in 44:18-34. However, he sees this connection in terms of character development and identifies Judah as "the first of Jacob's sons to recognize how God brought good out of evil" and whose speech leads Joseph to the same conclusion (45:48).[28] Since Judah seems to be consistently a character willing to commit crime and to make reparations, I prefer to speak of Judah's two speeches (38:26 and 44:18-34) as connected by foreshadowing rather than character development. Furthermore, Yui-Wing Fung has rightly questioned the usual assumption that Joseph's observation about God bringing good out of evil is the thematic statement of the story.[29]

Lambe has also examined Judah's role in some depth, but arrived at a different conclusion. He suggests that Judah has a preferential love for Shelah by which he develops sympathy for Jacob's preferential love for Joseph (and later Benjamin).[30] This sympathy derived from analogous experience is said to motivate Judah's offer to be a slave in Benjamin's place. There is no suggestion in the story, however, that Judah has a preferential love for Shelah. He is never said to love any of his sons more than the others. His concern for Shelah derives from the fact that of his three sons, only Shelah is left alive. Despite the problem of Judah's alleged preferential love, Lambe is correct in seeing Genesis 38 as an important element in the characterization of Judah that prepares for his speech in Gen 44:18-34. Judah's acknowledgement of his own wrongdoing in the case of Tamar foreshadows his willingness to suffer slavery rather than repudiate his promise to his father and injure his brother. Also, the fact that both Judah and Jacob suffer the bereavement of two sons (Gen 38:7-10; 42:36) further strengthens his motive for seeking to stand in place of Benjamin as surety (ערב).

Scholars generally note the similarities between the deceptions of Tamar and Joseph, but do not consider what these similarities suggest. Most often, commentators point out the repetitions of the root נכר ("to recognize") in both stories and find in this a sufficient reason for the

---

[28] Clifford, "Genesis 38," 520.

[29] Fung, *Victim and Victimizer: Joseph's Interpretation of his Destiny* (JSOTSup 308; Sheffield: Sheffield Academic Press, 2000).

[30] Anthony J. Lambe, "Judah's Development: The Pattern of Departure—Transition—Return," *JSOT* 83 (1999) 53-68.

placement of Genesis 38.[31] Joseph's brothers ask their father to "recognize" Joseph's blood-stained coat, and "he recognized" it (הכר־נא ... ויכירה, Gen 37:32, 33). Tamar asks Judah to "recognize" his seal, cord, and staff, and "he recognized" them (הכר־נא ... ויכירה, 38:25, 26). Both these exchanges involve sending (שלח) and speaking (אמר) and the recognitions concern "my son" (בני). Furthermore, Joseph later "recognizes" his brothers in Egypt (ויכר, ויכרם, Gen 42:7, 8), yet "treats them as foreigners" (ויתנכר אליהם, 42:7), and they do "not recognize him" (לא הכרהו, 42:8). This verbal repetition is a surface indication of a deeper connection. Major plot developments hinge on these recognitions, which are intertwined with deceptions. As noted above, Jacob's recognition and lament motivate Judah's speech in Gen 44:18-34. Judah's recognition leads to his confession and the reconstitution of his family. The difference between Joseph's recognition of his brothers and their ignorance of his identity make Joseph's elaborate deception possible.

The repetition of the root נכר has not led commentators to observe the parallel between the deceptions conducted by Tamar and Judah because the verbal echo invites comparison between Judah's recognition of his personal items and Jacob's recognition of the garment he made for Joseph. However, these episodes have little in common. Judah's recognition brings an end to Tamar's deception, but Jacob's recognition is only the beginning of his sons' deception. These two deceptions have opposite moral significance. Tamar's deception is justified (Gen 38:26), but that of Jacob's sons is not. Further consideration, however, indicates the importance deception and (non)recognition as motifs. Tamar's trick is a response to the realization that Judah lied to her as he had lied to Jacob. Judah thereby does not appear similar to Jacob (as the two dialogues involving נכר might suggest). Rather, he maintains the same role in Genesis 37 and 38, and indeed throughout the Story of Jacob's Line. He resorts to fraud in order to get what he wants. However, he is also willing to acknowledge his wrong and set things right when he sees the consequences of his behavior. Although

---

[31] Coats, "Redactional Unity," 17; Alter, *Art*, 10-11; Humphreys, *Joseph*, 37-38; Wenham, *Genesis 16–50*, 364; Hamilton, *Genesis 18–50*, 431; Jan P. Fokkelman, "Genesis 37 and 38 at the Interface of Structural Analysis and Hermeneutics," in *Literary Structure and Rhetorical Strategies in the Hebrew Bible* (ed. L. J. de Regt et al.; Assen: Van Gorcum, 1996) 177-79; Brodie, *Genesis*, 364; Waltke, *Genesis*, 507; Yairah Amit, *Reading Biblical Narratives: Literary Criticism and the Hebrew Bible* (trans. Yoel Lotan; Minneapolis: Fortress, 2001) 144.

Judah is deceptive, he is himself deceived twice by others: his daughter-in-law and his brother. Tamar and Joseph appear, therefore, as parallel characters in their response to the wrongs they suffer and the successful outcome of their machinations.

Recognition is also important in places where the root נכר does not appear. Tamar "sees" that Judah lied to her about marrying Shelah (ראתה, Gen 38:14) and therefore seizes an opportunity to initiate her own deception.[32] Judah does "not know" Tamar when he mistakes her for a prostitute (לא ידע, Gen 38:16), just as he will not recognize Joseph in Egypt. Like Jacob, Potiphar presumably recognizes Joseph's garment and accepts his wife's claim about Joseph (Gen 39:14). Joseph's brothers eventually realize who he is because Joseph "makes himself known" (בהתודע, Gen 45:1).

The repetition of נכר points to the broader motif of deception.[33] It indicates Judah's role in both narratives as a wrongdoer who comes to repentance through the deceptive stratagems of his victims. It also shows Tamar and Joseph as parallel characters who right the wrongs they suffer through justified trickery.

The verbal repetition of the root ערב also indicates the broad similarities between Genesis 38 and the Story of Jacob's Line. In both stories, Judah gives a pledge on which hinges the resolution of the plot. Tamar requests a "pledge" from Judah (ערבון, Gen 38:17) that he will send the promised payment. Judah asks her to name the "pledge" (ערבון, Gen 38:18), and she asks for his "cord, seal, and staff" (חתמך ופתילך ומטך, 38:18). After he returns home, Judah sends his friend Hira to retrieve the "pledge" (ערבון, Gen 38:20), but Hira is unable to locate Tamar. Later, Judah recognizes "the cord, seal, and staff" (החתמת והפתילים והמטה, 38:25) that Tamar sends him as his own and therefore realizes that he is the cause of Tamar's pregnancy. He then acknowledges his guilt for lying to Tamar, spares her life, and accepts her children as legitimate.

---

[32] Potiphar's wife has a similar realization when she "sees" that she has Joseph's garment and can use it to make others "see" that Joseph is an attempted rapist (Gen 39:13).

[33] Wilson (*Joseph*, 87-91) notes that the motifs of deceiver deceived are found in Genesis 38 and the larger narrative, but does not articulate the parallel in detail (for example, he does not note the parallel plots or repetitions of נכר beyond Gen 37 and 38). André Wénin ("L'aventura de Juda en Genèse 38 et l'histoire de Joseph," *RB* 111 [2004] 5-27) goes further and notes "la stratégie de dissimulation de Joseph pourrait bien être de la meme nature que celle de Tamar" (p. 20) and concludes that Genesis 38 "constitue une belle prolepse de dénouement de la crise familiale par Joseph" (p. 26).

The root recurs during the brothers' second trip to Egypt. Jacob does not want Benjamin to go to Egypt because he fears he will loose the only remaining child of Rachel. Judah assures his father that he will "stand as surety" for Benjamin (אערבנו, Gen 43:9), meaning that he will bear the blame forever if Benjamin does not return. In other words, he will spare no effort to insure Benjamin's safety. Indeed, when Benjamin is threatened, Judah tells Joseph how he "stood surety" (ערב, Gen 44:32) for Benjamin and offers himself as a slave in the place of his brother. This offer motivates Joseph's revelation of his deception and the reunion and salvation of the family in Egypt. The repetitions of ערב indicate that Judah has a similar role as one who gives pledges in Genesis 38 and in the Story of Jacob's Line. Both plots turn on the revelation of a deception by means of these pledges. This parallel points to the broader similarity between the stories and suggests Genesis 38 as a possible *mise-en-abyme* within Genesis 37–50.

Genesis 38 as *Mise-en-abyme*

The verbal repetitions noted above indicate the connection between Genesis 38 and the Story of Jacob's Line. The role of Genesis 38 as a *mise-en-abyme*, however, can be most clearly seen through the parallel plots of the two narratives. The parallels are sufficiently extensive that Genesis 38 represents the totality needed in a *mise-en-abyme*. In other words, it duplicates salient aspects of the whole Story of Jacob's Line, not just miscellaneous parts.

The chart below indicates the parallel plot developments in Genesis 38 and the Story of Jacob's Line. Both stories begin with a *problem* that motivates a *crime*. The victim resorts to *deception*, the *recognition* of which leads to *confession* of the crime and *reconciliation*.[34] Although

---

[34] These divisions are based on the plot developments that illustrate the *mise-en-abyme*, but others have offered outlines of the passage based on other criteria. Martin O'Callaghan ("The Structure and Meaning of Genesis 38—Judah and Tamar," *Proceedings of the Irish Biblical Association* 5 [1981] 82) divides the test into four major sections based on chronological notices (38:1-11, 12-23, 24-26, 27-30). Diane M. Sharon ("Some Results of a Structural Semiotic Analysis of the Story of Judah and Tamar," *JSOT* 29 [2005] 289-318) finds the same textual structure, but apparently without the benefit of O'Callaghan's article. Anthony J. Lambe sees five "phases": equilibrium (38:1-6); "descent" toward disequilibrium (38:7-11); disequilibrium (38:12a); "ascent"

prior scholarship has not identified Genesis 38 as a *mise-en-abyme*, a few scholars have hinted at this function.[35] Most importantly, Paul R. Noble indicates several similarities between the two narratives.[36] However, he focuses on inner-biblical allusions and how they can be separated from coincidental similarities. The following chart resembles Noble's illustration of these similarities, but my own illustration is confined to noting the parallel plots for purposes of the subsequent discussion:

	Genesis 38	**Genesis 37–50**
Problem	38:1-10, Judah should marry Tamar to his last surviving son, but he thinks she is somehow responsible for the deaths of his first two sons	37:1-11, Joseph's brothers hate him due to Jacob's preferential treatment and Joseph's tale-bearing

---

toward equilibrium (38:12b-26); and equilibrium (38:27-30). See Lambe, "Genesis 38: Structure and Literary Design," in *The World of Genesis: Persons, Places, Perspectives* (ed. Philip R. Davies and David J. A. Clines; JSOTSup 257; Sheffield: Sheffield Academic Press, 1998) 102-20.

[35] See Peter F. Lockwood, "Tamar's Place in the Joseph Cycle," *Lutheran Theological Journal* 26 (1992) 35-43; Humphreys, *Joseph*, 37. Both scholars hint at Genesis 38 as a summary of Genesis 37–50, but neither elaborates on this observation. Wilson (*Joseph*, 87-94) speaks of Genesis 38 as a "microcosm" of the larger narrative, noting common motifs ("life emerging from death," vindication of the wronged righteous person, the deceiver deceived) and elaborating somewhat on the observations of Lockwood and Humphreys. Wénin ("L'aventure," 19-27) may provide the fullest presentation of the parallel deceptions of Tamar and Joseph, although his discussion does not reach the breadth and specificity presented here. Also, Aaron Wildavsky was an influential political scientist who sometimes wrote on the Bible. For his interpretation of Genesis 37–50, see "Survival Must Not Be Gained through Sin: The Moral of the Jospeh Stories Prefigured through Judah and Tamar," *JSOT* 62 (1994) 37-48, revised with the same title in *Assimilation versus Separation: Joseph the Administrator and the Politics of Religion in Ancient Israel* (New Brunswick, NJ: Transaction Publishers, 1993) 31-67. He reads Genesis 38 and 37–50 as two stories with a common moral lesson: "Israel must seek its survival in abiding by the moral law, not in abandoning it" (*Assimilation*, p. 41). The analogy he finds between the two stories is limited to the moral that he derives from them.

[36] Paul R. Noble, "Esau, Tamar, and Joseph: Criteria for Identifying Inner-Biblical Allusions," *VT* 52 (2002) 219-52.

	Genesis 38	Genesis 37–50
Crime	38:11, Judah sends Tamar to live as a widow in her father's house with the false promise that he will marry her to Shelah	37:12-36, Joseph's brothers sell him into slavery and lead Jacob to believe that Joseph is dead
Deception	38:12-25, Tamar tricks Judah into fathering a child with her	42–44, Joseph tricks his brothers into bringing Benjamin to Egypt
Recognition of deception	38:26, Judah recognizes he is the cause of Tamar's pregnancy	45:1-4, Joseph reveals himself to his brothers because he is moved by Judah's speech
Confession	38:26, Judah acknowledges that Tamar's deception was justified because he was in the wrong	50:15-18, Joseph's brothers openly acknowledge their crime against him and ask that he let them live
Reconciliation	38:27-30, Judah embraces Tamar's twins as his own sons so that he again has three sons and Tamar is reintegrated into the family as the mother of two sons, and the younger usurps the elder.	50:19-21, Joseph forgives his brothers and provides for them and their families. Like Tamar, he also has two sons, and the younger surpasses the elder.

The above chart illustrates how the plots of Genesis 38 and the Story of Jacob's Line are parallel. Broadly speaking, Genesis 38 duplicates the whole of the larger narrative. However, there are several episodes in the Story of Jacob's Line that have no parallel in Genesis 38. A *mise-en-abyme* does not literally reproduce everything in the larger story, but only salient aspects. The above noted plot developments in Genesis 37–50 are central and important. Readers often refer to these chapters as "the Joseph Story" or "the story of Joseph and his brothers" precisely because the narrative interest resides primarily in the sibling conflict. The passages that are not duplicated are not central to the plot development of the Story of Jacob's Line. For example, Genesis 39–41 traces Joseph's rise to power. These chapters have intrinsic interest, but they are largely instrumental: they make Joseph's deception possible. Similarly, the family's move to Egypt (Gen 45:5–47:12) saves them from starvation and prepares for the following Exodus story, but does not contribute directly to the main plot. Joseph's policy toward the Egyptians also prepares for Exodus: Joseph magnifies the power of the monarchy that will enslave his descendants and his policy foreshadows the spoiling of the Egyptians. The narration of the deaths of Jacob and Joseph close the story of the ancestors and transition to the story of a nation (cf. Exod 1:7). The death of Jacob also prepares for the reconciliation between Joseph and his brothers. All these episodes in Genesis 37–50 that are not duplicated within Genesis 38 are subordinate to the central story line.

The major episodes in Genesis 38 and the Story of Jacob's Line are, as outlined above: problem, crime, deception, recognition of deception, confession, and reconciliation. These episodes may be discussed in detail to show how Genesis 38 duplicates its embedding narrative.

Problem

The narrative supplies motivation for the crimes committed against Joseph and Tamar. In each case, characters respond to a problem with a transgression that creates further complications. Joseph's brothers have cause to hate their younger brother. He habitually brings "bad reports" about them to his father (דבתם רעה, Gen 37:2). These reports may concern only the sons of Bilhah and Zilpah, whom Joseph is helping to shepherd the flock.[37] Joseph's tale-bearing does not endear him to his brothers, but his father seems to encourage it. Jacob sends Joseph to check on his brothers and the flock and bring him a report (דבר, Gen 37:14). Jacob's preferential love for Joseph intensifies the brothers' hatred of their young brother. Jacob gives Joseph a special garment as a visible token of his preference (37:3).[38] Joseph's brothers can there

---

[37] Westermann, *Genesis 37–50*, 36. He therefore concludes that Joseph's tale-bearing relates to the rivalry between Leah and Rachel rather than the conflict among the brothers. However, these rivalries cannot be fully separated.

[38] The garment has traditionally been explained as a coat of many colors (*KJV*, Luther's Bible) on the basis of LXX and Vulg. Scholars realize that this is a fanciful explanation, but lack any firm basis for a better suggestion. The same Hebrew word

fore see (in case they could not before) that Jacob loved Joseph more than his brothers (ויראו אחיו כי־אתו אהב אביהם מכל־אחיו 37:4). In their hatred (וישנאו אתו, 37:4), they are unable to speak peaceably with Joseph. The cold treatment he receives from his brothers does not stop Joseph from telling them about his first dream that suggests that he will rule over his older brothers (37:6-8).[39] His brothers begin to "hate him even more" because of his dream and his brazen report of it (ויוספו עוד שנא אתו, 37:5). Joseph tells his second dream to his brothers and his father (37:9-10). His father's reaction shows that the brothers have cause to be upset. Although he loves Joseph above all his children, Jacob rebukes him for relating his dream (37:10). The narrative describes a progressive tension within the family. The growing hatred and jealousy (ויקנאו־בו אחיו, 37:11) that the brothers have for Joseph must be resolved. The narrative offers ample motive for the serious crime that the brothers commit against Joseph.

Judah's crime against Tamar also develops out of a problem. The first part of the narrative establishes the necessary background to the problem: Judah marries and has three sons (Gen 38:1-5). Judah marries Er his firstborn to Tamar, but Er dies soon after. Onan likewise dies shortly after marrying Tamar. Judah does not know why his first two sons have died, but he assumes that their deaths are somehow related to their union with Tamar (cf. Tob 3:8; 6:14; 8:9-14).[40] Therefore, he is reluctant to marry Tamar to Shelah, his last remaining son (Gen 38:11). Judah's problem is that, according to custom, he should marry Tamar to Shelah, but he is afraid that Shelah will die as a consequence. In

---

describes the garment of a princess in 2 Sam 13:18. The significance of Joseph's garment concerns its special (expensive) quality. For further discussion, see David Noel Freedman and Michael O'Connor, "*kuttōnet*," in *TDOT* 7:383-87.

[39] Some commentators defend Joseph against the charge that by his reporting his dreams he shows himself imprudent or boastful. For example, von Rad (*Genesis*, 351-52) claims that "a vision was for the ancients so important and obligatory that a demand to keep it tactfully to oneself would not have occurred to them." Fung (*Victim*, 134 n. 17), however, points out that other characters in Genesis do not behave this way. Rebecca seems not to have reported her vision to Isaac (Gen 25:22-23), nor do Abraham or Jacob appear to share their various visions with others. The Egyptian prisoners only reluctantly tell Joseph their dreams, and Pharaoh reports his dreams because they trouble him.

[40] Similarly, Sarah's maid does not know why Sarah's husbands keep dying. She imagines that Sarah strangles them (Tob 3:8, reading ἀποπνίγουσα, "strangler," with LXX$^{A\,B\,319}$; LXX^{S} reads ἀποκτέννουσα, "killer, murderess"). Judah may or may not have such dark suspicions.

Genesis 38, as in 37, characters face problems that tempt them to illicit solutions.

Both stories begin with threats to the family. Jacob's family seethes with hatred and jealousy stemming from Jacob's preferential love, Joseph's dreams, and his tale bearing. Judah's family nears extinction as his sons die. Consequently, he does not trust his daughter-in-law, who appears to be associated with these deaths. Some characters have good reasons to harm Joseph and Tamar.

Crime

The solutions that characters find for the conflicts in both stories create further complications. These complications arise in part from the fact that the attempted solutions are crimes. When Joseph's brothers see him alone in an area remote from the protection of home, they decide to kill him (Gen 37:18-20). Later, they decide to sell him to Ishmaelite merchants as a slave instead (37:26-27). The second plan is a mitigation of the first, but kidnapping is still a serious crime, comparable to murder.[41] In the course of events, Midianites find Joseph and sell him to the same group of Ishmaelite merchants.[42] The brothers

[41] Albrecht Alt ("Das Verbot des Diebstahls im Dekalog," in *Kleine Schriften zur Geschichte des Volkes Israel* [3 vols.; Munich: C. H. Beck, 1953-59] 1. 333-40) suggests that the prohibition against theft in the Decalogue (Exod 20:15; Deut 5:17) originally outlawed kidnapping (similarly rabbinic exegesis, cf. *Sanh.* 86a). More recent exegesis holds that kidnapping may have been outlawed by the commandment as part of the wider crime of theft. Robert Gnuse (*You Shall not Steal: Community and Property in the Biblical Tradition* [Maryknoll, NY: Orbis, 1985) accepts Alt's "insight that the commandment against stealing was designed to protect persons and not property" (p. 9). Thus understood, the commandment equally protects the poor from capitalistic exploitation and the wealthy from large scale communistic redistribution of wealth (p. 123). See also Jeffery H. Tigay, *The JPS Torah Commentary: Deuteronomy* (Philadelphia: Jewish Publication Society, 1996) 71; Walter Brueggemann, "The Book of Exodus," in *NIB* 1. 848.

[42] The Ishmaelite/Midianite problem has long exercised commentators. It has been a basis for source division in Genesis 37. More recently, scholars employing a literary approach have tried to make sense of the text as it stands. Possibly, the brothers plan to sell Joseph to the Ishmaelites, but while they are at some distance from Joseph discussing the matter, Midianites find Joseph and sell him first to the Ishmaelites. See Adele Berlin, *Poetics and Interpretation of Biblical Narrative* (1983, reprint Winona Lake, IN: Eisenbrauns, 1994) 113-21; and Edward L. Greenstein, "An Equivocal Reading of the Sale of Joseph," in *Literary Interpretation of Biblical Narratives: Volume*

find only an empty pit instead of Joseph and must face Jacob without him. Joseph's disappearance leaves Jacob inconsolable and makes the rift between the brothers and Joseph seemingly irreparable. Thus, the brothers create further problems by their criminal attempt to resolve their conflict with Joseph. Jacob still loves Joseph most of all, but now he is plunged into inconsolable grief.

Judah also resolves his dilemma with respect to Tamar illegitimately. He sends her to live in her father's house as a widow with a false promise to marry her to Shelah when Shelah comes of age. Evidently, he plans to let Tamar languish in her widowhood and eventually to seek another female to continue his line through Shelah (Gen 38:11b). Since Judah has promised to give Tamar to Shelah, Tamar may not marry another man. Judah's crime against Tamar is similar to that of Onan's: both men would condemn Tamar to a life of childless widow-hood.[43] Tamar has no evident means by which she can have legitimate children.[44] Judah's attempted solution to his dilemma creates further

---

II (ed. Kenneth R. R. Gros Louis with James S. Ackerman; Nashville: Abingdon, 1982) 114-25.

[43] Onan's motive is greed (cf. a similar reluctance in Deut 25:7-10 and Ruth 4:5-6). As the second of three sons, he stands to inherit one fourth of his father's estate, since the firstborn receives a double portion. The death of Er means he will inherit one half of the estate, or two-thirds if he is accorded the status of firstborn (which may be a social status rather than a biological one, cf. Gen 25:29-34). Replacing Er by fathering a son with Tamar will only reduce his inheritance. By pretending to perform the levi-rate duty, while actually spilling his seed, Onan expects to cause Tamar to bear the stigma of apparent barrenness and thereby increase his own inheritance. Biblical texts present levirate marriage as an institution favored by widows and avoided by levirs. See Raymond Westbrook, "The Law of the Biblical Levirate," in *Property and Family in Biblical Law* (JSOTSup 113; Sheffield: Sheffield Academic Press, 1991) 69-89; Dvora E. Weisberg, "The Widow of Our Discontnent: Levirate Marriage in the Bible and Ancient Israel," JSOT 28 (2004) 403-429. On the ancient Near Eastern context, see also P. Cruveilhier, "Le Lévirat chez les Hébreux et chez les Assyriens," *RB* 34 (1925) 524-46; Eva Salm, *Judah und Tamar: Ein exegetische Studie zu Gen 38* (FB 76; Würzburg: Echter Verlag, 1996) 137-50. On the social status of first-born, see Frederick E. Green-spahn, *When Brothers Dwell Together: The Preeminence of the Younger Siblings in the Hebrew Bible* (Oxford: Oxford University Press, 1994) 58-69. Concerning the erro-neous ancient interpretation of Onan's crime as masturbation and its consequences for moral theology, see Michael S. Patton, ""Masturbation from Judaism to Victorian-ism," *Journal of Religion and Health* 24 (1985) 133-46; P. Grelot, "Le Péché de ʾÔnān" (Gn., XXXVIII,9)," *VT* 49 (1999) 143-55; Forrest L. Bivens, "Exegetical Brief: Genesis 38:8-10—the Sin of Onan," *Wisconsin Lutheran Quarterly* 98 (2001) 210-14.

[44] Weisberg ("Widow of Our Discontent," 414-15) notes "Genesis 38 offers no mechanism to dissolve the levirate bond; we are left with the sense that Tamar might

tension. He has placed Tamar in an impossible situation and abandoned hope of gaining offspring for Er and Onan through Tamar. The fertility of Jacob's family does not seem destined to continue through Judah.[45] The crimes committed against Tamar and Joseph create further problems not only for the victims, but also for the whole family.

---

be forced to remain a widow in her father's household indefinitely, unable to marry outside of Judah's family."

[45] Tamar, as a virtuous foreign women through whom the genealogy of David is traced, is explicitly compared to Ruth in Ruth 4:12. This point is explicit in Ruth 4:12, 18-22, but implicit in Genesis 38. The genealogy of David is connected to Tamar through Perez in Ruth 4:18-22; 1 Chr 2:3-15; Matt 1:3; Luke 3:33. Almost all commentators are agreed that Tamar is a Canaanite. See discussion by J. A. Emerton, "An Examination of a Recent Structuralist Interpretation of Genesis XXXVIII," *VT* 26 (1976) 90-93. John Calvin (*Commentaries on the First Book of Moses called Genesis* [2 vols.; trans. John King; Edinburgh: Calvin Translation Society, 1850] 2. 279) claims that Yhwh kills Er and Onan to punish Judah for marrying a Canaanite. Both women serve as counter-examples to the claim that foreign women threaten the integrity of the family and its traditions. See Thomas Krüger, "Genesis 38—ein 'Lehrstück' alttestamentlicher Ethik," in *Kritische Weisheit: Studien zur weisheitlichen Traditionskritik im Alten Testament* (Zurich: Pano, 1997) 1-22. Similarly, Bernhard Luther, "The Novella of Judah and Tamar and Other Israelite Novellas," in *Narrative and Novella: Studies by Hugo Gressman and Other Scholars 1906-1923* (trans. David E. Orton; ed. David M. Gunn; JSOTSup 116; Sheffield: Almond, 1991) 118. On the motif of exogamous marriage, see Thomas and Dorothy Thompson, "Some Legal Problems in the Book of Ruth," *VT* 18 (1968) 79-99; George W. Coats, "Widow's Rights: A Crux in the Structure of Genesis 38," *CBQ* 34 (1972) 461-66; J. A. Emerton, "Judah and Tamar," *VT* 29 (1979) 403-15; Esther Fuchs, "Status and Role of Female Heroines in the Biblical Narrative," in *Women in the Hebrew Bible* (ed. Alice Bach; New York: Routledge, 1999) 77-84; Fuchs, "The Literary Characterization of Mothers and Sexual Politics in the Hebrew Bible," in *Women and the Bible*, 127-39; Johanna W. H. Bos, "Out of the Shadows: Genesis 38; Judges 4:17-22; Ruth 3," in *Reasoning with the Foxes: Female Wit in a World of Male Power* (ed. J. Cheryl Exum and Johanna W. H. Bos; Semeia 42; Atlanta: Scholars, 1988) 37-67; Nelly Furman, "His Story Versus Her Story: Male Genealogy and Female Strategy in the Jacob Cycle," in *Women in the Hebrew Bible*, 119-26; Ellen van Wolde, "Texts in Dialogue with Texts: Intertextuality in the Ruth and Tamar Narratives," *BibInt* 5 (1997) 1-28; Katherine Doob Sakenfield, "Why Perez? Reflections on David's Genealogy in Biblical Tradition," in *David and Zion: Biblical Studies in Honor of J. J. M. Roberts* (eds. Bernard F. Batto and Katherine L. Roberts; Winone Lake, IN: Eisenbrauns, 2004) 405-416. Some scholars have read Genesis 38 in relation to the story of the rape of a different Tamar in 2 Samuel 13: Fokkelein van Dijk-Hemmes, "Tamar and the Limits of Patriarchy: Between Rape and Seduction (2 Samuel 13 and Genesis 38)," in *Anti-Covenant: Counter-Reading Women's Lives in the Hebrew Bible* (ed. Mieke Bal; JSOTSup 81; Sheffield: Almond, 1989) 135-56; Gary A. Rendsburg, "David and his Circle in Genesis XXXVIII," *VT* 36 (1986) 438-46; Craig Y. S. Ho, "The Stories of the Family Troubles of Judah and David: A Study of their Literary Links," *VT* 49 (1999) 514-31.

Those who perpetrate the crimes against Tamar and Joseph seek to protect the integrity and continuity of the family. However, the crimes result in the separation of each victim from the life of the family. Er and Judah would both condemn Tamar to a childless life that, at Judah's request, she will live out in her father's house away from Judah. Joseph's brothers spare his life, but commit him to slavery in a foreign land. Both Tamar and Joseph have good reasons to seize opportunities to correct the misfortunes they have suffered.

Deception

Tamar and Joseph both resort to deception as a means of repairing the damage done by the crimes of Judah and Joseph's brothers, respectively. As noted above, the deceptions in both stories involve a "pledge" (ערב). The deceptions share additional features.

Both deceptions are opportunistic: Tamar and Joseph see circumstances they can exploit to their benefit. Judah's wife dies and he leaves on a journey to shear his sheep, which was an occasion for celebration (cf. 2 Sam 13:23).[46] Tamar suspects that Judah will have a need for sex and places herself in a position to satisfy that need through her disguise as a prostitute and her presence along his path. Joseph's deception depends on appearing before him to buy grain. Like Judah, they have a need, but theirs is for food, not sex. Joseph satisfied their need and sends them away with plenty of grain.

Both deceptions hinge on disguise involving clothing. Tamar changes her clothes and wears a veil so that Judah will mistake her for a prostitute (Gen 38:14).[47] When Joseph's brothers come to Egypt, they do not recognize Joseph, the governor of the land (Gen 42:6). As part of his

---

[46] Jeffrey C. Geoghegan ("Israelite Sheepshearing and David's Rise to Power," *Bib* 87 [2006] 55-63) notes that the biblical evidence indicates that sheepshearing was also occasion for licentiousness, trickery, and revenge.

[47] Most commentators think that prostitutes wore veils, so Tamar's veil serves the double purpose of concealing her identity and leading Judah to believe she is a prostitute. For a full discussion of the issue and a contrary opinion, see John R. Huddlestun, "Unveiling the Versions: The Tactics of Tamar in Genesis 38:15," *The Journal of Hebrew Scriptures* 3 (2001) http://www.purl.org/jhs. The two different words used in the passage for "prostitute" (זונה, קדשה) likely represent the difference between private and public speech. Phyllis A. Bird (*Missing Persons and Mistaken Identities: Women and Gender in Ancient Israel* [OBT; Minneapolis: Fortress, 1997] 208) suggests the first

promotion from imprisoned slave to Pharaoh's vizier, Pharaoh clothes him in fine linen, gives him his own signet ring, a gold chain, and a new name (Gen 41:37-45).[48]

Both deceptions include an attempted payment by the deceived. Judah seeks to keep his promise of payment, but Tamar does not wait to accept it because her deception depends on keeping Judah's pledge. Joseph's brothers attempt to pay for the grain they acquire in Egypt, but Joseph has their money returned to them.

Both deceptions share a similar motive. Tamar and Joseph seek to repair the damage done by the crimes committed against them, especially their separation from their families. The motives, discussed in the next section on recognition of deception, are easier to discern when the deceptions are complete. Briefly stated, Tamar gets the children that Er and Judah sought to deprive her of. Joseph gets his family back (he seems especially concerned for Benjamin) and he is vindicated when his dreams of supremacy come true. Tamar and Joseph engage in deception in order to regain what they lost when their relatives harmed them.

Both deceptions are justified. Michael James Williams has examined all the major deceptions in Genesis and found that "deception is positively evaluated only when the perpetrators deceive one who has previously wronged them in order to restore their own situations to what they would have been had they not been disrupted."[49] Judah himself endorses this evaluation of Tamar's deception (Gen 38:26). Williams notes that Joseph's two deceptions of his brothers (Gen 42:7-28; 43:1-34) are not explicitly assessed, but the outcome of the deceptions suggests that they are justified.[50] Of the fifteen deceptions analyzed, only the deceptions of Joseph and Tamar are justified by the narrative.

---

might be translated "whore" and the second "courtesan." See also Speiser, *Genesis*, 300; Berlin, *Poetics*, 60-61; Hamilton, *Genesis 18-50*, 447.

[48] See Victor H. Matthews, "Anthropology of Clothing in the Joseph Narrative," *JSOT* 65 (1995) 25-36. The clothing that Joseph receives from Jacob and Pharaoh mark his status as a favorite of each. The seizure of his garments by his brothers and by Potiphar's wife indicate his change in status. Finally, Joseph gives clothing to his brothers to indicate his favor toward them, just as he gives extra clothing to Benjamin to show his preference for him (45:22).

[49] Williams, *Deception in Genesis: An Investigation into the Morality of a Unique Biblical Phenomenon* (Studies in Biblical Literature 32; New York: Peter Lang, 2001) 221. Williams does not treat minor deceptions, such as Judah's deception of Tamar.

[50] Williams, *Deception*, 27-28.

Tamar and Joseph are parallel characters in parallel plots. Their deceptions also share several specific similarities that reinforce the conclusion that Genesis 38 is a *mise-en-abyme* in the Story of Jacob's Line.

Recognition of Deception

The deceptions of Tamar and Joseph conclude with the recognition of the deception. In both cases, the deceiver reveals the deception. Furthermore, Judah instigates the revelation in both instances.

In Genesis 38, Tamar's deception ends when Judah recognizes his seal, cord, and staff and realizes that Tamar was the prostitute he encountered along the road to Enaim (Gen 38:26). Tamar's revelation is motivated by her impending execution. Her hope is that Judah will acknowledge paternity of her children and spare her life. Most translations render the report to Judah in Gen 38:24 (זנתה תמר כלתך וגם הנה הרה לזנונים) as "Your daughter-in-law Tamar has played the harlot; furthermore she is with child by harlotry" (*KJV*, similarly *NJPSV*, *NRSV*, *NAB*, *NJB*). This translation seems to be influenced by the fact that the translators know from the prior narrative that Tamar has been mistaken for a prostitute. The root זנה translated as "harlot/harlotry" indicates several forms of sexual misconduct. Tamar's pregnancy is evidence that she has had sex, not necessarily that she was paid for it.[51] Since Tamar is betrothed to Shelah, she is not free to have sex with anyone else. Judah assumes that she could not have had sex with Shelah and condemns her for her infidelity to her promised husband, even though Judah himself has no intention of keeping the promise of marriage. This constraint on Tamar explains why *only* her deception can save her from childlessness. She must acquire a child that Judah will acknowledge as legitimate, or no child at all. She is not free to contract another marriage. A suitable translation of the report in Gen 38:24 is thus: "Your daughter-in-law Tamar has been unfaithful;

---

[51] Bird, *Missing Persons*, 105: "What the Hebrew means . . . is that Tamar, who is bound by her situation to chastity, has engaged in illicit intercourse, the evidence of which is her pregnancy."

furthermore she is with child by her infidelity."[52] Her purpose is to acquire children and avoid the barren widowhood Judah plans for her. Judah certainly intends to marry Shelah to someone, just not Tamar. Judah's recognition of his cord, seal, and staff is immediately followed by his confession "She is righteous, not I," (צדקה ממני, Gen 38:26) and the reconciliation of the family, which I will discuss below.

In the case of Joseph and his brothers, there is more textual distance between the recognition of deception (Gen 45:4) and the confession and reconciliation (Gen 50:15-21). Joseph drops his deception and reveals himself to his brothers (Gen 45:4) as a result of Judah's selfless speech (Gen 44:18-34). Joseph designs his "test" not to discover whether the brothers are spies (since he knows they are not), but to determine whether they would repeat their crime against him by harming Benjamin. He discovers this by engineering a situation unmistakably analogous to that of Genesis 37. This time, Judah refuses to doom his father's favorite even at enormous cost to himself. This test depends on the close association of Joseph and Benjamin as the two sons of Rachel and Jacob's favorites. Benjamin takes the place of Joseph in a test to discover whether the brothers have repented of their prior crime against Joseph. Judah's speech is proof that Benjamin is safe from his brothers, who now repent of their crime against Joseph (cf. Gen 42:21-22).[53]

Judah's speech leads Joseph to bring Jacob's family down to Egypt that they may survive the famine (45:9-11). This family reunion, however, is only a partial resolution of the problems of the story. Since Judah does not recognize Joseph when he makes his climactic speech, he offers no apology or confession of guilt that might result in reconciliation among the brothers. His speech is therefore not comparable to his confession in Gen 38:26 ("She is righteous, not I"), but rather to his recognition of his seal, cord, and staff in the same verse (ויכר יהודה, "Judah recognized them"). Joseph encourages his brothers not to be distressed because of their crime against him, since this has put him

---

[52] See Bird, *Missing Persons*, 208.

[53] On this reading of Joseph's motives, see Meir Sternberg, *The Poetics of Biblical Narrative: Ideological Literature and the Drama of Reading* (Bloomington: Indiana University Press, 1987) 285-308.

in position to save the family (45:5). The immediate consequence of the revelation of Joseph's deception is the journey of Jacob to Egypt.

Judah is instrumental in both recognition scenes. Tamar shows the pledge to Judah for his acknowledgement because he is about to have her burned alive for infidelity. Joseph makes himself known because he is so moved by Judah's speech. Although Judah's actions in these two cases are different (cruel in Genesis 38, generous in Genesis 44), he instigates the end of the deception, which brings about the confession and reconciliation.

Confession and Resolution

The recognition of the deceptions of both Tamar and Joseph result in the resolution of the problems created by the crime committed against each of them. An important element of this resolution is the confession of wrong by those who sinned against them. When confronted with the evidence of Tamar's deceit, Judah acknowledges his paternity of Tamar's twins and admits, "She is righteous, not I, because I did not give her to my son Shelah" (Gen 38:26). Because of this admission on Judah's part, Tamar's twins are acknowledged as legitimate and become the fathers of two clans of the tribe of Judah. Tamar is thereby reintegrated into Jacob's family and liberated from her childless widowhood. Furthermore, her twins replace the two dead sons of Judah. Thus, the family problems that develop in the chapter are resolved through the confession of Judah elicited by the revelation of Tamar's deception.

Similarly, Joseph's deception of his brothers leads to a resolution of the problems that arise in the beginning of the Story of Jacob's Line. The resolution of the larger narrative is more complicated than Genesis 38. After Joseph's brothers are in prison, they betray their sense of guilt over their crime against Joseph (Gen 42:21-22). This admission does not lead to immediate reconciliation because the brothers do not realize who Joseph is or that he understands their conversation. The speech does indicate that the brothers experience remorse for their crime and so prepares for the later resolution. As noted above, Judah's speech in which he offers to be a slave in place of Benjamin is also not the final confession and resolution of the story.

The brothers do not fully acknowledge their crime openly until Gen 50:15-21.[54] The narrative of the family reunited in Egypt is silent concerning the conflict among the brothers. The problem that the crime created for Jacob (Gen 37:34-35; 42:36, 38) is resolved when Jacob meets Joseph (46:30), blesses Ephraim and Manasseh (48:11), and dies in the presence of his sons (49:33; cf. 46:4). The text does not describe a scene that resolves the conflict among the brothers until after Jacob is dead and buried. Joseph's brothers worry that only Jacob's presence has restrained Joseph from exacting vengeance for their treatment of him (50:15). They invoke their dead father to ask Joseph to forgive their crime against him and offer to be his slaves.[55] Joseph forgives them their offense, citing the good consequences of their plot. He does not make them slaves, but provides for them and their families. This scene (50:15-21) provides the closest analogue to Judah's confession in Gen 38:26 that resolves the problems within his own family.

After the recognition of the deceptions, those who wronged Tamar and Joseph admit their wrong to their victims. These are not confessions in the sense of revelations of secrets; Tamar already knows that she is righteous and Judah is not. The acknowledgement, however, facilitates the reconciliation that restores the family relationships. In the end, both Tamar and Joseph have two sons, whose priority becomes reversed. Thus, family relationships are repaired, the family survives the famine, and continues into the next generation.

---

[54] Contra Westermann (*Genesis 37–50*, 204), who says "the repetition of the reconciliation of Joseph with his brothers has no necessary function in the course of the narrative." Coats (*Genesis*, 311-12) thinks that "the Joseph novella ends in 47:27, with no strands of plot left open. Rather than a continuation of the story, with a new line of development for one or more of its principal motifs, this short section represent a recapitulation of the denouement." See similarly, Redford, *A Study*, 163; Sternberg, *Poetics*, 178; Fung, *Victim*, 32.

[55] Several commentators claim that Joseph's brothers lie about Jacob's request (50:17) because the text nowhere narrates this scene and the brothers' message is motivated by fear. So, Sternberg, *Poetics*, 379. This conclusion assumes an erroneous reading of biblical narrative and an overly harsh assessment of Joseph's brothers. Sternberg thinks that Jacob never discovers the crime that his sons committed, but Gen 45:25-28 suggests otherwise. It seems that the brothers could only persuade Jacob that Joseph lives by admitting their sin.

Mise-en-abyme: Pattern of Repetition

The *mise-en-abyme* represents a specific kind of textual repetition in which a whole text is duplicated within one of its own parts. In order to include a *mise-en-abyme*, a text must have a measure of sophisticated repetition. One would not expect to find the device in a simple chronicle. Several commentators have noticed a pattern of duplication in the Story of Jacob's Line. This pattern involves several forms of repetition, analogy, and correspondence. The repetitions are significant because they create an environment ripe for the application of the *mise-en-abyme*. As a *mise-en-abyme*, Genesis 38 fits into its embedding narrative not only by duplicating the whole story, but also by participating in its larger pattern of repetition. The following catalogue includes almost all the examples of doubling already observed in the narrative, as well as some additional observations.

Joseph has two dreams (Gen 37:5-7, 9), his two fellow prisoners each dream a dream (Gen 40:5, 9-11, 16-19), and Pharaoh has two dreams (Gen 41:17-21, 22-24). Joseph tells Pharaoh that his two dreams are one (Gen 41:25). He draws attention to the doubling of Pharaoh's dream and says it means that the events are fixed and will happen soon (Gen 41:32). The doubling of Joseph's dream may indicate the fixity of his future ascendancy over his brothers, but seems not to suggest that the event will happen in the near future, since the fulfillment is twenty-two years after the dreams.[56]

---

[56] Although the first dream predicts his ascendancy over his brothers, the second dream is problematic because his mother is already dead and his father never bows down to him. R. Pirson ("The Sun, the Moon, and Eleven Stars: An Interpretation of Joseph's Second Dream," in *Studies in the Book of Genesis: Literature, Redaction and History* [ed. A. Wénin; BETL 155; Leuven: Leuven University Press, 2001] 561-68) suggests that Jacob's interpretation (Gen 37:10) of Joseph's second dream (37:9) is mistaken. Joseph's second dream is not strictly a doubling of the first, like Pharaoh's, that signifies impending fulfillment. In fact, Joseph must wait over two decades for his brothers to bow down to him. Pirson argues that the second dream of Joseph indicates the time that will elapse before the first dream is fulfilled. The sun, moon, and eleven stars add up to thirteen, which is the number of years that Joseph spends as a slave and prisoner before he becomes Pharaoh's second in command (Joseph is seventeen years old in Gen 37:2, and thirty in 41:46). The celestial bodies may also refer to eleven years times two, which corresponds to the twenty-two years that elapse between Joseph's descent into Egypt and his ascendancy over his brothers (adding to the prior calculation the seven years of plenty and two of famine).

Joseph is sent to find his brothers first in Shechem (37:12-14), then in Dothan (37:15-17) and soon finds himself in the custody of Midianites, then Ishamelites (Gen 37:25-28).[57] Additional duplications include the brothers' two trips to Egypt (42:3; 43:15). During each visit, they have two audiences with Joseph (42:6-17, 18-24; 43:15-16, 26-34).[58] Joseph orders money placed in their bags both times (42:25; 44:1). On the second trip, the brothers bring double the money for the grain (43:12, 15). Reuben and Judah each attempt to persuade Jacob to allow Benjamin to go to Egypt with them (42:37; 43:8-9). Jacob's family is twice invited to stay in Egypt: first by Joseph (45:9-11), then by Pharaoh (45:17-20). Joseph twice accuses his brothers of spying (42:9, 14). The brothers formulate two plans for Joseph (37:20, 27) that correspond to the two plans that Joseph formulates for his brothers (42:15-16, 18-20). In each case, the second plan is more merciful than the first.

The several deceptions in the story fit into a similar doubling pattern. Joseph's brothers lead Jacob to believe that Joseph has been killed by a wild animal (Gen 37:20, 32-33). Joseph will later deceive his brothers (Gen 42:7-26; 44:1-17). There is symmetry in the brothers' deception of Jacob and Joseph's deception of his brothers. There is a similar poetic justice in Tamar's deception of Judah after he lied to her.

The favor that Joseph finds in the houses of Potiphar and the jailor are narrated in similar terms (39:2-6, 21-23). Both experiences foreshadow Joseph's elevation by Pharaoh (41:37-44). Of the many attempts of Potiphar's wife to seduce Joseph (39:10), two are narrated in detail: the first (39:7-9) and the last (37:11-12). She repeats her accusations against Joseph, first to the men of her household (39:14-15), then to her husband (39:16-18).

The doubling also occurs with offspring. Joseph himself is one of the two sons of Rachel. In Joseph's absence, his brother Benjamin becomes Jacob's favorite. Both are called the son of Jacob's old age (37:3; 44:20). In

[57] The Ishmaelite/Midianite problem may be a doubling of this kind if one accepts that the Midianite found Joseph and sold him to the Ishmaelites. See above n. 42.

[58] Some scholars understand the final audience (44:14–45:15) as separate from the two trips to Egypt. See Redford, *A Study*, 75; and James S. Ackerman, "Joseph, Judah, and Jacob," in *Genesis* (ed. Harold Bloom; Modern Critical Interpretations; New York: Chelsea House, 1986) 87, originally published in *Literary Interpretations of Biblical Narratives: Volume II* (ed. Kenneth R. Gros Louis with James S. Ackerman; Nashville: Abingdon, 1982) 85-113. Humphreys (*Joseph*, 97-98) counts it as a third audience and parallels it with the anticipated third audience during the brothers' first trip to Egypt (42:29-34).

the story, Judah and Reuben also form a kind of pair. Both are prominent characters among the brothers of Joseph who have competing ideas about what to do with Joseph (37:21-22, 26-27) and how to guarantee the safety of Benjamin (42:37; 43:8-9). Jacob and Joseph also form a pair. Both men wield authority over Joseph's brothers, die in Egypt, and are embalmed (Gen 50:2, 26). Judah and Jacob also have something in common: both believe themselves bereaved of two children. Jacob is mistaken (Gen 42:36); his sons are restored to him. Judah really looses two sons, but later fathers two new sons with Tamar.

The speeches of characters multiply the doubling of events. Several speeches recount events that were previously narrated. Some of these events are merely alluded to, such as Joseph's brothers recalling Joseph's dreams as they plan to kill him (37:19), and Joseph remembering the same dream when he first sees them in Egypt (42:9). Other repetitions, however, are more elaborate. Pharaoh's chief cupbearer narrates his imprisonment with the chief baker, and Joseph's accurate interpretation of their dreams (41:9-13). Pharaoh's dreams are first told by the narrator (41:1-7), then by Pharaoh (41:17-24). Joseph's brothers briefly present their family situation and the absence of two of their brothers (42:13). The brothers recall their treatment of Joseph in more detail while they are in prison (42:21), and Reuben brags of his attempt to save the boy (42:22). Jacob twice hears about his sons' encounter with the disguised Joseph: first from all the brothers (42:29-34), then from Judah (43:3-7). Judah's speech summarizes much of the preceding action (44:18-34).

The speeches that summarize events previously narrated frequently include extensive verbal repetition as well as variation. Only the double accusation of Potiphar's wife is so different from the actual course of events that it is recognizable as a lie. She relates her encounter with Joseph in a manner strikingly different from that given in the prior narrative. She has a different explanation of why she has Joseph's garment in her possession.

In addition to the major doubling mentioned above, the text includes minor repetitions. For example, gum, balm, and resin are twice brought down to Egypt (37:25; 43:11). Both Jacob and Judah speak of going to Egypt for grain "that we may live and not die" (ונחיה ולא נמות, Gen 42:2; 43:8). The Egyptians use the same phrase when they offer themselves as slaves to Pharaoh in exchange for food (ונחיה ולא נמות, Gen 47:19).

Scholars have offered various explanations for the pattern of doubling. Redford argues that the pattern of doubling serves several functions: emphasis, plot retardation (suspense), and characterization.[59] Waltke follows the lead of Joseph (Gen 41:32) and suggests that the doubling of plot elements point "to the unseen hand of Providence."[60] Westermann thinks the doubling emphasizes certain plot elements and provokes reflection through the diverse perspectives in which doubled events appear.[61] Similarly, Humphreys sees the doubling as a narrative technique by which the text provides commentary on itself.[62] Narrative doubling is not strictly commentary because it is not expository. It does create analogies, however, which invite the reader to consider the similarities and differences among elements of the text. Although commentators have noticed the repetitions in Gen 37:2–50:26, they have not yet recognized the full role of Genesis 38 within this pattern of doubling.

As a *mise-en-abyme* within the Story of Jacob's Line, Genesis 38 participates in this pattern of doubling. Tamar's twins form a pair corresponding to Joseph's two sons. Both sets of sons are born of a foreign woman. The symmetry of the brothers' deception of Jacob and Joseph's deception of the brothers is reduplicated in the symmetry between Judah's deception of Tamar and Tamar's deception of Judah. When she realizes that Judah has lied about marrying her to Shelah, she initiates her plan to become pregnant by Judah (Gen 38:13-14). Genesis 38 duplicates the Story of Jacob's Line and therefore fits into this pattern of doubling. Accordingly, Genesis 38 may be viewed as a *mise-en-abyme* of the Story of Jacob's Line. Both stories have a similar plot development from problem, crime, and deception, to confession and resolution. Judah is a prominent character in both stories and has the same role of one who does harm and is later deceived by his victim. Both stories involve threats to the integrity and continuity of the family. These similarities of plot, character, and theme bind the story of Judah and Tamar to the larger Story of Jacob's Line of which it is a part.

---

[59] Redford, *A Study*, 74-87. Redford includes several synoptic charts (in English) showing the variation within repetition between narrated events and their restatement in direct speech.

[60] Waltke, *Genesis*, 495.

[61] Westermann, *Genesis 37–50*, 246-47.

[62] Humphreys, *Joseph*, 99.

Conclusion

I have elucidated the major similarities between Genesis 38 and the Story of Jacob's Line in an effort to show that Genesis 38 is a *mise-en-abyme* of the larger narrative within which it occurs. These similarities involve two main aspects: the analogous plot structure and the role of Judah. In both stories, Judah wrongs a member of his family and is then deceived by his victim. The plot of both stories progresses from problem, crime, deception, to recognition of deception, confession and resolution. The analogy between the two narratives suggests that Genesis 38 is a *mise-en-abyme*. This observation leads to three major insights concerning the Story of Jacob's Line.

First, Genesis 38 fits into the pattern of doubling that commentators have observed in the Story of Jacob's Line. By duplicating the plot of the larger narrative, Genesis 38 highlights its most critical developments. The most important passages in the Story of Jacob's Line are Genesis 37, in which the problem and crime are articulated, Genesis 42–44 in which the deception is narrated, Gen 45:1-15 in which Joseph reveals the deception, and Gen 50:15-21 in which Joseph and his brothers are finally reconciled. The identification of Genesis 38 as a *mise-en-abyme* within the Story of Jacob's Line closely connects the chapter to its context and moves beyond prior attempts to discern the relationship between the two stories. Genesis 38 underscores the importance of justified deception in the larger story and accentuates the narrative concern with the survival and continuity of the family, which is the goal of both deceptions.

This first consideration leads to a second. The similarity of plot suggests a close relationship between Gen 45:1-15 and 50:15-21. These two passages have sometimes been understood as repetitive. As I have shown above, however, Gen 45:1-15 is the recognition of the deception by which Joseph and his brothers are reunited, but it does not include any expression of repentance on the part of Joseph's brothers. Therefore, Gen 50:15-21 does not repeat any supposed reconciliation in Gen 45:1-15.

A third interpretive problem in the Story of Jacob's Line is highlighted by this comparison with Genesis 38. Joseph's motives for his elaborate deception are not stated. Commentators are left to fill this gap on their own. Joseph has been variously characterized as desiring revenge or generously plotting to reconcile his family without particular concern for his own suffering. Tamar's motives in Genesis 38 are also not stated, but the motive in her case is easier to discern. She wants children, not revenge.[63] Her scheme is not designed to educate Judah as much as to gain her own ends. Genesis 38 thus suggests that Joseph does not simply want revenge. He tells his brothers when he first sees them that he will "test" them to see whether they are spies. His deception may indeed be a test, although he knows that they are not spies. If they happily leave Benjamin to his fate and run home, then Joseph knows them to be as dangerous to Benjamin as they were to him. The fact that Judah offers himself in place of Benjamin proves that his brothers are not prepared to repeat their jealous crime in light of the fact that it did not solve the problem of Jacob's preferential love. They collectively express their sense of guilt for what they did to Joseph (Gen 42:21-23), and Judah's offer shows what he is willing to endure in order that he may not repeat his crime. Thus Joseph's deception may be a test. Like Tamar's deception, it may be neither a matter of malicious revenge nor selfless charity.

The recognition that Genesis 38 is a *mise-en-abyme* within the Story of Jacob's Line is based on the similarities between the narratives as discussed above. Comparison of the two stories, however, also illuminates several differences that should not be overlooked. Three major contrasts may be noted.

First, the most obvious difference between the deceptions of Joseph and Tamar concerns a difference of power. Joseph is able to engineer an elaborate deception that depends on his undisputed power over his brothers and the servants who plant false evidence at Joseph's direction. Joseph may do whatever he wishes to his brothers. Tamar's situation is entirely different. She has no power over Judah. Her daring deception depends on Judah's honesty in recognizing his own guilt, sparing Tamar, and acknowledging her children as legitimate. Judah evidently has the power to order her execution should he be base enough to deny his paternity or claim that it is irrelevant. This difference with respect

---

[63] Weisberg ("Widow of Our Discontent," 414) discusses Tamar's motives: "What is unclear is whether Tamar acts to preserve her husband's name and lineage, to preserve her connection to Judah's family, or simply to secure for herself a child and a future." The last of these motives seems the most compelling and entails the first two. Similarly, Rahab desires a future for herself and therefore allies with the Israelites (Josh 2:8-13).

to power in the two deceptions likewise creates a difference between Judah's statement to Tamar and the brothers' statement to Joseph. In Genesis 38, Judah's own statement creates the resolution of the story. In Gen 50:15-21, the brothers are in Tamar's powerless position and depend on Joseph to have mercy and reconcile the family. Therefore, whereas the guilty party ultimately resolves the problems by acknowledging his guilt in Genesis 38, it is the victim who has the power to restore the peace of the family in the Story of Jacob's Line.

Second, the difference of power between Joseph and Tamar corresponds to a difference of gender. Deception is the favorite weapon of the powerless, and women may be constrained to employ it in a patriarchal society. Powerlessness, however, does not justify deception. As discussed above, the key to a positive evaluation of deception in Genesis is motive: the deception is justified if the deceiver acts against someone who has previously wronged him or her in order to restore his or her situation to what it was before the wrong.

A final difference between Joseph and Tamar is worth noting. As indicated above, the text assigns Joseph some responsibility for his own victimization. The crime of his brothers is partly motivated by Joseph's own conduct. Tamar, by contrast, is totally exonerated. The narrative tells us what Judah does not know: Yhwh kills Er and Onan dies because of his own sin; they do not die because of Tamar. Judah's crime against Tamar is motivated by his own understandable but mistaken suspicions about Tamar's role in his sons' death. Joseph, by contrast, is not exonerated in this way.

As these differences indicate, the similarity between a *mise-en-abyme* and its context does not obfuscate the differences. I have focused on the resemblance between Genesis 38 and the Story of Jacob's Line in order to show that the former is a *mise-en-abyme* within the latter. The contrasts, however, also illuminate the texts. The variations between the texts have generally encouraged the idea that the two stories are not related. Once their relationship is appreciated, however, the contrasts emerge as potentially interesting aspects for exegetical consideration. For example, the difference of gender between Tamar and Joseph may indicate ways in which the narrative presents gender. Contrary to what some commentators suppose, deception is not practiced only by women, nor are women always justified in their deceptive practices. Gender may be an important element in biblical stories of deception, but future work on this question will need to build on Williams' work or show where it is mistaken.[64]

To return to the initial question: what is Genesis 38 doing in the Story of Jacob's Line? It functions as a *mise-en-abyme* that accentuates the centrality of family continuity and Joseph's justified deception of his brothers. Episodes that do not advance this topic appear comparatively secondary (e.g., Joseph's rise in Genesis 39–41). Furthermore, the *mise-en-abyme* indicates Joseph's justification for the deception and his self-interested (rather than vengeful or charitable) motive. Genesis 38 also clarifies the separate functions of Gen 45:1-15 (recognition) and Gen 50:15-21 (reconciliation). Finally, the recognition of Genesis 38 as a *mise-en-abyme* accounts for both the evident isolatability of the passage and its relation to the larger story.

---

[64] In her response to the articles in *Reasoning with the Foxes: Female Wit in a World of Male Power* (ed. J. Cheryl Exum and Johanna W. H. Bos; [Semeia 42; Atlanta, GA: Scholars, 1988] 133-55), Mieke Bal anticipates some of Williams's findings concerning deception in Genesis. She criticizes Bos for defining deceptive characters as female (p. 136), suggests that it is "a bit risky to attribute the feature of trickery, with its moral ambivalence, to female characters only" (p. 147), and realizes the significance of the fact that Tamar's deception works to the benefit of Judah. She also observes that Judah himself deceived Tamar (p. 148-49), which Williams fails to note. These same criticisms apply to Melissa Jackson, "Lot's Daughters and Tamar as Tricksters and the Patriarchal Narratives as Feminist Theology," *JSOT* 98 (2002) 29-46.

CHAPTER THREE

1 Samuel 25

What is the story of David and Nabal doing in the narrative of David's rise? This question has drawn much less attention than the comparable problem of Genesis 38. The story poses no chronological problem of the kind that fascinates biblical scholars. However, its awkward placement is no less problematic. Like Genesis 38, the story of David and Nabal introduces a change of setting and a new set of characters (Nabal and Abigail). This side story about David's encounter with Nabal and Abigail seems not to advance the plot. David's marriage to Abigail may explain the origin of his kingship in Hebron, since she is the widow of a wealthy Calebite (cf. Josh 14:13-14).[1] However, this connection would require only a brief notice of the marriage, not the involved story of 1 Samuel 25. The larger narrative of the Story of David and the House of Saul (1 Sam 13:1– 2 Sam 5:3) consistently seeks to present David as a better man (and therefore king) than Saul.[2] David

---

[1] For further discussion of David's use of women for political purposes, see Jon D. Levenson and Baruch Halpern, "The Political Import of David's Marriages," *JBL* 99 (1980) 507-18.

[2] This delimitation of the connected narrative grounds the limits in the (corrupted) regnal notice for Saul in 1 Sam 13:1 and the similar regnal notice concerning David in 2 Sam 5:4, which indicates that the narrative section concludes with 2 Sam 5:3 (and therefore 2 Sam 5:1-5 is not a unit as imagined by many translations [e.g., *NAB*; *NRSV*; *NJB*] and commentators [P. Kyle McCarter, *I Samuel* (AB 9; Garden City, NY: Doubleday, 1984), 130-34; A. A. Anderson, *2 Samuel* (WBC 11; Dallas: Word Books, 1989) 74-75]). I refer to the section as the Story of David and the House of Saul, because David's conflict with Saul and Ishbaal constitutes the major theme of the story, not merely David's rise (note that David's presence is assumed as early as 1 Sam 13:13-14 and 15:27-28). The Rise of David source was first proposed by Leonard Rost, *The Succession to the Throne of David* (trans. Michael D. Rutter and David M. Gunn; Historic Texts and Interpreters in Biblical Scholarship 1; Sheffield: Almond, 1982) 6-34, originally published in 1926. This view was followed with modifications by Martin Noth, *Überlieferungsgeschichtliche Studien* (Tübingen: Max Niemeyer,

is presented as closer to God, more popular with the people, and a better warrior.[3] This thematic concern, however, recedes from view along with Saul himself in 1 Samuel 25. Therefore, the chapter does not obviously contribute to the plot or theme of its larger context.

This chapter will argue that 1 Samuel 25 is a *mise-en-abyme* within the Story of David and the House of Saul. Nabal and Saul are parallel characters, just as Tamar and Joseph are parallel characters. In 1 Samuel 25, as in Genesis 38, the one character who is prominent in the larger narrative and the *mise-en-abyme* (David and Judah, respectively) has a similar relationship with a character in the shorter story and its surrounding narrative. Specifically, David serves both Saul and Nabal, but suffers harm in return from each man. David does not avenge himself on either man, but is ultimately vindicated by Yhwh.

1957), originally published in 1943; in English as *The Deuteronomistic History* (trans. J. Doull et al.; 2nd ed.; JSOTSup 15; Sheffield: Sheffield Academic Press, 1991). The source theory has been further developed by H. U. Nübel, *Davids Aufstieg in der frühe israelitischer Geschichtsschreibung* (Bonn: Rheinische Friedrich-Wilhelms-Universität, 1959); Artur Weiser, "Die Legitimation des Königs David: Zur Eigenart und Entstehung der sogen. Geschichte von Davids Aufstieg," *VT* 16 (1966) 325-54; Rolf Rendtorff, "Beobachtungen zur altisraelitischen Geschichtsschreibung anhand der Geschichte vom Aufstieg Davids," in *Probleme biblischer Theologie: Gerhard von Rad zum 70. Geburtstag* (ed. Hans Walter Wolff; Munich: Kaiser, 1971) 428-39; J. H. Grønbaek, *Die Geschichte vom Aufstieg Davids (1. Sam. 15–2. Sam 5): Tradition und Komposition* (Acta Theologica Danica 10; Copenhagen: Munksgaard, 1971); P. Kyle McCarter, "The Apology of David," *JBL* 99 (1980) 489-504; reprinted in *Reconstructing Israel and Judah: Recent Studies on the Deuteronomistic History* (ed. Gary N. Knoppers and J. Gordon McConville; Sources for Biblical and Theological Study 8; Winona Lake, IN: Eisenbrauns, 2000) 260-75; Antony F. Campbell, *Of Prophets and Kings: A Late Ninth-Century Document (1 Samuel 1–2 Kings 10)* (CBQMS 17; Washington, DC: The Catholic Biblical Association of America, 1986) 125-38. For summaries of scholarship, see Brevard S. Childs, *Introduction to the Old Testament as Scripture* (Philadelphia: Fortress, 1979) 263-80; Walter Dietrich and Thomas Naumann, "The David-Saul Narrative" (trans. Peter T. Daniels), in *Reconsidering Israel and Judah* (ed. Gary N. Knoppers and J. Gordon McConville; Sources for Biblical and Theological Study 8; Winona Lake, IN; Eisenbrauns, 2000) 276-318.

[3] See, for example, Dominic Rudman, "The Commissioning Stories of Saul and David as Theological Allegory," *VT* 50 (2000) 517-30; Johannes Klein, *David versus Saul: Ein Beitrag zum Erzählsystem der Samuelbücher* (BWANT 158; Stuttgart: Kohlhammer, 2002) 64-70. The comparison can extend beyond the Story of David and the House of Saul. Klein (*David versus Saul*, 84-85) contrasts Saul's treatment of Jonathan and David's treatment of Absalom. K. L. Knoll (*The Faces of David* [JSOTSup 242; Sheffield: Sheffield Academic Press, 1997] 117) similarly notes David's loyalty even to those who may stand in his way, such as Saul, Jonathan, and Absalom.

The short narrative in 1 Samuel 25 duplicates pertinent aspects of the whole of the Story of David and the House of Saul.

The following discussion will explain how scholars have understood the story's connection to its context. It will indicate further how 1 Samuel 25 reduplicates the Story of David and the House of Saul. Finally, some consequences of recognizing 1 Samuel 25 as a *mise-en-abyme* will be noted.

1 Samuel 25 in Context: Toward the *Mise-en-abyme*

As with Genesis 38, the characters that appear in 1 Samuel 25 may parallel characters from the larger context. Some scholars have observed that Nabal parallels Saul and therefore that the story of David and Nabal serves as a miniature representation of David's struggle with Saul. With few exceptions, the observation that Nabal serves as a stand-in for Saul is normally briefly stated and not explored.[4]

Robert Gordon's article is the most detailed discussion of this connection. Gordon treats 1 Samuel 25 as part of the sequence of chapters that deal with the motif of "grievance, revenge, and bloodguilt" (1 Samuel 24–26).[5] Each of the three chapters forms an "incremental

---

[4] For example, David M. Gunn, *Fate of King Saul: An Interpretation of a Biblical Story* (JSOTSup 14; Sheffield: JSOT, 1980) 97, 101-2; Alice Bach, "The Pleasure of Her Text," *USQR* 43 (1989) 44; reprinted in *The Pleasure of Her Text: Feminist Readings of Biblical and Historical Texts* (ed. Alice Bach; Philadelphia: Trinity, 1990) 28-29; Diana Vikander Edelman, *King Saul in the Historiography of Judah* (JSOTSup 121; Sheffield: Sheffield Academic Press, 1991) 206; Jacques Vermeylen, "La maison de Saül et la maison de David: Un écrit de propagande théologico-politique de 1 S 11 à 2 S 7," in *Figures de David à travers la Bible: XVIIᵉ congrès de l'ACFEB (Lille, 1ᵉʳ-5 septembre 1997)* (ed. Louis Desrousseaux and Jacques Vermeylen; LD 177; Paris: Cerf, 1999) 46-47; Vermeylen, *La loi du plus fort: Histoire de la rédaction davidique de 1 Samuel 8 à 1 Rois 2* (Leuven: Leuven University Press, 2000) 150; Cynthia Edenburg, "How (not) to Murder a King: Variations on a Theme in 1 Sam 24. 26," *SJOT* 12 (1998) 64-83.

[5] Gordon, "David's Rise and Saul's Demise: Narrative Analogy in 1 Samuel 24-26," *TynBul* 31 (1980) 57; reprinted in *Reconsidering Israel and Judah*, 319-39. Gordon's article is the basis for the elaborations of Moshe Garsiel (*First Book of Samuel: A Literary Study of Comparative Structures, Analogies and Parallels* [Ramat-Gan, Israel: Revivim, 1985] 125-33, cf. p. 160 n. 52), who adds discussion of intertextual connections between 1 Samuel 25 and Genesis. Mark E. Biddle ("Ancestral Motifs in 1 Samuel 25: Intertextuality and Characterization," *JBL* 121 [2002] 617-38) takes up Garsiel's intertextuality and pursues it in detail. Robert Polzin's remarks on 1 Samuel 25 (*Samuel and the Deuteronomist: A Literary Study of the Deuteronomistic History Part Two: 1 Samuel* [Indiana Studies in Biblical Literature; Bloomington: Indiana University

repetition" of the same motif in different narratives. Gordon understands the function of chap. 25 primarily in terms of David. David
learns that Yhwh will exact vengeance on David's enemies. The difference in David's behavior during his two opportunities to kill Saul
manifests the difference that his experience with Nabal has created
in David. Whereas David symbolically takes the kingdom from Saul
by cutting off the corner of his garment, he refrains from any such
action during his second encounter with a vulnerable Saul. Gordon
understands that Nabal is a substitute for Saul and that the narrative
adumbrates subsequent developments (e.g., Saul's death). However,
Gordon primarily confines the function of 1 Samuel 25 to its immediate context in 1 Samuel 24–26 and does not develop the full range of
parallels between chapter 25 and the Story of David and the House of
Saul. Also, his claim that David's character develops in these chapters
is dubious. David's theft of Saul's spear is not obviously less serious
than his cutting of Saul's cloak.

Gordon indicates several textual features that connect Saul and
Nabal.[6] Like Nabal (1 Sam 25:2), Saul is associated with Maon (1 Sam
23:24) and Carmel (1 Sam 15:12).[7] Both men enjoy wealth and high social
status: Nabal's banquet is "like the banquet of a king" (1 Sam 25:36).
Both experience resistance to their "anti-David" attitudes from within
their own houses. Saul's servants do not cooperate in Saul's slaughter
of the priests at Nob who assisted David (1 Sam 22:6-10, 17-19). Even
Saul's own son Jonathan is presented as in league with David (1 Sam
18:1-4; 20:30-31; 23:17-18), as is his daughter Michal (1 Sam 19:11-17).
Similarly, Nabal's servants speak ill of him to Abigail (1 Sam 25:17).

Press, 1993] 205-15) partially parallel Gordon, although he seems not to be familiar
with Gordon's work and he adds little to what Gordon says. Barbara Green ("Enacting Imaginatively the Unthinkable: 1 Samuel 25 and the story of Saul," *BibInt* 11 [2003]
1-23) argues that 1 Samuel 25 is a "sideshow of the action" in chaps. 24 and 26. Green's
reading seems to suggest that the story duplicates its context, but primarily in negative
terms; it indicates ways in which Saul's kingship will not end. Paul Borgman (*David,
Saul, and God: Recovering an Ancient Story* [Oxford: Oxford University Press, 2008]
79-95) follows Gordon's argument with a focus on the theme of receiving evil for good.
Borgman similarly confines his attention to 1 Samuel 24–26.

[6] Gordon, "David's Rise," 43-51. See also Jacques Briend, "Les figures de David en
1 S 16, 1–2 S 5, 3: Rapports entre literature et histoire," in *Figures de David á travers
la Bible: XVIIe congrès de l'ACFEB (Lille, 1er–5 septembre 1997)* (Lectio Divina 117;
Paris: Cerf, 1999) 25.

[7] Reading with LXX Maon in 1 Sam 25:2.

Abigail herself shows kindness to David (which she at first conceals from Nabal) and finally becomes his wife.[8] David suffers harm from Saul and Nabal, but does not avenge himself on either yet ultimately triumphs over both. This similar relationship of each man to David explains what the story about Nabal is doing in the Story of David and the House of Saul.

Ellen van Wolde has followed Gordon's lead.[9] She makes a distinction between the "literal" and "metaphorical" aspects of Abigail's speech. Abigail speaks literally about the immediate situation between David and Nabal, but she metaphorically addresses the larger conflict between David and Saul. Abigail begins by discussing Nabal (1 Sam 25:25), but soon shifts to David's enemies in general (25:26). She mentions enemies of David that pursue him and seek his life (25:29). This reference can only mean Saul, because Nabal does not pursue David or seek to kill him. Abigail also involves Yhwh and Israel in her speech. She says that David is fighting the battles of Yhwh and that Yhwh

---

[8] Jon D. Levenson argues for a close parallel between Saul and Nabal in "1 Samuel 25 as Literature and History," *CBQ* 40 (1978) 28; similarly, Levenson and Halpern, "Political Import," 507-18; Marti J. Steussey, *David: Biblical Portraits of Power* (Studies on Personalities of the Old Testament; Columbia, SC: University of South Carolina Press, 1999) 11. Levenson suggests that David marries the wives of both men. He speculates that the Ahinoam mentioned in 1 Sam 25:43 as the wife of David is the same Ahinoam mentioned as Saul's wife in 1 Sam 14:49-50. The suggestion is interesting it might explain several features of the text. In addition to providing an antecedent to Nathan remark that Yhwh gave to David his master's wives (2 Sam 12:8) the marriage would account for Saul's persecution of David, including the notice that Saul gave Michal to Palti (1 Sam 25:44) placed immediately after David's marriage to Ahinoam (25:43). Perhaps the move was retaliatory. It may also explain why Saul calls Jonathan the "son of a perverse, rebellious woman" (1 Sam 20:30). The proposal may be combined with McKenzie's suggestion (*King David: A Biography* [Oxford: Oxford University Press, 2000] 86-88) that David attempted a coup against Saul. It would not be the first time that a wife conspired with her lover against her husband. This suggestion is interesting, but speculative, and most commentators understandably keep the two Ahinoam's separate (McCarter, *I Samuel*, 400; David Toshio Tsumura, *First Book of Samuel* [NICOT; Grand Rapids, MI: Eerdmans, 2007] 594; Stanley Isser, *The Sword of Goliath: David in Heroic Literature* [Studies in Biblical Literature 6; Atlanta: Society of Biblical Literature, 2003] 39-40). David's Ahinoam appears to come from a Jezreel near Maon, Ziph, and Carmel (cf. Josh 15:55-56) and is mentioned here because of geographic proximity of the story, the topic of marriage (which also explains the notice about Michal being given to Palti), and perhaps because this marriage took place around this time. Indeed, Abigail and Ahinoam are normally mentioned together (1 Sam 27:3; 30:5; 2 Sam 2:2).

[9] Ellen van Wolde, "A Leader Led by a Lady: David and Abigail in I Samuel 25," *ZAW* 114 (2002) 355-75.

has appointed David leader over Israel. She characterizes David as a leader (25:30), in contrast to her husband, who calls him a runaway servant (25:11). Since Yhwh appointed David and David is fighting Yhwh's battles, David must not murder his own enemies. He needs to guard himself against bloodguilt and allow Yhwh to destroy his enemies. On the literal level, her speech persuades David not to kill Nabal. On the metaphorical level, she persuades David not to kill Saul. She places David's immediate circumstances in the larger framework of his election by Yhwh and his path to the throne. Like Gordon, van Wolde strives to understand the story in terms of the psychology of the characters rather than the development of the narrative. This approach seems misplaced since David does not need Abigail to persuade him (even metaphorically) not to kill Saul because he never has any intention of killing Saul. Also like Gordon, van Wolde limits the similarity between 1 Samuel 25 and the Story of David and the House of Saul to the immediate context of 1 Samuel 24–26, with particular emphasis on chapter 26.[10]

Several terms develop the primary similarity between Nabal and Saul: each man receives favors from David, but responds with harm. As Gordon indicates, David does good (יטב/טוב) for each man, but receives evil (רע) in return (1 Sam 24:18; 25:21, 31; cf. Gen 44:4; Pss 35:12; 38:20; 109:5; Prov 17:13; Jer 18:20). These terms establish the main theme of justice in David's relations with each Saul and Nabal. In 1 Sam 24:18, Saul says to David what Judah says to Tamar: "You are righteous, not I" (ממני צדיק אתה) and explains "because you did good (טוב) for me and I repaid you with harm (רע)." Similarly, David complains of Nabal, "he has returned me evil (רע) for good (טוב)" (1 Sam 25:21), a complaint supported by the statement of Nabal's own servants (טוב, 25:15). With this proverbial expression, David presents himself as the innocent victim of

---

[10] Van Wolde, "A Leader," 373: "The function of this correspondence between Nabal and Saul lies in David's future decisions." I will argue that it is equally applicable to previous events. Due to her emphasis on Abigail's anticipation of subsequent developments, van Wolde sees Abigail as a prophetess (p. 367). However, her prescience is the result of her "good sense" (25:3, 33), not prophetic inspiration. On the history of interpreting Abigail as a prophetess, see John Jarick, "The Seven (?) Prophetesses of the Old Testament," *Lutheran Theological Journal* 28 (1994) 116-21. Josephus does not make Abigail out to be a prophet, but his unqualified positive portrayal of her contrasts both with other Jewish sources and Josephus' portrait of other women. See Christopher T. Begg, "The Abigail Story (1 Samuel 25) according to Josephus," *EstBib* 54 (1996) 5-34.

wicked men in his relationship to Saul and Nabal. David would seem to be justified in avenging himself, since he would only be seeking justice. Instead, he spares each man's life: Saul because he is Yhwh's anointed, and Nabal because of Abigail intervention. The language of good and evil extends more widely than Gordon indicates. It is not confined to chapters 24–26, but extends through the larger story, as when David makes Saul "better" (טוב) by easing Saul's torment from the "evil" (רע) spirit (1 Sam 16:23). Also, Jonathan claims that David has not sinned against Saul, but David's deeds "have been extremely good for you" (טוב־לך מאד, 1 Sam 19:4). Nabal's servant similarly indicates to Abigail that David and his band "were very good to us" in the highland (טבים לנו מאד, 1 Sam 25:15). These uses of good and evil amplify the thematic statement in 1 Sam 25:21, "he has returned to me evil for good" (וישב־לי רעה תחת טובה, cf. 1 Sam 24:18).

Gordon also notes that the theme of justice articulated by the good/ evil language is advanced by the repetition of "cause" or "lawsuit" (ריב). In 1 Samuel 24:16, David asks that Yhwh may "plead my cause (וירב את־ריבי) and vindicate me against you." His plea evokes Saul's acknowledgement of wrongdoing in 24:18. Similarly, when David learns of Nabal's death, he interprets it as Yhwh's action on his behalf: "Blessed be Yhwh who has prosecuted the case of my insult (רב את־ריב חרפתי) from the hand of Nabal" (25:39). The repetitions of Yhwh judging a case for David with respect to Saul and Nabal further highlight the theme of justice in David's dealings with both men. David expresses the hope that Yhwh will strike Saul as Yhwh struck Nabal (נגף, 1 Sam 25:38; 26:10). Thus, Nabal's fate foreshadows that of Saul, as Abigail seems to suggest (25:26).[11]

The text places David in the relationship of a son to both Saul and Nabal. David instructs his messengers to ask Nabal to give provisions "to your son David" (לבנך לדוד, 25:8). David had similarly addressed Saul as "my father" (אבי, 24:12). Saul reciprocates by addressing David as "my son David" (בני דוד, 24:17) and uses the same mode of address without David's invitation in 26:17, 21, 25. Although Gordon observes

---

[11] The meaning of Abigail's words ("Let your enemies be as Nabal along with those who seek evil for my lord," v. 26) is uncertain, since Nabal is alive and well as she speaks. Either she foresees the death of Nabal (and Saul) or she means that David's enemies are as wrong-headed as her husband. Right-thinking people support David's inevitable rise to the throne. McCarter (*I Samuel*, 394) relocates the verse between vv. 41 and 42.

this textual connection that places David in a similar relationship to each man, he does not develop the implications of these terms. David situates himself as the heir to each man. When Nabal dies, David evidently inherits Nabal's wealth and status in the clan of Caleb by marrying his widow Abigail. Similarly, David seeks to inherit Saul's throne through marriage with Saul's daughter Michal and a covenant with the heir-apparent Jonathan. The text even shows Jonathan giving his birthright to David 1 Sam 23:16-18. The father-son language indicates David's similar relationship to Nabal and Saul and his eventual inheritance from each man.

The connections between David and Saul and Nabal involve the language of servant as well as son. David identifies himself as Nabal's son and his followers as Nabal's servants (עבדיך, 1 Sam 25:8).[12] He identifies himself as the servant of Saul (עבד, 17:34, 36; 26:18, 19), and others understand David to be Saul's servant (19:4; 29:3; 22:8). David presents himself as a servant who has been abused by his master. Nabal, however, voices the Saulide interpretation of David as a traitorous runaway servant: "These days many servants are breaking away from their masters" (המתפרצים איש מפני אדניו היום רבו עבדים, 25:10). The servant language describing David's relationships with Saul and Nabal brings these two relationships into parallel with each other and heightens the issue of justice. If David is the innocent sufferer, then Saul's injustice is heightened by David's close relationship to him (as "son," son-in-law, and servant). If Saul is the innocent sufferer, then David's disloyalty is intensified to treason or worse by Saul's closeness to David (as his "father," father-in-law, and king).

Other motifs and vocabulary common to 1 Samuel 25 and the Story of David and the House of Saul develop the central claim that David suffers injustice. Jonathan reminds Saul how David slew (ויך) Goliath and Saul rejoiced (1 Sam 19:5). Abigail also appears to allude to the slaying of Goliath by a slung stone (קלע, 1 Sam 17:40, 49, 50) when she says to David, "If a man arises to pursue you and seek your life, then may the life of my lord be bound up in the bundle of the living with Yhwh your God, but as for the life of your enemies, may he sling

---

[12] Reading MT (LXX^A, Vulg, Syr). A few medieval Hebrew MSS read עבדך, "your servant." This reading seems to show David identifying himself as both son and servant to Nabal.

them (יקלענה) from the hollow of a sling (הקלע)" (1 Sam 25:29).[13] Abigail's speech also includes a stronger connection to Saul in the expression "If a man arises to pursue you and seek your life..." (ויקם אדם לרדפך ולבקש את־נפשך). Saul consistently "pursues" David (רדף, 1 Sam 23:25, 28; 24:15; 26:18, 20) and "seeks" him (בקש, 1 Sam 19:2, 10; 20:1; 23:14, 15, 25; 24:3; 26:2, 20; cf. "hunt" [צדה] in 24:12) to take his life (נפש, 1 Sam 19:11; 20:1; 23:15; 24:12). Abigail also contrasts the life (נפש) of David and his ene-mies (איב). As Jonathan points out, David had risked his life for Saul (נפש, 1 Sam 19:5), yet Saul consistently seeks to take the life of David, as does his successor Ishbaal (נפש, 2 Sam 4:8). When he spares Saul the second time, David tells Saul "just as your life (נפשך) was precious in my eyes today, so may my life (נפשי) be precious in the eyes of Yhwh, and may he rescue me from all distress" (ויצלני מכל־צרה, 1 Sam 26:25). Later, David reflects that Yhwh "has redeemed my life from all distress" (פדה את־נפשי מכל־צרה, 2 Sam 4:9).

As van Wolde notes, the enemy (איב) of David that Abigail has in mind must be Saul, who is often identified as David's enemy (איב, 1 Sam 18:29; 19:17; 24:5, 19; 26:8).[14] Later, Ishbaal inherits this role (איב, 2 Sam 4:8). Like Abigail, Jonathan wishes that Yhwh may seek (בקש) the ene-mies (איב) of David (1 Sam 20:16). Abigail specifically likens Saul and Nabal through the language of enmity, evil, and seeking: "now let your enemies (איביך) be like Nabal along with those who seek evil for my lord" (והמבקשים אל־אדני רעה, 1 Sam 25:26). Abigail uses language that strongly connects Saul and Nabal and points toward the function of 1 Samuel 25 as a *mise-en-abyme* within the Story of David and the House of Saul.

The motif of bloodguilt is especially frequent in 1 Samuel 24–26. The issue of bloodguilt bears directly on the question of whether David is more righteous than Saul or *vice-versa* (cf. 1 Sam 24:18; 25:21). Abi-gail identifies David as one whom "Yhwh has prevented from entering into bloodguilt and gaining your victory with your own hand" (מבוא בדמים והושע ידך לך, 1 Sam 25:26). She asks, "Let this not be for you a qualm of conscience or faltering courage for my lord to have shed

---

[13] A similar image of slinging out a person occurs in Isa 22:17-18 concerning Shebna. However, the difficult passage does not use vocabulary from 1 Sam 25:29 or 17:40, 49-50: "See, Yhwh is about to hurl you away, great man, and he will surely seize you firmly, whirl you around, and throw you like a ball into a wide land. There you will die and there your splendid chariots will lie, a disgrace to your lord's house."

[14] van Wolde, "A Leader," 363.

blood in vain (ולשפך־דם חנם) and for my lord to have gained his victory for himself" (25:31). David blesses her because "you have today prevented me from entering into bloodguilt (מבוא בדמים) and gaining my victory with my own hand." (25:33). Abigail's speech identifies David as one in the right, but asks him to stay in the right by not killing Nabal. Similarly, Jonathan identifies Saul as the guilty party when he asks his father, "Why would you sin against innocent blood (ולמה תחטא בדם נקי) by killing David for nothing (חנם)?" (1 Sam 19:4-5).

Both Jonathan and Abigail identify a killing as "for nothing" (חנם), a term that suggests both a lack of cause for the killing and a lack of profit from the act. Abigail seeks to mitigate Nabal's insult by indicating that Nabal is beneath David's consideration. Jonathan identifies David as "innocent" (נקי) and therefore killing David is "without cause" (חנם). David tries to maintain his innocence by not killing Saul (ונקה, 1 Sam 26:9). He also maintains that he is innocent (אנכי נקי) of the blood of Abner (מדמי אבנר, 2 Sam 3:28). While Saul seeks to kill David, David refuses to "raise his hand against Yhwh's anointed" (1 Sam 24:7, 11; 26:9, 11, 23; cf. 2 Sam 1:14; 1 Sam 22:17). Instead, he complains to Saul of his exile as a wrong comparable to murder: "Do not let my blood (דמי) fall to the ground away from the presence of Yhwh" (1 Sam 26:13). He also executes the assassins who killed Saul's son Ishbaal: "Shall I not seek his blood (דמו) from your hand?" (2 Sam 4:11). The language concerning bloodguilt and innocence serves to highlight the moral contest between David and Saul's house and show its parallel in that between David and Nabal.

Abigail's use of Nabal's name to characterizes her husband as foolish also serves to characterize Saul, since she places the two men in parallel. Also, Nabal's folly may be related to Saul's admission, "I have acted foolishly" (הסכלתי, 1 Sam 26:21).[15] Scholars normally treat the name Nabal as a transparent name meaning "fool." There are two problems with this assumption. First, "fool" is a strange name to give a child. Second, Abigail related his name to the abstract noun "folly" (נבלה). If the name transparently means "fool," however, then the second half of her statement in 1 Sam 25:25 is unnecessary. James Barr has argued that the name Nabal does not primarily mean "fool." His article, published forty years ago, seems unknown to those who argue

---

[15] Gordon, "David's Rise," 50-51. See below.

for this equivalence of Nabal and fool.[16] Barr suggests four possibilities for the meaning of Nabal's name.[17] First, it may derive from a word meaning "fire, flame" (cf. Akkadian *nablu*, Ugaritic *nblat*). Nabal's name would thereby be analogous to "several other well-established Hebrew names connected with fire, flame and light, such as Uriel, Uri, Uriah, Jair, Neriah, Ner, Baraq, Lapidoth."[18] Second, the name may derive from a word meaning "to send forth" (cf. South Arabian *nbl*, "one sent," and Eithiopic *tänbälä*,"one sent as an envoy"). The suggestion is strengthened by the Common Semitic root *ybl* or *wbl*, "bring, carry." Third, the name may be explained in reference to the Arabic *nabl*, *nabula* ("to be noble, noble-minded, generous"). Fourth, it may be related to the Lihyanite name *ʾanbal* ("skilled, clever"), and to the Dathina *nebel* ("wide-awake, nimble, alert"). To Barr's four suggestions, may be added Punic *nbl*, which is attested as a personal name. The name occurs in an inscription from Algeria that is to be dated "between Carthaginian and Neopunic" texts.[19] In the fourth century C.E., a certain *nbl* was a powerful prince in North Africa, whose name may be Neopunic.[20] Neopunic *nbl* is also a noun meaning "cup" or "jar" (cf. Hebrew נבל, "skin, jar, pitcher" in 1 Sam 25:18).[21]

Barr points out that Nabal's name "did not mean 'churlish fool', and that there is ample room for suggestions that it meant something else."[22] From this different starting point, Barr briefly examines the narrative in a way that differs from most previous and subsequent scholarship.

[16] Barr, "The Symbolism of Names in the Old Testament," *BJRL* 52 (1969) 11-29. Levenson's article ("1 Samuel 25") rather than Barr's has formed the opinion of most subsequent scholarship. Gunn (*Fate of King Saul*, 155 n. 9) disagrees with Levenson independently of Barr. Barr's view is followed by Moshe Garsiel ("Wit, Words, and a Woman: 1 Samuel 25," in *On Humor and the Comic in the Hebrew Bible* [JSOTSup 92; Sheffield: Sheffield Academic Press, 1990] 164 n. 2) and Victor Hamilton (*Handbook on the Historical Books* [Grand Rapids, MI: Baker, 2001] 279-80).

[17] Barr, "The Symbolism," 25-26.
[18] Barr, "The Symbolism," 25.
[19] *KAI* 105; Frank L. Benz, *Personal Names in the Phoenician and Punic Inscriptions: A Catalog, Grammatical Study and Glossary of Elements* (Studia Pohl 8; Rome: Biblical Institute Press, 1972) 358.
[20] Ammianus Marcellinus, *Rerum gestarum libri*, 29.5.2; Edward Gibbon, *Decline and Fall of the Roman Empire*, chaps. 25 and 29. Gibbon renders the Latin *Nubel* as Nabal.
[21] *KAI* 137; Charles R. Krahmalkov, *Phoenician-Punic Dictionary* (Orientalia Lovaniensia Analecta 90; Studia Phoenicia 15; Leuven: Peeters, 2000) 324.
[22] Barr, "The Symbolism," 26.

Most commentators assume that Nabal's name means "fool" and that Abigail is merely commenting on the fact that the man and the name fit one another. This conclusion is based on the assumption that ancient Israelites believed that there was an intrinsic connection between a name and the character of the person named. Barr's article is devoted in some measure to disproving this assumption. Barr's understanding of Abigail's play on Nabal's name "depends on the play of homonyms against one another; it is a recognition story, working through the discovery that a name is fitting for a person when it is understood in a sense other than that in which it was applied."[23] Abigail's word play becomes additional evidence of her cleverness.

Barr also comments on another aspect of Abigail's paronomasia. She connects the name of her husband with the noun נבלה rather than the more obvious adjective נבל. This is significant because "the negativity and unfavourableness of the noun is very much stronger than that of the adjective."[24] The adjective means "foolish, ungenerous, stupid, ungracious." The noun, though cognate, is used of a category of serious sins of the kind that are "not done in Israel." The noun characterizes rape in Gen 34:7; Judg 20:6, 10; 2 Sam 13:12 and attempted homosexual rape in Judg 19:23, 24. It describes Achan's violation of the ban in Josh 7:15 and, in legal material, the crime of a bride found not to be a virgin in Deut 22:21. Other commentators on 1 Samuel 25 have discussed the semantic range of נבל, but curiously ignore נבלה.[25] Although the name of Nabal does not serve the purpose of characterization in the way that most commentators suppose, it does serve as the occasion for Abigail's clever word play, which characterizes both her and her husband.[26]

---

[23] Barr, "The Symbolism," 27. One may imagine homophonous wordplays on such English names as Matt, Dick, or Harry.

[24] Barr, "The Symbolism," 27.

[25] Levenson, "1 Samuel 25," 13-14. Levenson has elaborated on the meaning of נבל. However, he overestimates the relevance of the information he provides and neglects the force of נבלה.

[26] Nabal is also identified as כלבי ("a Calebite") in MT (Q), although LXX reads κυνικός "dog-like." The Hebrew may or may not reflect a play on Caleb/dog. Tova L. Forti (*Animal Imagery in the Book of Proverbs* [VTSup 118; Leiden: Brill, 2008] 92-99) notes that Prov 26:11 correlates the fool (נבל) with the dog (כלב). MT (K) reads כלבו (perhaps "according to his heart").

Since Saul and Nabal are parallel characters, the expression may also characterize Saul. When David spares Saul the second time, Saul recognizes that his persecution of David is mistaken. He expresses it three ways (1 Sam 26:21): "I have sinned" (חטאתי); "I have acted fool-ishly" (הסכלתי); and "I have made a serious mistake" (ואשגה הרבה מאד). In connection with the other two expressions, the term הסכלתי appears to express the serious folly indicated by נבלה in other contexts. Like נבלה, the root סכל is associated with moral failure (Gen 31:28; 1 Sam 13:13; 2 Sam 24:10), not merely intellectual incapacity. Both terms are related to folly and occur more often in narrative than wisdom literature. However, the terms are never connected to each other, so it is difficult to discern whether Saul's admission connects to Abigail's word play on her husband's name.[27]

In sum, some scholars perceive a basic parallel between Saul and Nabal, but this parallel has not been fully explored. Those who have pursued it in some depth have confined their attention primarily to 1 Samuel 24–26, although it can be expanded to the whole Story of David and the House of Saul.[28] The limited view of the context of 1 Samuel 25 is due in part to the attempt to discern character development in David between chapters 24 and 26. Also, the motif of bloodguilt is particu-larly focused in this sequence of three chapters which are reasonably discussed together.[29] Indeed, the connections between 1 Samuel 25 and the Story of David and the House of Saul are particularly concentrated in this sequence because it presents two confrontations between David and Saul after David flees Saul's court. These encounters allow the narrator to develop the theme of justice in the conflict between David and Saul in ways that are impossible when the two men are not in contact.

[27] Gordon ("David's Rise," 50-51) tentatively suggests that the two are connected.

[28] So also Walter Brueggemann, *Power, Providence, and Personality: Biblical Insight into Life and Ministry* (Louisville, KY: Westminster John Knox, 1990) 52-65. Brueggemann does not develop the parallel between Saul and Nabal, but notes that all three chapters "focus the David story on the troubling issue of the violence, murder, and vengeance that normally accompany a seizure or transfer of public power" (p. 64) and portray David as destined to "arrive at royal power unencumbered by guilt" (p. 65).

[29] Brueggemann (*Power, Providence & Personality*, 52-65) also discusses these chapters together under the heading "Bloodguilt Avoided."

1 Samuel 25 as *Mise-en-abyme*

Saul and Nabal appear to be parallel characters as suggested by the observations made above. Verbal repetitions point to the motif of justice in David's relationship to Saul and Nabal. These repetitions occur with particular frequency in 1 Samuel 24–26 because chaps. 24 and 26 present encounters between David and Saul. However, the repetitions extend well beyond 1 Samuel 24 and 26. Furthermore, 1 Samuel 24 and 26 both assume prior narratives and anticipate David's eventual enthronement (1 Sam 24:10, 19, 21; 26:18, 24-25). The parallels between Saul and Nabal are so extensive that 1 Samuel 25 represents a *mise-en-abyme* of the Story of David and the House of Saul.

As indicated by the verbal connections noted above, the story in 1 Samuel 25 and its surrounding narrative both develop the injustice suffered by David who helps, yet suffers harm from Saul and Nabal. This theme is most clearly summarized in 1 Sam 24:18, in which Saul acknowledges to David, "you did good for me and I repaid you with harm" (אתה גמלתני הטובה ואני גמלתיך הרעה), and 1 Sam 25:21 in which David echoes Saul and claim about Nabal, "he has returned me evil for good" (וישב־לי רעה תחת טובה). Even Nabal's name is used by Abigail to indicate that he is in the wrong.

The argument that David is the just sufferer of injustice does not agree with modern scholarship on David. Modern critical scholars frequently understand the narratives in Samuel as propaganda that seeks to defend David against a variety of accusations leveled by his enemies.[30] For example, one may reasonably doubt the narrative claim that David made peace with Abner and Joab killed Abner without David's

---

[30] Although this critical tradition is centuries old (see Pierre Bayle, "David," in *Dictionnaire historique et critique* [4 vols.; Amsterdam: P. Brunal, 1720] 2. 1-7), it has achieved strong support in recent years. See Baruch Halpern, *David's Secret Demons: Messiah, Murderer, Traitor, King* (Grand Rapids, MI: Eerdmans, 2001); McKenzie, *King David*; Briend, "Figures"; Vermeylen, "La maison de Saül"; André Wénin, "David roi, de Goliath à Bathsabée: La figure de David dans la livres de Samuel," in *Figures de David à travers la Bible: XVIIᵉ congrès de l'ACFEB (Lille, 1ᵉʳ-5 septembre 1997)* (ed. Louis Desrousseaux and Jacques Vermeylen; LD 177; Paris: Cerf, 1999) 75-112; Walter Dietrich, "Das Biblische Bild der Herrschaft Davids," in *Von David zu den Deuteronomisten: Studien zu den Geschichtsüberlieferungen des Alten Testaments* (BWANT 156; Stuttgart: Kohlhammer, 2002) 9-31. These works owe a debt to McCarter, "Apology of David." For a more nuanced view of David, see Steussy, *David*. For discussion of this scholarship, see David Bosworth, "Evaluating King David: Old Problems in Recent Scholarship," *CBQ* 68 (2006) 191-210.

order or consent.[31] The circumstances of Abner's death during peace talks with David are suspicious. And Joab, as David's right-hand man (and nephew according to 1 Chron 2:15), might have been entrusted to do David's bidding while allowing David to maintain plausible deniability. Furthermore, the people notice David's public mourning for Abner and it pleased them (וכל־העם הכירו וייטב בעיניהם, 2 Sam 3:36). "And all the people and all Israel knew that day that the king did not order the killing of Abner" (וידעו כל־העם וכל־ישראל ביום ההוא כי לא היתה מהמלך להמית את־אבנר, 3:37). This notice raises the question of whether David's mourning was an act for public consumption rather than a sincere expression of sorrow.[32] In several places, the text implies that David is not the pious hero he appears to be. An attentive reader might wonder whether David does anything in Saul's service to provoke Saul's enmity.[33] Indeed, some doubt that David ever served in the court of Saul, and that he was always a brigand with an eye on Saul's throne.[34] Saul expresses concern for his dynasty and recognizes the threat posed by David, which motivates his persecution of David and makes Saul a sympathetic character.[35] The story of David and Nabal also duplicates this aspect of the text. Nabal expresses the Saulide view of David as a

---

[31] Halpern (*David's Secret Demons*, 308) thinks that Abner came to David at Ishbaal's instruction to offer him marriage to Michal in exchange for loyalty to Ishbaal. Since Halpern does not think that David ever served in Saul's court, this meeting was the first discussion of David's marriage to Saul's house. McKenzie (*King David*, 117-22) stays closer to the text by accepting the reasons for David's meeting with Abner, but agrees that David ordered Joab to kill Abner.

[32] As Steussey (*David*, 56) asks, "Does David feel bad about Abner's death? Or does his initial agitation arise more from fear of bloodguilt (see his initial reaction in 3:28-29) and loss of Abner's help in rallying Israel? How much of his lament is a public-relations ploy?"

[33] McKenzie (*King David*, 86-88) suggests that David may have attempted a coup against Saul.

[34] Halpern (*David's Secret Demons*, 280-82) thinks the whole narrative of David in Saul's court is a fabrication.

[35] Consequently, some scholars have read Saul as a tragic character. See W. Lee Humphreys, "The Tragedy of King Saul: A Study of the Structure of 1 Samuel 9–31," *JSOT* 6 (1978) 18-27; Humphreys, "The Rise and Fall of King Saul: A Study of an Ancient Narrative Stratum in 1 Samuel," *JSOT* 18 (1980) 74-90; Gunn, *Fate of King Saul*; John A. Sanford, *King Saul, the Tragic Hero: A Study in Individuation* (New York: Paulist, 1985); J. Cheryl Exum, *Tragedy and Biblical Narrative: Arrows of the Almighty* (Cambridge: Cambridge University Press, 1992) 16-44; Sarah Nicholson, *The Three Faces of Saul: An Intertextual Approach to Biblical Tragedy* (JSOTSup 339; Sheffield: Sheffield Academic Press, 2002). Edelman (*King Saul*) treats the story of Saul (1 Samuel 8–2 Samuel 1) as a unit, but without recourse to the genre of tragedy.

traitorous servant (25:10). The following discussion will highlight the text's explicit claim that David unjustly suffers, but also consider how the text provides another reading of David that is more congruent with critical scholarship. Both the positive and negative views of David are duplicated in 1 Samuel 25.

The verbal links noted above show that 1 Samuel 25 presents David in a relationship to Nabal that closely resembles his relationship to Saul described in the Story of David and the House of Saul. David does favors for, yet suffers harm from Saul and Nabal. The shorter narrative is a *mise-en-abyme* within the longer story since both accounts articulate identical relationships. The relationships have four common elements: the two narratives show David *doing good* for Saul and Nabal, *receiving evil* in return, *declining to avenge* himself, and being *vindicated* by God. These four points will organize the discussion of 1 Samuel 25 as a *mise-en-abyme*.[36] The parallel relationship David has with each man is illustrated in the chart below:[37]

---

[36] The notice of Samuel's death in 1 Sam 25:1a has no apparent relation to what precedes or follows. If it explains David's movement from his stronghold (24:23) to Maon (reading LXX, 25:1b), the connection is not clear. Edelman (*King Saul*, 204; similarly Walter Brueggemann, *First and Second Samuel* [IBC; Louisville, KY: John Knox, 1990] 175) suggests that Samuel's removal indicates that there will be "no further developments in the divine plan" since Yhwh's prophet is removed from the story (and so can not anoint another king). The problem with this suggestion is that God can raise up new prophetic kingmakers (1 Kgs 11:29-39; 2 Kgs 9:1-13). David Jobling (*1 Samuel* [Berit Olam; Collegeville, MN: Liturgical Press, 1998] 253-54) notes that Samuel's death seems postponed beyond expectations that he might die after his defeat of the Philistines (1 Samuel 7) or his farewell speech (1 Samuel 12) in order to make kingship seem like an organic development from judgeship. Jobling does not indicate why Samuel finally dies when he does, but his observation may be combined with Edelman's suggestion that Samuel's function only ends when Saul acknowledges that David will be king (1 Sam 24:21).

[37] The outline offered by Biddle ("Ancestral Motifs," 621-23) claims a "roughly parallel" structure: In the first part (vv. 3-13), David "hears" (v. 4) about Nabal's sheep shearing and "sends" (v. 5) messengers, just as in the third part (vv. 39-42) he "hears" (v. 39) about Nabal's death and "sends" (v. 39) messengers to propose marriage to Abigail. In the second intervening part (vv. 14-38), Abigail "is told" (v. 14) about the conflict between David and Nabal and "sends" the requested provisions to David (vv. 18-19). I am not confident that the rather common verbs he cites indicate the structure of the story. J.P. Fokkelmann (*Narrative Art and Poetry in the Books of Samuel* [4 vols.; Assen: Van Gorcum, 1986] 2. 477-80) opts for a slightly different structure grounded in the plot: the exposition (vv. 1b-13) and consequences (vv. 39-44) bracket the main story (vv. 14-38), which may be divided into crisis (vv. 14-17), confrontation (vv. 20-35), and solution (vv. 36-38).

	David and Nabal	David and Saul
David does good	David protects Nabal's property and treats his servants well	David slays Goliath, defeats Philistine armies, and soothes Saul's madness with music. David mourns the deaths of Saul, Abner, and Ishbaal and avenges the deaths of Saul and his son.
David receives evil	Nabal refuses reciprocal hospitality to David and insults his messengers	Saul seeks to kill David at court, and even his apparent kindness (offering Michal as David's wife) is a trap. When David flees, Saul pursues him and David suffers exile and persecution.
David declines vengeance	Abigail restrains David from avenging himself on Nabal	David refrains from taking vengeance against Saul. He does not make war against Saul and twice spares his life. He executes those who claim to have killed Saul or his heirs.
Yhwh vindicates David	Yhwh kills Nabal, and David marries Nabal's wife	Saul dies in battle, and David becomes king of Judah and then of all Israel.

As distinct from the discussion of Genesis 38, the *mise-en-abyme* in 1 Samuel 25 is not dependent on parallel plots. In Genesis 38, the parallel relationships of Judah with Tamar and Joseph unfold in specific narrative segments. In the present case, aspects of the relationship do not correlate with segments of the plot. The good done by David and the harm suffered by him are both distributed throughout the narrative. Saul begins to turn on David as early as 1 Samuel 18:8-9 and tries to kill him in 18:11. David continues to show kindness to the house of Saul in his lament for Saul and Jonathan (2 Samuel 1:19-27), and his vengeance for Ishbaal's murder (4:9-12). Similarly, Nabal's servants confirm David's kindness to them (1 Sam 25:15-16) after Nabal has insulted David (25:10-11). Thus, David's favors are recalled after Nabal's insult. Since the major concern in both stories is reciprocal justice, the various aspects of David's relationship to each man are recalled throughout the stories and the relevant aspects of the relationships do not fit into neat textual units.

Although the *mise-en-abyme* in the case of 1 Samuel 25 does not depend on parallel plots, the parallel relationships still suggest how the *mise-en-abyme* places emphasis on some passages over others. The two times David spares Saul's life highlight David's kindness and the harm he has suffered from Saul (1 Samuel 24 and 26). As noted above, the *mise-en-abyme* is especially focused in these chapters because these are the only two occasions when Saul and David meet face to face after David flees Saul's court. The connections are also frequent in David's career in Saul's court, where David's faithful service contrasts with Saul's persecution (1 Samuel 16–20). During David's sojourn in the wilderness, the two men can only be implicitly compared. For example, David seeks and receives divine guidance (וישאל דוד ביהוה, 1 Sam 23:2, 4; 30:8; cf. 1 Sam 22:5, 10, 15), but "Saul inquired of Yhwh, but Yhwh did not answer him by dreams, urim, or prophets" (וישאל שאול ביהוה ולא ענהו יהוה גם בחלמות גם באורים גם בנביאם, 1 Sam 28:6). Also, Saul massacres the priestly city of Nob (1 Sam 22:11-23), but David refrains from massacring the house of Nabal (1 Sam 25:34).

The motif of receiving good for evil binds 1 Samuel 25 to the larger Story of David and the House of Saul. In both stories, David refrains from exacting vengeance for the evil done to him by men whom he has aided. I will describe David's relationship to Saul and Nabal in detail by discussing its parts: the favors that David does for each man; the harm he receives from each in return; his restraint in the face of this injustice; and Yhwh's final vindication of David in each case. The second part is particularly lengthy because the narrative of Saul and David includes several relevant episodes and because Nabal's insult to David has not been widely appreciated and needs to be discussed in detail.

David Does Good

In both narratives, David performs some benefit for another man but is mistreated in return. The Story of David and the House of Saul includes ample testimony to the good deeds that David does for the benefit of Saul, all of which modern scholars have doubted. According to one account, David gains entrance into Saul's court by playing the harp to soothe Saul when the evil spirit torments him (1 Sam 16:23). An alternative account indicates that David comes to Saul's attention only when David slays Goliath.[38] The Goliath story appears dubious given that elsewhere Elhanan, one of David's men, is credited with killing Goliath (2 Sam 21:19). The story, however, has become well established in Samuel, and Jonathan (1 Sam 19:5) and Ahimelech (21:9) refer to it and Abigail alludes to it (25:29). Some scholars argue that the story was originally about Elhanan, but was later elaborated with David as the hero of the story.[39] If the battle with Goliath could not have gained David entry into Saul's court (since it never happened), maybe David's musical skill did. Although some scholars concede that David may have played the lyre, the image of David soothing Saul's madness is not widely accepted.[40] One may wonder, then, how David came to serve Saul. Halpern argues that David never did, but the entire sojourn in Saul's court is an invention to address a variety of apologetic concerns about David. For example, it establishes David's credentials as a killer of Philistines and counteracts the admission that he served as a Philistine vassal. It also claims for David some positive connection to the house of Saul through Jonathan and Michal, which mitigates the

---

[38] Although single combat between champions is common in Homer's *Iliad*, it is unusual in ancient Near Eastern literature. Possible examples include the battle of the young men in 2 Sam 2:12-17, Marduk and Tiamat in *Enuma Elish*, and Hattusili III and a champion of the tribes north of the Halys river before Hattusili became king. See Harry A. Hoffner, "A Hittite Analogue to the David and Goliath Contest of Champions?" *CBQ* 30 (1968) 220-25.

[39] Isser (*Sword of Goliath*, 34-37) employs this detail in his argument that the David stories grew as legends analogous to stories about King Arthur.

[40] Since Halpern (*David's Secret Demons*, 280-82) does not accept that David served in Saul's court, he has no use for David's musical skill. McKenzie (*King David*, 56-57) is skeptical, but not dismissive. Others note the textual representation of David as musician without passing historical judgment. Thus, Vermeylen, "La maison de Saül," 39-40 and Walter Dietrich, *David: Der Herrscher mit der Harfe* (Biblishe Gestalten 14; Leipzig: Evangelische Verlagsanstalt, 2006) 277-309; Dietrich, "Das biblische Bild," 10-11.

statement that he nearly exterminated Saul's house.[41] Halpern's skepticism has a basis in the text. When David flees Saul's court, no one from court joins David's band in the wilderness even though David was Saul's most famous and beloved officer.

After David vanquishes Goliath, Saul appoints him a military commander, and he succeeds on every mission Saul sends him to accomplish (18:5). He demonstrates his military prowess against the Philistines on several occasions (18:30; 19:8), and he earns a martial reputation that exceeds Saul's (18:7). David manages to bring Saul two hundred Philistine foreskins as the bride-price for Michal (18:27).[42] If Halpern is correct and David never served Saul, then he could not have performed any of these favors. Even after he flees from Saul, David twice spares Saul's life when he has the opportunity to kill him (1 Samuel 24; 26). David's mercy may be called a favor if declining to kill a man qualifies as kindness. The text presents Saul accepting David's restraint as generosity (1 Sam 24:18-19; 26:21). After Samuel anoints David as king, David pursues a middle course or policy of restraint between two extremes. He might "hide among the baggage" as Saul did (1 Sam 10:22-23) and wait for Yhwh to thrust him onto the throne, or he might immediately set out to kill Saul and take his throne, as Jehu did following his anointing (2 Kings 9–10). Instead, David serves Saul and rises in his court in order to position himself for Yhwh to complete his ascension to the throne. David's policy of restraint seeks a middle path that both trust in Yhwh to act on his behalf, but still makes efforts to facilitate Yhwh's plan.[43]

In addition to David's many actions, the narrator reports that "David was successful in all his ways and Yhwh was with him" (18:14).

---

[41] Halpern, *David's Secret Demons*, 181-82.

[42] LXX reads one hundred.

[43] Borgman (*David, Saul, and God*, 91-91) asks, "Does God simply make David king, after the secret anointing through Samuel? Does God ever do anything for David without David doing what he can, which includes asking for help?" He answers his questions by observing "David goes so far, asks God for direction, gets it, and then moves on. Or, when David goes in completely the wrong direction and is confronted [e.g., by Abigail], he almost always responds in such a way as to move in a different and better direction." Claire Matthews McGinnis ("Swimming with the Divine Tide: An Ignatian Reading of 1 Samuel," in *Theological Exegesis: Essays in Honor of Brevard S. Childs* [ed. Christopher Seitz and Katheryn Greene-McCreight; Grand Rapids, MI: Eerdmans, 1999] 266) similarly argues that "while David's success is attributable to the divine favor he receives, David's general willingness to place YHWH's interests above his own, his desire to discern the direction of God's activity and to act in accordance with it, play an integral role in the favorable outcome of events."

David's success as a military leader serves both as a favor that David does for Saul while in his service (1 Sam 19:4; 22:14), and as a problem that engenders Saul's animosity (1 Sam 18:7-12). The expression "Yhwh was with David" (יהוה עם־דוד, 18:28; cf. vv. 12, 14; 16:18) means that he was successful, not necessarily good or pious.[44] Various individuals explicitly characterize David positively. Saul's servant calls him "brave" (גבור חיל) and "well spoken" (נבון דבר, 16:18). Ahimelech characterizes David as "faithful" (נאמן, 22:14; cf. 26:23) to Saul and "honored" (נכבד) in the king's house (22:14). Saul calls him "righteous" (צדיק, 24:18; cf. 26:23). The text repeatedly claims that David is good and that he does good for Saul. However, he also does good for Israel's Philistine enemy. The king of Gath "trusts" (נאמן, 27:12) David and finds him "honest" (ישר, 29:6), and "good in my eyes like an angel of God" (טוב אתה בעיני כמלאך אלהים, 29:9). A few characters are less sanguine about David's virtues. Nabal sees him as a rebellious servant (25:10) and Shimei calls him a "man of blood and son of Belial" (איש הדמים ואיש הבליעל, 2 Sam 16:7, cf. v. 8), and his own brother tells David, "I know your insolence and the evil of your heart (אני ידעתי את־זדנך ואת רע לבבך), for you have come down to see the battle" (1 Sam 17:28). Modern scholars have tended to agree with Nabal and Shimei. Also, David is not uniformly popular. The Ziphtes twice try to assist Saul in killing David (23:19-24; 26:1) and the people of Keilah were ready to hand him over to Saul (23:12).

The good that David does for Nabal consists in guarding his servants and property. David invites Nabal to verify his favor by consulting his servants (1 Sam 25:8). David claims that he did no injury to Nabal's shepherds and no sheep went missing (25:7). This claim implies that David and his men helped Nabal's servants guard the sheep from human and animal predators. Although Nabal does not ask his servants about David's conduct, one of these servants does confirm David's testimony when speaking to Abigail. He affirms that David and his men "were extremely good to us" (25:15). The servant's passive, "We were done no injury" (25:15), draws attention to the fact that not

---

[44] The meaning of the expression "Yhwh was with PN" appears to mean "PN was successful" (Gen 39:2, 3, 23; Judg 1:22; 2:18; 1 Sam 18:12, 14, 28; 2 Kgs 18:7). See McKenzie, *King David*, 65-66; Steussy, *David*, 87-91; Yiu-Wing Fung, *Victim and Victimizer: Joseph's Interpretation of His Destiny* (JSOTSup 308; Sheffield: Sheffield Academic Press, 2000) 12-14; Bosworth, "Evaluating King David," 200.

merely did David not harm them, but he allowed no one else to do so. He confirms that nothing went missing "while we were living among them in the highland" (25:15). The reference to the "highland" (בשדה) emphasizes the exposed position of Nabal's flock and the ease with which it might have been plundered, for the "highland" or "open country" can be a place of danger where none can help.[45] The servant also says that they were living among David's men, not *vice versa* (התהלכנו אתם, 25:15; cf. v. 7). This expression suggests that they were in a sense guests near David's encampment, not that David sought them out and solicited their friendship.[46] The servant further emphasizes the kindness done by David by saying that the men "were a wall around us night and day the whole time we were with them shepherding the sheep" (כל־ימי היותנו עמם רעים הצאן חומה היו עלינו גם־לילה גם־יומם, 25:16).[47] This statement again implies that Nabal's servants were guests of David and his men went to some length to protect them from all mischief. However, the story does not narrate any specific threats to Nabal's property. The narrative does not claim that David killed any lions or bears (cf. 1 Sam 17:34-36) or drove off any thieves. David may be asking Nabal to spend his wealth on strangers who have not rendered him any significant service.

In sum, the narrative presents many favors David does for which Saul should be grateful. He slays Goliath, plays the harp to soothe Saul when the evil spirit torments him, and achieves many victories against the Philistines. In short, he is a good and faithful servant of his king.

---

[45] Cf. בשדה in Gen 4:8; Exod 22:30; Deut 21:1; 22:27; 2 Sam 14:6. William H. Propp ("Hebrew *śāde(h)*, 'Highland,'" *VT* 37 [1987] 230-36) argues that the term (related to Akkandian *šadû*) may denote specifically mountains or highlands in addition to land or a cultivated plot. He also notes the semantic connection between the meanings "out of doors" and "mountain, highland" is natural in contexts referring to mountainous terrain. Propp's suggested meaning of "highland" appears to fit the present context.

[46] T. R. Hobbs ("Hospitality in the First Testament and the 'Teleological Fallacy'," *JSOT* 95 [2001] 25-28) has explored the motif of hospitality in 1 Samuel 25. He argues that the servant's testimony verifies that David qualified for Nabal's hospitality as reciprocation for his kindness to Nabal's servants (p. 26). Hospitality seems to be operative in the story, but as Hobbs notes, the issue is complicated by David's outlaw status and the murky political situation. Significantly, Abigail offers David hospitality outside the house. Abigail's actions preserve her household and satisfy David's request and restore his honor. Marjorie O'Rourke Boyle also touches on hospitality in "The Law of the Heart: The Death of a Fool (1 Samuel 25)," *JBL* 120 (2001) 417.

[47] Andrea L. Weiss, *Figurative Language in Biblical Prose Narrative: Metaphor in the Book of Samuel* (VTSup 107; Leiden: Brill, 2006) 47-50, 100-105.

The text includes alternative views of David, including his service to Achich of Gath, Israel's enemy and Nabal's interpretation of David as a traitorous servent. When he flees to the hill country, David guards the servants and sheep of Nabal when they were exposed in the highlands where David and his men were staying. However, the text does not lay heavy stress on David's kindness, perhaps because it may have been unnecessary since the story does not narrate any serious threat to Nabal's house.

David Receives Evil

As noted above, David's relationships to Saul and Nabal are characterized in proverbial terms: David does good for each man, but receives evil in return (1 Sam 24:18; 25:21; cf. Gen 44:4; Pss 35:12; 38:20; 109:5; Prov 17:13; Jer 18:20). The ways in which Saul wrongs David are well understood, although the differences between versions (LXX and MT) require some sorting out of Saul's motives and actions.[48] The manner in which Nabal harms David, however, is not well understood, so I will discuss the issue in detail.

There are three major reasons why Saul begins to persecute David, one of which is unique to MT: (1) Saul fears David's military success (1 Sam 18:7-9, 15-16); (2) in the MT only, Saul is tormented by an evil spirit and openly attacks David (1 Sam 18:10-11); (3) Saul's subtle plan to kill David backfires, and David marries Michal, leading Saul to realize that Yhwh is with David. Saul therefore fears David even more (1 Sam 18:12a), and, according to MT, becomes David's enemy (18:12b).

The evil spirit that afflicts Saul is normally interpreted to mean that Saul became insane.[49] Saul's "ranting" (1 Sam 18:10) and subsequent

---

[48] On the text-critical issues, see *The Story of David and Goliath: Textual and Literary Criticism, Papers of a Joint Research Venture* (eds. Dominique Barthélemy et al.; OBO 73; Göttingen: Vandenhoeck & Ruprecht, 1986); Emanuel Tov, "The Composition of 1 Samuel 16-18 in the Light of the Septuagint Version," in *Empirical Models for Biblical Criticism* (ed. Jeffrey H. Tigay; Philadelphia: University of Pennsylvania Press, 1985) 97-130; Stephen Pisano, *Additions or Omissions in the Books of Samuel: The Significant Pluses and Minuses in the Massoretic, LXX and Qumran Texts* (OBO 57; Göttingen: Vandenhoeck & Ruprecht, 1984) 78-86; Arie van der Kooij, "The Story of David and Goliath: The Early History of Its Text," *ETL* 68 (1992) 118-31.

[49] Ancients often interpreted mental illness in terms of spirits. However, commentators generally recognize that the text presents Saul's suffering as theological

"prophesying" (both ויתנבא, 19:23-25; cf. 10:10) indicate his mental insta-
bility, which seems to be a consequence of the spirit of Yhwh departing
from Saul (16:14).[50] This madness explains Saul's attempts on David's
life in 18:10-11 and 19:9-10 and may shed light on his general hostility to David even when his mind is not afflicted. The wider narrative indicates, however, that Saul's hostility to David is not madness,
but insight. Saul accurately perceives that David threatens his dynasty
(18:8; 20:31) and acts to remove the threat. Saul is not paranoid; David
really is out to get him.

Scholars and translators sometimes claim that Saul was jealous of
David. The unusual verb in 1 Sam 18:9 (עוין, Q; עון, K) appears to be the
only basis on which scholars say that Saul is "jealous" of David.[51] But
Saul is never characterized as jealous (קנא, cf. Gen 26:14; 30:1; 37:11). It
is better to interpret the meaning of the present verb, which occurs
nowhere else, in the context of Saul's anger (ויחר לשאול מאד, 18:8) and
fear (וירא שאול מלפני דוד, 18:12) rather than appeal to a jealousy which is
nowhere expressed.[52] The verb עוין is denominative from עין "eye." Otherwise unattested in biblical Hebrew, the verb is known from Ugaritic,
Phoenician, and post-biblical Hebrew. The Ugaritic verb means "to
see, look (at), watch, spy."[53] For example Baal observes Anat coming to

---

rather medical. In Judges, legitimate leadership is indicated by the spirit rushing on an
individual. The expression in 16:14 seems to indicate the moment that Saul's divinely
sanctioned rule comes to an end. See McCarter, *I Samuel*, 280-81; Tsumura, *The First
Book*, 246-47.

[50] Unlike the later references to Saul's madness, this first indication is present in
LXX.

[51] Thus, for example, *BDB*, 745a; Gunn, *Fate of King Saul*, 116-19; McCarter,
1 Samuel, 312-13; John van Seters, *In Search of History: Historiography in the Ancient
World and the Origins of Biblical History* (New Haven: Yale University Press, 1983;
repr., Winona Lake, IN: Eisenbrauns, 1997) 266; Briend, "Les Figures," 18; Vermeylen,
"La maison de Saül," 43.

[52] Mayer I. Gruber (*Aspects of Nonverbal Communication in the Ancient Near
East* [2 vols.; Studia Pohl: Dissertationes Scientificae de Rebus Orientis Antiqui
12/1-2; Rome: Pontificio Instituto Biblico, 1980] 2. 371-74) argues that the expression
ויחר לשאול מאד means "Saul became very depressed" rather than "angry." Gruber's
argument assumes a greater distinction between depression and anger than actually
exists. Anger is a common manifestation of depression, and Saul's casting his spear
appears to be an angry gesture. Since many people mistakenly imagine that depressed
people are quiet and sullen, his proposed translation might be misleading. However,
he is right to note the depth of Saul's emotions here; Saul is not merely angry, but suffers a complex set of emotional responses to David's success.

[53] Gregorio del Olmo Lete and Joaquín Sanmartín, *A Dictionary of the Ugaritic*

meet him: "the advance of his sister Baal eyes" (*hlk.aḫth.bʿl.yʿn*, CAT 1.3 IV 39).[54] The term occurs in parallel with other verbs of seeing: "Baal sees (*wtmr*) his daughters, / eyes (*yʿn*) Pidray, Daughter of Light, / Then Tally, [Daughter] of Rain" (CAT 1.3 I 22-25).[55] The Ugaritic evidence suggests the unusual Hebrew verb most likely indicates seeing or eyeing without specific connotations of jealousy.

The Phoenician verb may be known from an amulet found at Arslan Tash and dated to the 7th century. The protective amulet frequently repeats the noun "eye" and may include one example of the denominative עין, although some scholars read it as another noun.[56] Although the Arslan Tash inscription seems concerned with the evil eye, McCarter notes that "there appears to be no suggestion of the Evil Eye" in 1 Sam 18:9.[57] In post-biblical Hebrew, the verb resembles the Ugaritic meaning.[58] Considering the context and the comparative evidence of Ugaritic and post-biblical Hebrew, the meaning "to keep an eye on" seems most appropriate in 1 Sam 19:6. The reasonable LXX translation reads ὑποβλεπόμενος, "to eye scornfully, suspiciously, or angrily."[59] Due to fear for his life and throne, Saul keeps an eye on his too-successful officer. Saul reasonably fears that a high-ranking, successful, and popular soldier is well positioned to take the throne.[60]

Language in the Alphabetic Tradition (trans. Wilfred G. E. Watson; 2 vols.; HO 67; Leiden: Brill, 2003) I. 167-68.

[54] Translation by Mark S. Smith, "The Baal Cycle," in *Ugaritic Narrative Poetry* (ed. Simon B. Parker; SBLWAW 9; Atlanta, GA: SBL, 1997) 114.

[55] Smith, "Baal Cycle," 106. The word also occurs with *wyšu.ʿnh.wyʿn* "he lifted his eyes and saw" and parallel to *hnh* "see" in CAT 1.3 I 15.

[56] John C. L. Gibson (*Textbook of Syrian Semitic Inscriptions* [3 vols.; Oxford: Clarendon, 1982] 3. 90) reads the word as a participle meaning "caster of the evil eye." Frank Moore Cross ("Leaves from An Epigrapher's Notebook," *CBQ* 36 [1974] 486-90) and Y. Avishur ("The Second Amulet Incantation from Arslan-Tash," *UF* 10 [1978] 32) read the word as a noun. This reading preserves parallelism and seven occurrences of "eye" in the amulet.

[57] McCarter, *I Samuel*, 313.

[58] Marcus Jastrow, *A Dictionary of the Targumim, the Talmud Babli and Yerushalmi, and the Midrashic Literature* (New York: Judaica Press, 1996) 1053-54. Jastrow glosses the verb "to look in, to look carefully, to search."

[59] LSJ, 1876a.

[60] As examples of this principle, the books of Samuel and Kings offer David, Zimri (1 Kgs 16:9-10), Omri (1 Kgs 16:15-22), Jehu (2 Kings 9–10, N.B. 9:31), Menahem (2 Kgs 15:14), and Pekah (2 Kgs 15:25). It is not clear whether Baasha (1 Kgs 16:27-28), Shallum (2 Kgs 15:10), and Hoshea (2 Kgs 15:30) were officers. Imperial Roman history provides especially abundant examples.

David flees the court after he has established that Saul is trying to kill him. Saul's constant attempts on David's life leave David no choice but to escape. David complains bitterly of this exile because he has "no share in Yhwh's inheritance" (1 Sam 26:19). Certain speeches summarize this motif of injustice with language of sin, guilt, innocence, good, and evil. Jonathan speaks "well" (טוב) of David to his father in 1 Sam 19:4-5: "Let not the king sin (אל־יחטא) against his servant David, since he has not sinned against you (לוא חטא לך), and his deeds have been extremely good for you (טוב־לך מאד). He risked his life when he slew the Philistine, and Yhwh accomplished a great victory for all Israel. You saw and rejoiced. Why would you sin against innocent blood (ולמה תחטא בדם נקי) by killing David for nothing?" This speech specifically claims that not only has David not harmed Saul, but that he has helped him. In support of his argument, Jonathan cites David's slaying of the Philistine and the consequent victory over the Philistines. Jonathan presents this action as a benefit to Israel, but especially to Saul, who had been afraid of the Philistine like everyone else (17:11). He also stresses that David risked his life and that Saul rejoiced in David's victory.

The conclusion of the speech stresses David's innocence and indicates the bloodguilt that would come to Saul if he were to kill David. Jonathan's speech appears to be successful, since Saul solemnly swears that David will not die.[61] Saul, however, violates this oath and tries twice more to kill David (19:10, 15). David escapes, goes to Jonathan, and reemphasizes his innocence in the form of a rhetorical question, "What have I done? What is my guilt or my sin (מה־עוני ומה־חטאתי) before your father that he is seeking my life?" (1 Sam 20:1).[62] Later, Ahimelch echoes Jonathan's speech by recollecting how David has been a faithful servant of Saul's: "Who among your servants is as faithful as David? He is son-in-law to the king and honored in your house" (1 Sam 22:14).

---

[61] For a detailed discussion of Jonathan's speech, see François Rossier, *L'intercession entre les hommes dans la Bible hébraïque: L'intercession entre les hommes aux origines de l'intercession auprès de Dieu* (OBO 152; Göttingen: Vandenhoeck & Ruprecht, 1996) 75-99.

[62] Steussey (*David*, 71) answers David's question for him: "David has accepted the heir apparent's sword and robe (18:4), married into the royal family, developed popular support (including particularly the army), and publicly flaunted his relationship with the kingmaker Samuel (19:18), who declared Saul's downfall. David's intentions may only have been hinted at, but his actions point steadily to the throne."

The motif of Saul's unjust treatment of David achieves its clearest expression in the chapters bracketing the story of David and Nabal. In these episodes, David and Saul meet in person following the final rift in their relationship. Their encounter provides the narrator an opportunity to review the issues between the two men and to add legal language into the presentation. The first time David spares Saul's life, he shows the evidence of his mercy to Saul (1 Sam 24:12). He argues that his mercy is proof that he has never plotted against Saul. David generously attributes Saul's animosity to bad counsel: "Why do you listen to the words of a man saying, 'David seeks to do you harm'?" (דוד מבקשׁ רעתך, 24:10). He offers proof of his mercy to Saul as evidence that "there is no wrong or rebellion in my hand and I have not sinned against you" (אין בידי רעה ופשע ולא־חטאתי לך, 24:12). David invokes Yhwh to judge (ישׁפט, 24:13; cf 24:16) between David and Saul, to avenge (ונקמני, 24:13) David, and decide his case (את־ריבי וירב, 24:16). Saul responds by acknowledging the justice of David's case: "You are righteous (צדיק); I am not. You have done good (הטובה) to me, but I have done evil (הרעה) to you" (24:18; cf. Prov 17:13). Saul even says that David will become king of Israel and asks that David spare his children (24:22). The second time David spares Saul, David asks him, "What have I done? What evil is in my hand (מה עשׂיתי ומה־בידי רעה, 1 Sam 26:18)?"[63] Saul again acknowledges his wrong and says, "I have sinned" (חטאתי, 26:21), and promises "I will not harm you again" (לא־ארע לך עוד, 26:21), and admits, "I have acted foolishly and made a serious mistake" (26:21). For sparing Saul's life, David hopes for a reward, for "Yhwh rewards a man for his righteousness and his fidelity" (ויהוה ישׁיב לאישׁ את־צדקתו ואת־אמנתו, 26:23).

The Story of David and the House of Saul presents David as unjustly persecuted by Saul. Saul is angry, afraid, and insane. Saul and several other characters recognize that the treatment of David is unfair and even Saul and Jonathan acknowledge that David will become king. Scholars understandably dismiss the historical reliability of Saul's extraordinary acknowledgement, especially considering that Saul con-

---

[63] Steussey (David, 72) answers the question of what David has done: "David has now had multiple secret meetings with Saul's son, gathered a fighting force, gotten a corner on priestly support, developed contacts in neighboring kingdoms (see especially 22:3), demanded support from landowners (25:8), married into riches (25:42), and possibly run off with Saul's wife (25:43). The Philistines speak of him as king already (21:11)."

tinues to pursue David. Although Saul's inconsistent behavior might be explained by his madness, Saul looks less insane considering that he presciently foresees the danger that David poses to his house. The narrative's dubious claims bring its central argument into question, complicate the presentation of the dispute between Saul and David, and imply that Saul's animosity may be sane and rational.

Like Saul, Nabal treats David unjustly. The wrong that Nabal does to David has not been widely appreciated. The narrative introduces Nabal as an evil man (מעללים קשה ורע in 1 Sam 25:3). Nabal's servant, Abigail, and David enrich this view (1 Sam 25:17, 21, 25).[64] Still, several readers have asserted that Nabal's actions may be both reasonable and prudent. They claim that David extorts money from people using his armed followers as an implicit threat of harm to those who refuse to pay. He is a "racketeer."[65] One might understand why Nabal might not want to finance David's activities. A still more compelling motive for Nabal is simple self-preservation. Nabal may know what Saul did to the priests of Yhwh at Nob for their unwitting support of David. He might expect a similar fate if he supplies David and his men with provisions. These considerations may be sufficient to explain why Nabal refuses David's request.

The racketeering analysis of David's activity neglects a critical aspect of the text. The claim that David is merely a criminal neglects the political thrust of his activities. Older scholarship likened David's

---

[64] The note that Nabal is a Calebite would help to explain the beginning of David's kingship in Hebron, which was the center of the clan of Caleb (Josh 14:13-15; Judg 1:10-20). If David acquired Nabal's wealth along with his wife, then he would have also acquired status in Hebron. A few commentators (e.g., van Wolde, "A Leader," 357) follow LXX and read "doglike" rather than "Calebite" and therefore see the expression as casting Nabal in a negative light, since dogs were allegedly despised ancient Near East. However, Geoffrey David Miller ("Attitudes towards Dogs in Ancient Israel: A Reassessment," *JSOT* 32 [2008] 487-500) argues that dogs were esteemed in ancient Israel as helpers and companions (Job 30:1; Tob 6:2; 11:4). Such esteem may be consistent with pejorative uses of the term "dog" (1 Sam 17:43; 2 Sam 3:8; Lachish Letters, *KAI* 193:4; 196:4; 197:4, also in Johannes Renz, *Handbuch der Althebräischen Epigraphik* [3 vols.; Darmstadt: Wissenschaftliche Buchgesellschaft, 1994] 1. 409-12, 419-22, 425-27.). Similarly, one might mistakenly think that English-speakers despise female dogs because of similar pejorative references. See also Oded Borowski, *Every Living Thing: Daily Use of Animals in Ancient Israel* (Walnut Creek, CA: AltaMira, 1998) 133-40.

[65] Gunn, *Fate of King Saul*, 96; Brueggemann, *First and Second Samuel*, 176; McKenzie, *King David*, 97; Halpern, *David's Secret Demons*, 284.

activities to those of the *ḫabiru*.[66] The *ḫabiru* occur in the Amarna letters and Mari texts as peripheral people who may be brigands or mercenaries. Like some of the *ḫabiru*, David appears as a raider, who operates on his own, then under Philistine protection. Such raiders appear elsewhere in the text and do not seem to be regarded as criminals (1 Sam 27:8-12; 30:1-2; 2 Sam 3:22; 4:1-4). A closer parallel to David's wilderness career is the rise of Idrimi.[67] Idrimi was forced to leave Aleppo when a coup displaced his father. He set out into the desert to raise a force of loyal followers who helped him to his throne in Alalah. Although David's father was not a king, his anointing by Samuel prepares for a story about David's rise to the throne. The anointing and eventual ascension of David casts the intermediate stories in a political rather than only criminal light. The narrative does not reduce David to a racketeer. Elsewhere, David does not punish the Judeans who are hostile to him (1 Sam 23:12, 19-20; 24:2; 26:1). Therefore, it seems that he would not slaughter a household merely for refusing him provisions. Also, the criminal analogy overlooks the political thrust of David's actions. The distinction between organized crime and political opposition is not always clear, and governments may have an interest in obscuring the difference. (For example, the labor organizers in the United States have been treated as criminals.[68]) The characterization of David as a criminal, therefore, is grounded in aspects of the text,

[66] For example, John Bright, *A History of Israel* (4rd ed.; Philadelphia: Westminster John Knox, 2000) 193.

[67] On Idrimi's inscription, see Edward L. Greenstein and David Marcus, "The Akkadian Inscription of Idrimi," *JANES* 8 (1976) 59-96; *ANET* 159-61; *Contexts of Scripture: Canonical Compositions, Monumental Inscriptions and Archival Documents from the Biblical World* (ed. William W. Hallo et al.; 3 vols; Leiden: Brill, 1997-2002) 1. 479-80. Also, James W. Flanagan (*David's Social Drama: A Hologram of Israel's Early Iron* Age [JSOTSup 73; Sheffield: Almond, 1988] 327-331) notes that Ibn Saud, the founder of the Saudi dynasty, established his dynasty after a period of raiding his rival from the periphery of the Arabian peninsula. His raids were directed at his rivals (the Rashids), and he won the support of the people after his daring capture of Riyadh. Like the actions of David and Idrimi, Ibn Saud's political and military exploits are not reducible to criminal activity.

[68] Several nations (but not the United States) recognize a category of specifically political crime, as distinct from other crime and protect political criminals from certain kinds of punishment. Nations without such a category of laws can claim to have no political criminals because such persons are treated as "common criminals." For a substantial catalogue of examples of how criminal and political behaviors have overlapped and become confused in American history, see *The Tree of Liberty: A Documentary History of Rebellion and Political Crime in America* (ed. Nicholas N. Kittrie

but oversimplifies the issue. David aims at kingship. He is not merely a highway robber or extortionist; he is a usurper.

David's reaction to Nabal does not indicate that David was a racketeer. Nabal does more than decline to feed David and his men. He insults David in a manner that David cannot ignore, as seen in the dialogue between David and Nabal. The passage emphasizes the role of the messengers in this context. Moses conducts diplomatic correspondence with Edom (Num 20:14-21) and Sihon (Num 21:21-23) through messengers, but the messengers are not an important element of the story. Similarly, the dialogue between Jephthah and the Ammonites (Judg 11:12-28) does not require the narrator to describe the messengers. In contrast, the disgraceful treatment of David's messengers at the hands of Hanun king of the Ammonites (2 Sam 10:1-5) is cause for war.[69] Therefore, the messengers are a significant part of that story. Similarly, the treatment of David's messengers is an issue in 1 Samuel 25. Although Nabal does not seem to strike the servants, he mistreats them (ויעט, 1 Sam 25:14).[70] David resolves to kill Nabal and the males of his household not because Nabal refuses to supply him with provisions, but rather because Nabal abuses his messengers. Several unusual elements in the story emphasize the presence of the messengers because of their treatment at the hands of Nabal is an issue: the narrator shows David addressing the messengers (25:5-8); the messengers are identified as ten young men (25:5); David's message is quoted when he presents

---

and Eldon D. Wedlock, Jr.; rev. ed.; Baltimore, MD: Johns Hopkins University Press, 1998).

[69] Ancient Near Eastern diplomatic texts frequently note concern for the hospitable treatment of messengers. See Raymond Westbrook, "International Law in the Amarna Age," and Geoffrey Berridge, "Amarna Diplomacy: A Full-fledged Diplomatic System?" both in *Amarna Diplomacy: The Beginnings of International Relations* (ed. Raymond Cohen and Raymond Westbrook; Baltimore: Johns Hopkins University Press, 2000) 33-34 and 213-14, respectively.

[70] The root of this verb is related to the Hebrew word for a bird of prey (עיט). *BDB* (p. 743) and *HALOT* (p. 816) both understand the verb to mean "to shout, scream" with ב and "to swoop down on" with אל as in 1 Sam 14:32 (reading ויעט, Q; ויעש, K) and 15:19. The cognates in Arabic (ʿyṭ, "to scream"; ġyẓ, "to inflame with anger") and Syriac (ʿyṗ, "anger") seem to support "scream." However, the *Diccionario biblico hebreo-español* (2d ed.; eds. Luis Alonso Schökel et al.; Madrid: Trotta, 1999) 557, which relies less heavily on cognate words in languages attested much later than biblical Hebrew, offers the translation "maltratar" ("to mistreat, abuse, misuse") for 1 Sam 25:14. This interpretation draws on the present context of the verb and captures its pertinent meaning. For a full discussion of the language here, see Weiss, *Figurative Language*, 50-58, 93-100.

it to the young men, rather than when Nabal hears it (25:9); the narrator superfluously states that the messengers addressed Nabal "in the name of David" (25:9); the messengers wait (25:9); a servant of Nabal characterizes Nabal's conduct as mistreatment (25:14). All of these elements are absent from the dialogues of Moses and Jephthah mentioned above, where the reception of the messengers is not important to the story.

The content of David's message is calculated to elicit a positive response from a reasonable person. It begins with a threefold "peace" greeting. The repetition of the term "peace" (שלום, 1 Sam 25:6) seems designed to put Nabal at ease and dispose him toward a positive response. David then mentions the reason he is sending to Nabal now: he has heard that he is shearing his sheep. Nabal is celebrating a festival and may have extra provisions at hand. Sheep-shearing, like the harvest of crops, was an occasion for celebration (1 Sam 25:8, 36; 2 Sam 13:23-28).[71] Nabal's prosperous harvest is occasion for hospitality and generosity. David claims that he is partly responsible for this rich harvest. David recalls a past favor he has done for Nabal. David guarded the flock of Nabal at Carmel so that nothing went missing. David and his men did not steal anything and ensured that no one else did. David invites Nabal to ask his own servants for confirmation of this service. He specifically requests that the messengers be treated well and that the request be granted since they come during the sheep-shearing celebration. Finally, David makes the request for provisions. David's message is polite and respectful. The indication of past favors is designed to make Nabal well disposed to the request and provoke some sense of obligation. Since Nabal's refusal is not as judicious as David's request, we have no way of knowing whether David would have taken a polite no for an answer. It is even possible that he would have left Nabal alone if Nabal had pleaded fear of Saul in light of events at Nob (cf. 1 Sam 22:22-23).

In addition to mistreating David's messengers, Nabal also manages to insult David directly. He derisively asks, "Who is David?" (25:10).

[71] Jeffery C. Geoghegan ("Israelite Sheepshearing and David's Rise to Power," *Bib* 87 [2006] 55-63) finds that the biblical evidence indicates the sheepshearing was occasion for trickery, licentiousness, and revenge. Nabal may have processed his wool at Timnah, where excavations have uncovered loom weights indicative of the textile industry (cf. Gen 38:12). On the use of goats and sheep in ancient Israel, see Borowski, *Every Living Thing*, 61-71.

Although Nabal pretends not to know who David is, his next question, "Who is the son of Jesse?" indicates that he does in fact know David.[72] The phrase "the son of Jesse" is most commonly found on the lips of Saul in a distinctly negative sense (1 Sam 20:27, 30, 31; 22:7, 8, 13), but these negative contexts do not mean that David's patronymic is inherently negative (cf. 1 Chr 10:14; 12:18; 29:26; Ps 72:20; and Jesse in Isa 11:1, 10).[73] Nabal's question expresses his doubts about the status of David and explains his mistreatment of David's messengers.

Nabal comments, "These days many servants are breaking away from their masters" (היום רבו עבדים המתפרצים איש מפני אדניו, 25:10). This remark further indicates that Nabal knows about David, and it reveals Nabal's interpretation of recent events. The hithpael of פרץ seems to indicate an unlawful act on David's part. The hithpael in general is a rare stem which is generally used as the reflexive and reciprocal of the piel (although it is to be noted that פרץ does not occur in the piel).[74] In the qal, פרץ has a wide range of meanings, but violence is a common thread. For example, when David fights the Philistines after he becomes king, he remarks after his victory, "Yhwh has burst forth (פרץ) against my enemies before me, like a bursting flood" (כפרץ מים, 2 Sam 5:20). The root also expresses urgent persuasion as when his servants urge Saul to eat (ויפרצו־בי, 1 Sam 28:23; cf. 2 Sam 13:25, 27). The verb expresses the importunate manner of the request with a verbal root that indicates violence or other crossing of boundaries. Nabal's use of the reciprocal hithpael of this violent root indicates his view that David has *illegitimately* broken *himself* away from the rule of his king, or persuaded himself that he no longer owed loyalty to his king. Nabal thinks Saul is the victim of David's unjust treatment, not *vice versa*. Nabal's understanding is the exact opposite of the voices of the narrator and most characters in the text. If Saul is the innocent sufferer of injustice, then David is a traitor and brigand whom Yhwh should

---

[72] Hobbs ("Hospitality," 26) argues that Nabal denies knowledge of David to justify his denial of provisions: "David was outside his moral community and a wanderer."

[73] *Pace* some commentators, for instance, Ralph W. Klein, *1 Samuel* (WBC 10; Waco, TX.: Word Books, 1983) 208-9. Isser (*Sword of Goliath*, 124) thinks that most occurrences of "the son of Jesse" occur in parallelism. Although true of some striking instances (1 Sam 25:10; 2 Sam 20:1; 1 Kgs 12:16), this observation does not hold for most occurrences (e.g., 1 Sam 16:18; 20:27, 31; 22:9).

[74] Bruce K. Waltke and Michael O'Connor, *An Introduction to Biblical Hebrew Syntax* (Winona Lake, IN: Eisenbrauns, 1990) 428-29.

defeat and Abigail is more foolish than her husband. Modern scholars largely concur with Nabal's interpretation of David, although they are reluctant to reevaluate Abigail's character.

Jeffrey C. Geoghegan notes the recurrence of פרץ in contexts of sheep-shearing and the house of David.[75] He suggests that פרץ expresses something about the nature of the house of David, which is descended from Perez (פרץ). Perez is so named because he managed to usurp his twin brother's position as firstborn. The midwife remarked, "How you have breeched a breech for yourself" (מה־פרצת עליך פרץ, Gen 38:29). Absalom similarly urges his father to attend his sheep shearing, or at least allow his brothers to come (ויפרץ־בי, 2 Sam 13:25, 27). Absalom also tries to usurp his brother's position as firstborn and later his father's throne. Nabal characterizes David as a usurper like his ancestor and his son.

If Nabal, considering the example of the priests of Yhwh at Nob (1 Sam 22:17-19), is concerned about the consequences of helping Saul's enemy, he might have found a more diplomatic way of declining. Instead, he incites the rage of the leader of an extrajudicial armed band. There may be truth in Nabal's reading of David, but this interpretation would seem to further urge a more circumspect response to David's request.

The text shows that both Saul and Nabal reciprocate David's favors with evil (1 Sam 24:18; 25:21). David has provided favors to both men, but Saul persistently tries to kill David and Nabal insults him. The unjust offense might be grounds for David to avenge the injury, but in both cases he refrains. However, the text also gives voice to another interpretation. Nabal, like Saul, sees David as a traitorous servant with designs on his master's throne. David may deserve punishment from Saul if he has been disloyal, or if he was only ever an outlaw with Philistine support. Indeed, Nabal's remark may be so insulting because it is true.

David Declines Vengeance

David refrains from taking vengeance against Saul and Nabal for his mistreatment. David twice spares Saul when he has the opportunity to

---

[75] Geoghegan, "Israelite Sheepshearing," 55-63.

kill him, even though his companions urge him to the deed. In the case of Nabal, David sets out to avenge the insult, but Abigail restrains him by reminding him of the seriousness of bloodguilt.[76]

In the course of David's flight from the court, there is no sign that David sees regicide as a possible solution to his problem. David insists on the sanctity of Yhwh's anointed (1 Sam 24:7; 26:9). David does not want the stain of bloodguilt or the political inconvenience of ascending to the throne by means of regicide. If David establishes the principle that men can be kings by committing regicide, then his throne and dynasty will not be safe. David is himself Yhwh's anointed and therefore has an interest in establishing the sanctity of the king's person by publicly declining to kill Saul or Ishbaal.[77] By executing the Amalekite who claims to have killed Saul, David distances himself from Saul's death and upholds the principle that no one may kill Yhwh's anointed (2 Sam 1:14-16; cf. 1 Sam 24:7, 11; 26:9, 11, 23).[78] Although Ishbaal may or may not be Yhwh's anointed, David executes his assassins because they are base men who slaughtered a righteous man in his bed (2 Sam 4:11).

Unlike Saul, Nabal does not enjoy the protection of Yhwh's anointing. Consequently, David feels free to abandon his policy of restraint and kill him and his house for his insult: "May God to thus and more to David if I leave a single male from all those who are his by morning" (1 Sam 25:22).[79] Abigail dissuades him from this murder on the grounds

---

[76] That the text seeks to distance from David from bloodguilt in the deaths of those standing between him and the throne is widely recognized. For detailed discussion of how the text achieves this distance, see James C. VanderKam, "Davidic Complicity in the Deaths of Abner and Eshbaal: A Historical and Redactional Study," *JBL* 99 (1980) 521-39; Leo G. Perdue, "'Is there anyone left of the house of Saul . . .?' Ambiguity and the Characterization of David in the Succession Narrative," *JSOT* 30 (1984) 67-84; C. F. Cryer, "David's Rise to Power and the Death of Abner: An Analysis of 1 Samuel xxvi 14-16 and its Redaction-Critical Implications," *VT* 35 (1985) 385-94; Tomoo Ishida, "The Story of Abner's Murder: A Problem Posed by the Solomonic Apologist," *ErIsr* 24 (1993) 109*-113*; Halpern, *David's Secret Demons*, 73-103.

[77] Polzin, *Samuel*, 210; Steussey, *David*, 56. David makes this self interested logic explicit in 1 Sam 26:24: "just as your life was precious in my eyes today, so may my life be precious in the eyes of Yhwh."

[78] David's dynasty enjoys remarkable stability in comparison with the northern kingdom, which experiences many regicides and changes of dynasties.

[79] David's oath, which he fails to fulfill on Abigail's advice, includes three noteworthy features. First, the MT reads לאיבי דוד, "to the enemies of David" rather than simply לדוד, "to David" as in LXX τῷ Δαυιδ. Scholars generally assume that LXX reflects an earlier stage of the text and that the MT addition is a theological correction

that Nabal is not worthy of such vengeance (1 Sam 25:25) and that he may become a source of bloodguilt for David (25:31). David recognizes the "good sense" (טעם, 25:33; cf. טובת־שׂכל in v. 3) in Abigail's petition and blesses her for restraining him from bloodguilt (25:33). Abigail assures David that since he is Yhwh's elect, Yhwh will destroy his enemies (25:29). Abigail's plea for restraint seems to partially foreshadow David's treatment of the house of Saul after Saul's death. David refrains from killing Yhwh's anointed (Saul and Ishbaal) and shows mercy to a remnant of Saul's line (2 Samuel 9) to fulfill his promises to Saul and Jonathan (1 Sam 24:22-23; 20:14-15). However, David also creates this remnant by executing the other sons of Saul (2 Sam 21:1-14).

Abigail's intercession manifests her intelligence. Her persuasiveness rests in part on the provisions she supplies; she does not ask David to turn back empty-handed. Before she speaks, she shows her deference by falling to the ground at David's feet (cf. Gen 33:3-7; 1 Sam 24:9; 2 Sam 14:4, 22, 33). Her opening statement ("Let the guilt be mine," v. 24) is "a polite way of initiating conversation with a superior" and refers to any potential blame that may arise as a result of the conversation, and not to the prior insult of Nabal's (cf. 2 Sam 14:9).[80] The similar expression in v. 28 indicates the second part of the speech. Abigail's prostration and first words establish the deferential tone that persists throughout her speech.[81] In the first part of her speech (vv. 25-27), Abigail admits

---

motivated by the fact that the threat is not carried out. See S. R. Driver, *Notes on the Hebrew Text and the Topography the Books of Samuel* (2nd ed.; Oxford: Clarendon Press, 1913) 199; McCarter, *I Samuel*, 349. Tsumura (*First Book*, 85-86), who generally adheres closely to MT, thinks the MT expression is original, but euphemistic. Second, the self-imprecatory oath evidently expressed a firm intention without necessarily including the idea that the imprecation would take effect. It may have been accompanied by a gesture of touching the throat. See Paul Sanders, "So May God Do To Me!," *Bib* 85 (2004) 91-98. Third, the expression "anything that pisses against a wall" is a circumlocution for "male" and a stereotyped phrase used in contexts in which the extermination of all the male members of a household is contemplated (1 Sam 25:34; 1 Kgs 10:14; 16:11; 21:21; 1 Kgs 9:8). The expression includes euphony of בקר ("morning") and בקיר ("against a wall"). Joshua Schwartz ("Dogs, "Water" and Wall," *SJOT* 14 [2000] 100-116) thinks the expression refers to dogs as well as humans, as Nabal would have had dogs to guard and shepherd his many sheep.

[80] McCarter, *I Samuel*, 398; followed by Rossier, *L'intercession*, 126.

[81] Many commentators have remarked on the amount of deferential language in Abigail's speech. Recently, Yael Ziegler ("'As the Lord Lives and as Your Soul Lives': An Oath of Conscious Deference" *VT* 58 [2008] 117-30) argues that Abigail's dual oath formula creates a parallel between David and Yhwh which is deferential, but may also be "designed to remind the addressee of his responsibilities" (p. 122). Lydie Kucová

that Nabal is guilty of insulting David, but cleverly mitigates the insult by indicating that Nabal is not so considerable a person as his wealth may suggest through a reinterpretation of his name.[82] She also distances herself from Nabal's insult by suggesting that she would have treated David's messengers differently. Since she portrays Nabal as a person of no account, she can argue that he does not merit death and that to kill him would incur bloodguilt. Her reference to "shedding blood without cause" (לשפך־דם חנם, 25:31) does not mean that there was no insult from Nabal, but that Nabal and his insult are not serious enough to merit incurring bloodguilt. This rhetorical strategy allows her to defend the interests of her household even as she admits Nabal's guilt.[83] It also enables her to convince David that he will be serving his own interests by granting her request. Since Nabal is not worthy of consideration, Abigail focuses attention on David instead. Specifically, she focuses on the future greatness of David's house and Yhwh's defeat of his enemies.

The purpose of Abigail's intercession is to persuade David that his interests and hers coincide, and his campaign against Nabal, like regicide, is counterproductive. Abigail directs David's attention to the future and to Yhwh. Abigail realizes that Yhwh will establish for David a lasting dynasty because he is a good man who fights Yhwh's battles (25:28) and that Yhwh has promised success for David and appointed him "leader" (נגיד) over Israel (25:30).[84] In the future, when

("Obeisance in the Biblical Stories of David," in *Reflection and Refraction: Studies in Biblical Historiography in Honor of A. Graeme Auld* [ed. Robert Rezetko et al.; VTSup 113; Leiden: Brill, 2007] 241-60) observes that David appears to introduce prostration. Like his policy on regicide, David's behavior toward Saul's house prepares for his own rule. As Kucová (p. 249) states, "Since David initiates courtly etiquette and does obeisance to the dynasty he is about to succeed [1 Sam 24:20; cf. 23:17], his acts pave the way for people to behave similarly when he is on the throne." The self-humiliation that David uses to his advantages is also used by others (such as Abigail) to gain something from David.

[82] See above and Barr, "The Symbolism, 11-29.

[83] For discussion of Abigail's sophisticated use of metaphor, see Weiss, *Figurative Language*, 58-72, 105-115

[84] The meaning of this term both historically and in its present context has been much discussed, but with no firm conclusion. Halpern surveys previous scholarship and concludes that "*nāgîd* was the correct term in a dynastic setting for the designated heir" (*The Constitution of the Monarchy* [HSM 25; Chico, CA: Scholas, 1981] 9). See also Albrecht Alt, "The Formation of the Israelite State in Palestine," in *Essays on Old Testament History and Religion* (trans. R. A. Wilson; Garden City, NY: Doubleday, 1966) 245-55; Martin Noth, *The History of Israel* (trans. Peter R. Ackroyd; 2d. ed.;

he sits securely on his throne, he may have cause to regret his unnecessary vengeance. Also, since he is fighting the battles of Yhwh, he has no need to pursue personal vengeance; Yhwh will take care of his interests. In sum, she argues convincingly that David's plan to slaughter the males of Nabal's house is not good policy. She concludes by laying claim to David's future kindness.

David follows the sagacious advice of Abigail and credits her and Yhwh with restraining him from bloodguilt (25:32-34). Although the unjust treatment David receives from Saul and Nabal might seem to warrant a violent reaction from David, David maintains his policy of restraint and abstains from violence. When he is tempted to vengeance, Abigail providentially intercedes to prevent him from shedding blood needlessly.

Yhwh Vindicates David

By refraining from bloodguilt, David achieves victory over the enemies who wronged him. Both Nabal and Saul die, and David's war with Saul's successor ends successfully and David becomes king of Israel. His progress toward the throne appears to be assisted by the wealth and status he inherited in the clan of Caleb by marrying the widow of Abigail, which enabled him to begin his rule over Judah in Hebron (2 Sam 2:1-4; cf. 2 Sam 25:3; Josh 14:13-14). David's status as heir to Nabal seems to be hinted in David's self-identification as Nabal's son (לבנך לדוד, 25:8) and solidified by his marriage to Abigail. Similarly, David and Saul speak to each other as father and son (אבי, 24:12; בני דוד, 24:17; 26:17, 21, 25) and Jonathan surrenders his inheritance to David (23:17-18; cf. 20:30-31). The familial language and David's marriage to Michal suggest that David has a legitimate claim to Saul's throne. As

New York: Harper & Row, 1960) 169; Roland de Vaux, *Ancient Israel* (trans. John McHugh; Grand Rapids, MI: Eerdmans, 1997) 70, 94; originally published in 2 vols. in 1958-60, English translation published in 1961; William F. Albright, *The Biblical Period from Abraham to Ezra* (2d ed.; New York: Harper, 1963) 47-48; Wolfgang Richter, "Die *nāgîd*-Formal," *BZ* 9 (1965) 71-84; Bright, *History of Israel*, 190; Frank Moore Cross, *Canaanite Myth and Hebrew Epic: Essays in the History of the Religion of Israel* (Cambridge: Harvard University Press, 1973) 220-21; G. F. Hasel, "*nāgîd*," in *TDOT* 9, 187-202; Wolde, "A Leader," 367-72.

an heir of sorts to both Nabal and Saul, David need only wait for these men to die.

Both Nabal and Saul die and their deaths bring David closer to the throne. In the case of Nabal's death, Yhwh's intervention is explicit (ויגף יהוה את־נבל, 1 Sam 25:38). Here too, some scholars suspect the account glosses over some foul play. David may have killed him outright or trusted Abigail to kill him.[85] Nabal's reaction to Abigail's news of his near extermination is normally interpreted in a medical sense (i.e., he has a heart attack or stroke), in which case David may be said to have scared him to death.[86] Marjorie O'Rourke Boyle instead argues that "Nabal's petrification is obduracy to the law, a moral, not a physical, hardening of the heart. This [hardening] renders him like stone, to be slung away by Yhwh as an enemy [cf. 1 Sam 25:29], as he had once hurled the Egyptians into the sea [Exod 15:5] and petrified the Canaanites on the land [Exod 15:16]."[87] Nabal's moral obtuseness is a comment on the enemies of David in general, and on Saul in particular. The narrative discredits Nabal's interpretation of David as a rebellious servant by characterizing Nabal as a brutal and immoral man whom Yhwh struck down.

The death of Saul is not explicitly the result of divine intervention. David expects to ascend to the throne by means other than regicide. It is not easy to discern what these means might be. He tells Abishai not to slay the sleeping Saul because "Yhwh will strike him (יהוה יגפנו, cf. 25:38), or his death will come and he will die, or he will go down in battle and be destroyed" (1 Sam 26:10). Saul does die in the course of battle, but David does not immediately replace him. After Saul's death, David becomes king of Judah in Hebron (2 Sam 2:4), but Saul's son Ishbaal becomes king of Israel (2:8-9). David cannot become king of the northern tribes while Ishbaal is alive. Still, David seems to benefit from Yhwh's activity on his behalf. The narrative saves him from the awkward position of making war on Ishbaal by stating that Ishbaal makes war on him. Abner's expedition from Mahanaim to Gibeon

---

[85] Since both Abigail and David benefit from Nabal's death, McKenzie (*King David*, 101) suggests a conspiracy. He also suggests that David's questions, "Should Abner die as a fool (נבל) dies?" (2 Sam 3:33) alludes to Nabal's death by violence (p. 122).

[86] See Boyle, "Law of the Heart," 403-5 for various attempts to understand the expression.

[87] Boyle, "Law of the Heart," 423. See also Weiss, *Figurative Language*, 74-76, 115-19.

looks like a war of aggression by which Ishbaal seeks to establish his rule over Judah (2 Sam 2:12). The text presents the civil war in which David becomes involved as not of his own making. Many interpreters are reasonably suspicious of the biblical presentation of David's blameless self-defense. David clearly aims to be king. The text legitimates his ambition with Samuel's anointing (1 Sam 16:1-13) and David's activities have a definite political purpose. He seeks to act as a king by protecting Israelites from their enemies even during his outlaw life (23:1-5) and his sojourn under Philistine protection (27:8-12). He also protects the last surviving priest of Nob from Saul (22:10-23). David's ambition and aggressiveness, especially in contrast to Ishbaal's weakness (2 Sam 2:8; 3:8-11), cast doubt on the depiction of David as the passive defender against Saulide attack.

David's cause is further favored by Abner's defection from Ishbaal. Abner realizes that Yhwh promised the throne to David and that the northern tribes know of this promise and favor David over Ishbaal (2 Sam 3:9-10, 17-18). Abner's death during a peace conference is presented as Joab's responsibility and an act that works against David's interests. The text further distances David from the murder by showing David publicly mourning for Abner, which pleases the people (2 Sam 3:31-37). After Ishbaal's murder, the northern tribes willingly submit to David's rule on the basis of their kinship with him, his success as Saul's officer, and Yhwh's promise to David (2 Sam 5:1-2). David's kingship over all Israel is ultimately established or ratified by consent.

David's rise to the throne parallels his experience with Nabal. In both cases, David pursues a policy of restraint that seeks a middle path between acting on his own and relying entirely on Yhwh. By listening to Abigail and refraining from his intended murder, David acquires the provisions he needs and later acquires Nabal's wife, presumably with all his property. By not destroying Nabal's house, David becomes the head of Nabal's household. Similarly, by not committing regicide, David enhances his kingship. While he is a usurper, his good conduct enables him to avoid the moral stigma of usurpation and gain a measure of legitimacy. The legitimacy that the text seeks to afford him, however, is undermined or tarnished by the dubious nature of some of its claims and the voice it gives to alternative interpretations of David. For example, the text shows Saul recognizing David's imminent reign (1 Sam 24:20), yet continuing to try to kill David (1 Sam 26:2). Although the text distances David from the profitable deaths of Saul and Ishbaal (among other loyal Saulides), scholars understandably suspect David's complicity and culpability. Even the text acknowledges that Ishbaal dies because his assassins expect David to reward them for their regicide (2 Sam 4:8). These alternative views of David are also duplicated in 1 Samuel 25, which presents Nabal's interpretation of David as a rebellious servant (1 Sam 25:10). The story of David and Nabal duplicates the larger story of David and the House of Saul by presenting the relationship between David and Saul in miniature. Although both texts focus on David as the just sufferer of injustice who refrains from vengeance and gains recompense from Yhwh, both stories also duplicates the textual ambiguities about the character of David and the justice of his cause.

Mise-en-abyme: Pattern of Repetition

As with Genesis 37–50, the Story of David and the House of Saul manifests a pattern of repetition into which 1 Samuel 25 fits as a *mise-en-abyme*. This pattern indicates the sophisticated texture of the narrative. One would not expect a *mise-en-abyme* in a simple work of propaganda or chronology. The books of Samuel, like biblical narrative generally, include frequent analogy and repetition either as the result of deliberate artistry, a complex history of composition, or (most likely) both. The Story of David and the House of Saul includes several noteworthy repetitions of stories ("doublets") and smaller textual elements. The song of the women is quoted three times (1 Sam 18:7; 21:12; 29:5).[88] David's military prowess is mentioned throughout the narrative. He defeats Goliath (1 Sam 17:48-51) and summaries of his success occur several times (1 Sam 18:5, 13-19, 27, 30; 19:8). He continues to be victorious over Israel's enemies after his flight into the wilderness (23:1-5), during his refuge with Achish of Gath (27:8-12; 30:9-20), and in the war against Saul's son Ishbaal (2 Sam 2:17; 3:1). Jonathan's friendship for David is mentioned three times (1 Sam 18:1-4; 20:41 42; 23:16-18). David twice receives a sword and armor belonging to members of the royal house (1 Sam 17:38-39; 18:4).

---

[88] Concerning the poetry of the song and its relation to the narrative, see Michael O'Connor, "War and Rebel Chants in the Former Prophets," in *Fortunate the Eyes that See: Essays in Honor of David Noel Freedman in Celebration of His Seventieth Birthday* (ed. Astrid B. Beck et al.; Grand Rapids, MI: Eerdmans, 1995) 322-37.

Scholars generally think that the doublets in Samuel share a common purpose and reinforce one another: to legitimate David's rise to the throne. Halpern, however, discerns differences between the doublets, which he divides into source A and source B.[89] The A source seems to be a document that focuses on Saul and presents him as a tragic figure. It evidently ends with 1 Samuel 31 and presents kingship in continuity with judgeship. The B source, which includes material unique to MT, focuses on Samuel, then on David, and takes place almost entirely in Judah. According to Halpern, it continues as the main source for the Davidic succession. Both sources begin within 1 Samuel 8–12, where there are two stories of Saul's rejection: one for illegitimate sacrifice (A: 1 Samuel 13–14) and one for failing to execute the ban on the Amalekites (B: 1 Samuel 15). David enters Saul's court by two different means: as a musician whose music soothes Saul (A: 1 Sam 16:14-23) and as a shepherd who slays Goliath (B: 17:55–18:5).[90] Saul twice tries to kill David while he plays the lyre (B: 1 Sam 18:10-11; A: 19:9-10).[91] David has opportunities to marry two daughters of Saul: Merab (A: 18:17-19) and Michal (B: 18:20-27).[92] Jonathan twice speaks with Saul in defense of David (B: 19:1-7; A: 20:28-33). David twice flees Saul's court: once with the help Michal (B: 19:11-24), and once with the help of Jonathan (A: 1 Samuel 20). The Ziphites twice inform on David (A: 23:19-24; B: 26:1). David twice spares Saul's life when his men urge him to kill Saul (A: 1 Samuel 24; B: 1 Samuel 26). On two occasions, David seeks to enter the court of Achish: once unsuccessfully (A: 1 Sam 21:10-15), and once successfully (B: 1 Sam 27:1-7). There are two accounts of the death of Saul: one by the narrator (A: 1 Samuel 31) and one by the Amalekite (B: 2 Samuel 1). David twice executes those who claim to have assassinated his enemies: Saul's killer and Ishbaal's assassins (2 Sam 1:14-16; 4:8-12, both included in Halpern's B source).

---

[89] Halpern, *The Constitution*, 149-74. Halpern (*David's Secret Demons*, 277-79) indicates the parallel sources in a synoptic chart. The classic source division is that of Karl Budde, *Die Bücher Samuel* (Kurzer Handcommentar zum Alten Testament 8; Tübingen: J. C. B. Mohr, 1902) xii-xxi. For a survey of scholarship, see Hans Joachim Stoebe, *Das erste Buch Samuelis* (KAT VIII/1; Gütersloh: Mohn, 1973) 35-52; Halpern, *The First Historians: The Hebrew Bible and History* (New York: Harper & Row, 1988) 181-94.

[90] LXX omits the passage from Halpern's B source.

[91] LXX omits the passage from Halpern's B source.

[92] LXX omits the passage from Halpern's B source.

Although the narrative in Samuel does seem to incorporate prior sources, Halpern's source divisions are problematic. He relies on doublets as opposed to "ideological" criteria because "a consistent, variant narrative is the only sure criterion for establishing the existence of more than one original source."[93] However, he does look for ideological differences between doublets in order to establish that the two passages originate from separate sources (as opposed to the repetitive technique of a single author).[94] Furthermore, his source division creates the same kinds of problems it is supposed to solve. For example, Halpern thinks 1 Sam 25:1 originally followed directly on 19:24 in the B source. If so, then where does David find his followers (he gains them in the A source in 22:2, but they also appear in the B source in chaps. 25; 27; 30)? The mention that David gained followers is an example of the kind of story that should be repeated if two separate documents were combined. Also, some of the doublets that justify Halpern's source division are not really doublets. For instance, the death of Samuel in 1 Sam 25:1 and 28:3 are not doublets: the first narrates Samuel's death ("Samuel died," וימת שמואל), while the second recalls this death as pertinent to the current episode ("Samuel had died," ושמואל מת). These kinds of problems indicate that either the narrative is not a combination of two sources or that the sources were sufficiently reworked that they cannot be reliably separated. The problems with the source division, however, do not imply that the narrative was composed by a single author. If the source division is problematic, so is the present form of the text.

In addition to the above doublets, the narrative includes doubling of characters and relationships. The text includes detailed narratives concerning how David acquires two of his wives (Michal and Abigail), and both wives are related to his enemies (Saul and Nabal, respectively). The two anointed leaders (Saul and David) each have a faithful adherent (Abner and Joab, respectively) whose contest with each other anticipates the outcome of the larger conflict. In the course of the story, David serves two masters, one of whom appreciates David's qualities (Achich) and one who proves ungrateful

---

[93] Halpern, *Constitution of the Monarchy*, 151-52.
[94] For example, he argues that 1 Sam 9:1–10:16 presents kingship in continuity with judgeship, while 1 Samuel 8 and 10:17-27 view monarchy as an innovation in government and theology.

(Saul). The narrative also includes several deceptions. For example, David deceives Ahimelech (1 Sam 21:1-6), Achish (21:10-15), and enrolls Michal (19:11-17) and Jonathan (20:3-34) to help him deceive Saul. Saul deceives the medium at Endor (28:8-14) and misleads David by offering his daughters in marriage, since the women are really bait for a trap (18:17-29).

Finally, 1 Samuel 25 fits into this larger pattern of repetition within the Story of David and the House of Saul. As a *mise-en-abyme*, the chapter duplicates pertinent aspects of the whole Story of David and the House of Saul and thereby illuminates the larger history. The *mise-en-abyme* functions by duplicating David's relationship with Saul in his relationship with Nabal. David performs favors for both men, but receives harm in return from each. David refrains from vengeance and is rewarded with success over each man. Although both narratives indicate that David is the just sufferer of injustice, both also acknowledge other possibilities. Nabal characterizes David as a traitor (1 Sam 25:10), which echoes Saul's interpretation (1 Sam 20:13; 22:8, 13) and possibly that of the Ziphites (23:10; 26:1) and Philistines (29:4).[95]

Conclusion

I have described the relationship between 1 Samuel 25 and the Story of David and the House of Saul (1 Sam 13:1–2 Sam 5:3) as a *mise-en-abyme*. The story of David and Nabal duplicates the larger narrative. In his relationship to both Saul and Nabal, David does good and receives evil in return. The good that David does for Saul consists of his military service and musical skill, but Saul attempts to kill David and drives him into the arms of the Philistines. The good he does for Nabal involves the protection he extends to Nabal's sheep and shepherds, but Nabal insults David and his messengers and refuses to reciprocate David's hospitality. Despite the treatment David receives from Saul and Nabal, he does find allies within their households. Saul's son Jonathan and his daughter Michal both help David in opposition to Saul's policy

---

[95] From their fear that David might seek to reconcile himself to Saul by betraying the Philistines, it is not clear whether the Philistines see David as a traitor to Saul or an innocent victim of Saul.

and Nabal's anonymous servant and his wife Abigail similarly favor David. Due to the unjust treatment he receives from Saul and Nabal, David might be justified in killing them. However, David refuses to kill Saul when he has the opportunity to do so because Saul is Yhwh's anointed. David does plan to kill Nabal, but Abigail restrains him with the considerations that he should not expose himself to bloodguilt and that Yhwh will destroy his enemies. David's conflicts with the houses of Saul and Nabal are resolved without incurring bloodguilt. Thus, 1 Samuel 25 reproduces the pertinent aspects of the Story of David and the House of Saul. Recognizing 1 Samuel 25 as a *mise-en-abyme* explains both the evident isolatability of the passage and accounts for its relation to its context.

Although scholars have generally recognized the basic similarity between Nabal and Saul, the above discussion expands the parallel in three major ways. First, discussion of the relationship between 1 Samuel 25 and its context has been largely confined to the sequence of 1 Samuel 24–26. The *mise-en-abyme* is focused in this sequence because it presents David and Saul together after David's flight from court. David spares Saul's life in chapters 24 and 26, and Nabal's life in the intervening chapter. The claim that David has received evil (רע) in exchange for good (טוב) appears in 24:18 and 25:21. Also, David's expectation that Yhwh will kill (נגף) Saul (26:10) follows Abigail's speech to this effect (25:24-31) and Yhwh's slaying of Nabal (נגף, 25:38). These three chapters focus on the theme of justice and particularly the motif of bloodguilt and David's innocence. The issue of justice in David's relation to Saul is focused here because 1 Samuel 24 and 26 are the only episodes in which Saul and David meet following David's escape from Saul's court. However, 1 Samuel 25 also relates to its larger context, as the references to receiving evil for good indicate. David's conflict with Nabal repeats his conflict with Saul. The good that David does for Nabal and the evil he receives recall the good (טוב) he does for Saul as early as 1 Sam 16:14-23 and evil (רע) he receives as early as 18:10-11. Nabal's death without David's intervention adumbrates the death of Saul and the collapse of his house. David's marriage to Abigail and presumable inheritance of Nabal's wealth and status foreshadows his "inheritance" of Saul's kingdom. The parallel between 1 Samuel 25 and the Story of David and the House of Saul embraces the whole story, not only 1 Samuel 24–26.

Second, the motif of bloodguilt prominent in 1 Samuel 24–26 pertains to the larger issue of kingship, which embraces the whole Story of David and the House of Saul. The link between bloodguilt and kingship is justice. As Saul remarks to David, "You are righteous (צדיק), not I" (1 Sam 24:18; cf. 2 Sam 23:3) because David spared his life. He continues: "Now I know that you will surely be king (מלך תמלוך) and the kingdom of Israel (ממלכת ישראל) will be established in your hand" (24:21). The thrust of this passage and Abigail's speech is that David will be king because he is, as Samuel told Saul, "better than you" (ממך הטוב, 1 Sam 15:28). One of the major responsibilities of the king is to establish justice. Absalom uses David's failure to appoint adequate judges as a means of gathering support for his rebellion (2 Sam 15:2-5, employing the roots צדק, שפט, מלך, and ריב). David's complaint about Nabal, "he has returned me evil (רע) for good (טוב)" (1 Sam 25:21), echoes Saul's statement "you did good (טוב) for me and I repaid you with harm (רע)" (1 Sam 24:18). Finally, Abigail's implicit comparison of Nabal and Saul ("let your enemies be as Nabal along with all those who seek evil for my lord," 25:26) brings 1 Samuel 25 in relation to the larger problem of David's conflict with the House of Saul.

Third, the claim that David has received evil from Nabal in payment for good has not been adequately appreciated. The Story of David and the House of Saul generally presents David as a better man than Saul and more qualified to be king. The story of David and Nabal is not a strange interruption in this story, but rather an integral part of it. The presentation of David in this chapter is consistent with the surrounding narrative and clarifies the fundamental issue surrounding David's conflict with Saul: "He has repaid me evil for good" (1 Sam 25:21). Nabal, as discussed above, is guilty of a serious offense against David in violation of justice and hospitality. He mistreats his messengers and insults David personally, even though David had shown hospitality to his servants. Scholars have often overlooked the seriousness of Nabal's offence in their effort to read David negatively as a racketeer. Although the modern critical reading of David as a murdering usurper has merit, it sometimes distracts from what most voices in the text actually say. Although the text includes negative statements and implications about David, most characters echo the narrator's statement that David is a better man than Saul (1 Sam 15:28) and a man after God's own heart (1 Sam 13:14). The negative implications about David should not be mistaken for the whole truth; the text holds together both positive and negative interpretations of David. The mixed and sophisticated portrait of David does not seem consistent with the claim that these narratives are "propaganda," because propaganda does not evince such complexity.[96]

Fourth, the *mise-en-abyme* highlights certain aspects of the larger story over others. The language of 1 Samuel 25 connects to the Story of David and the House of Saul especially in the sections involving direct contact between David and Saul. These include the stories of David in Saul's court and the two stories of David sparing Saul's life. This focus of duplication places stress on David as a just sufferer of injustice with respect to Saul and Nabal. The larger story employs multiple methods for indicating the legitimacy of David's rise. For example, it presents David as closer to Yhwh than Saul, who finds himself abandoned by Yhwh (1 Sam 14:37; 16:14; 28:6). David also appears to be a man with greater personal merits including musical and martial skills and superior leadership. While David inspires loyalty in his followers, Saul makes poor decisions and looses the loyalty of his troops (1 Sam 14:24; 39; 43-45; 22:16-19). By focusing on the specific issue of reciprocity, the *mise-en-abyme* emphasizes the importance of David's moral legitimacy over other elements that legitimate his rule. However, the *mise-en-abyme* also includes an alternative reading expressed by the character Nabal that shows Saul as an innocent suffer of injustice at David's hand. Thus, the story duplicates the ambiguity in the larger narrative presentation of David's character and focuses the conflict on the issue of justice.

The role of 1 Samuel 25 as a *mise-en-abyme* depends on the extensive similarities between the chapter and the Story of David and the House of Saul discussed above. These similarities also serve to highlight certain differences between the stories that are also important for recognizing how the analogous stories function together. Three major points of contrast may be noted.

First, David's refusal to kill Saul in chaps. 24 and 26 contrasts with his readiness to kill Nabal in chap. 25. David explains the contrast by noting that Saul, unlike Nabal, is Yhwh's anointed (1 Sam 24:7;

---

[96] For discussion of how the Samuel narratives do and do not resemble ancient Near Eastern propaganda, see Dietrich, "Das Biblische Bild," 17-23; Bosworth, "Evaluating King David," 204-9.

26:9-11). Abigail, however, persuades David that his policy of refraining from regicide should be expanded to encompass Nabal. David's magnanimous conduct will ensure his kingship and peace of mind, but killing Nabal may endanger both. She encourages David to be generous and upright in his relations with private citizens, not just Saul's royal house. David recognizes Abigail's good sense and sees the hand of Yhwh behind her intervention (1 Sam 25:32-33). In this story, David appears for the first time capable of wholesale slaughter and personal vengeance (like Saul at Nob), and both traits will appear again later, such as when he slaughters Judah's neighbors (1 Sam 27:8-12) and has the sons of Saul impaled at Gibeon (2 Sam 21:1-14). In the present context, Abigail broadens David's narrow understanding of just conduct and shows David as a man capable of taking good advice. By showing David both willing to massacre Nabal's house and refraining from the slaughter, the text duplicates the wider portrait of David as both a good and pious hero and a "man of blood." Also, Abigail's argument that David would incur bloodguilt for killing Nabal echoes Jonathan's argument that Saul would incur bloodguilt for killing David. David's murderous rage makes him resemble Saul, but unlike Saul, David can take advice.

Although David does favors for both Saul and Nabal, these favors, like the harm David suffers from each man, are not equal. The narrative gives significant testimony to David's service to Saul as a military leader and musician that should move Saul to gratitude and generosity. However, David's kindness in guarding Nabal's sheep seems comparatively insignificant. The text does not indicate that David had to fight any predatory animals or thieves to protect the flock. David's kindness seems to consist in declining to steal what he could have easily taken. Furthermore, Nabal does not ask for David's help as Saul does (1 Sam 16:19; 18:2, 5). Thus, Nabal does not seem moved to gratitude or generosity. Similarly, the harm David suffers from Saul and Nabal are not equal. Saul consistently seeks to kill David. Nabal merely insults David's messengers. Furthermore, Nabal's insult is not as serious at the affront to David's messengers by king Hanun of the Ammonites (2 Sam 10:1-5). Since David is king of Israel when he sends messengers to Hanun, the offense is necessarily an international incident. Furthermore, while Nabal stops at verbal abuse, Hanun physically assaults and humiliates David's messengers. The harm Nabal does to David seems trifling compared to the danger posed by Saul. Therefore, David's eagerness to slaughter Nabal's house while refraining from killing Saul seems out of balance, as Abigail perceives.

To return to the initial question: what is the account of David and Nabal doing in the Story of David and the House of Saul? It serves as a *mise-en-abyme* that highlights the theme of justice in David's relationship with Saul and his house with particular emphasis on bloodguilt. Consequently, episodes that do not contribute to this central theme seem secondary by comparison (e.g., Saul at Endor in 1 Samuel 28). Furthermore, the *mise-en-abyme* emphasizes David's moral legitimacy over other aspects of the narrative that tend to legitimate his rule (e.g., his anointing by Samuel and his military skill). Finally, the recognition of 1 Samuel 25 as a *mise-en-abyme* explains both the isolatability of the chapter and its relation to the larger narrative.

CHAPTER FOUR

1 Kings 13

What is the story of the man of God and the old prophet doing at
the beginning of the History of the Divided Kingdom? Scholars have
generally not asked this question. When commentators have turned
to 1 Kings 13, they have been interested in the strangeness of the story
rather than its relationship to its context. The story involves one prophetic figure lying to another. It seems strange because the reader
expects the liar to be punished for his deception, but instead the
deceived is punished for his credulity. However, the strange story can
only be explained by appeal to its context.

Apart from the peculiar nature of the story, several commentators
have detached 1 Kgs 13:11-32 from its context and argued that it was
inserted at a late date, along with its conclusion in 2 Kgs 23:15-20. The
tale of two prophetic figures has no obvious connection to the surrounding context, which concerns the political separation of Israel
and Judah after Solomon's death. Amidst these political concerns, the
prophetic story seems to be an interruption with entirely different concerns.[1] Like Genesis 38 and 1 Samuel 25, the story of the two prophetic
figures is isolatable from its context.

This chapter will explore the story in 1 Kgs 13:11-32 and 2 Kgs 23:15-20
as a *mise-en-abyme* in the History of the Divided Kingdom. Understood in these terms, the story's placement is less problematic. The
prophetic story stands at the beginning and end of the History of the
Divided Kingdom, specifically connected to the institution of the cult
at Bethel by Jeroboam and its destruction by Josiah. In this signifi-

---

[1] Jules Francis Gomes (*The Sanctuary at Bethel and the Configuration of Israelite
Identity* [BZAW 368; Berlin: Walter de Gruyter, 2006] 36) notes that 1 Kings 13:1 is a
separable unit "with a new narrative, new plot, new form, and a new set of characters" (excepting Jeroboam).

cant context, the two anonymous prophetic figures represent the two nations from which they come. The relationship that unfolds between these men adumbrates the relationship that unfolds between their nations during the History of the Divided Kingdom. The individuals, like their nations, begin the narrative in a state of mutual hostility. Later, the prophetic figures share a common meal in violation of a divine command. Similarly, the two nations will be in alliance despite divine disapproval. Through a role-reversal, the lying prophet speaks a true word of God to the disobedient man of God. Similarly, the apostate Israel returns to God with Jehu's coup while Judah engages in Baal worship under the rule of Athaliah. The hostility returns, but the man of God saves the old prophet's bones from desecration as Josiah acts to destroy the Bethel altar and remove the cause of Israel's sin. Ultimately, both nations share the same grave as their two nations share a common exile.

The present chapter begins by briefly indicating the current state of scholarship concerning the connection between 1 Kings 13 and its context. Then the *mise-en-abyme* is described in detail on the basis of the parallel plot structures. Finally, some consequences for the present reading of 1 Kings 13 are noted.

1 Kings 13 in Context: Toward the *Mise-en-abyme*

I have discussed the history of scholarship on 1 Kings 13 in detail elsewhere.[2] I will here note two major considerations that have detracted scholars from recognizing the role of 1 Kings 13 in the History of the Divided Kingdom (1 Kings 11–2 Kings 23).[3] First, most commentators

---

[2] David Bosworth, "Revisiting Karl Barth's Exegesis of 1 Kings 13," *BibInt* 10 (2002) 360-83.

[3] Gary N. Knoppers (*Two Nations Under God: The Deuteronomistic History of Solomon and the Dual Monarchy* [2 vols.; HSM 52-53; Atlanta: Scholars, 1993-94] 1.135, 137) persuasively argues that "1 Kings 11 clearly marks a new and negative phase in Solomon's rule" and that the chapter "is critical to understanding the Deuteronomist's perspective on the division [of the kingdom], a decisive turning point in the history of Israel." Consequently, 1 Kings 11:1 begins the period of the Divided Kingdom. Furthermore, although this period would seem to end with the destruction of the Northern Kingdom in 2 Kings 17, the problems created at the start of the division are not finally resolved until Josiah destroys Jeroboam I's Bethel cult (2 Kgs 23:15-10) and the high places Solomon built that led to the division (2 Kgs 23:23-24). Therefore, as Knoppers

regard the narrative of 1–2 Kings as a composite work compiled from diverse sources by different redactors working at different times. Consequently, scholarly interest has centered on source and redaction criticism. Source critics have sought to reconstruct the pre-Dtr source behind the chapter.[4] Redaction critics have examined the means by which Dtr incorporated the sources into his history.[5] Commentators have concerned themselves with the history of composition more that the result of the compositional process. Consequently, there has been little appreciation of 1 Kings 13 in relation the History of the Divided Kingdom.

Second, many commentators focus on the chapter's didactic purpose regarding the nature of true and false prophecy. These scholars therefore try to deduce from the story a rule by which true and false prophecy may be differentiated.[6] In 1651, Thomas Hobbes succinctly stated why the story offers no such guidance: "If one prophet deceive another, what certainty is there of knowing the will of God, by other way than that of reason?"[7] According to Crenshaw, the story shows

---

(*Two Nations*, 2. 240) argues, the period of the divided monarchy extends through 2 Kings 23.

[4] Thomas B. Dozeman, "The Way of the Man of God from Judah: True and False Prophecy in the Pre-Dtr Legend of 1 Kings 13," *CBQ* 44 (1982) 379-93; Uriel Simon, "I Kings 13: A Prophetic Sign—Denial and Persistence," *HUCA* 47 (1976) 98-103; revised and reprinted as "A Prophetic Sign Overcomes Those Who Would Defy It: The King of Israel, the Prophet from Bethel, and the Man of God from Judah," in Simon, *Reading Prophetic Narratives* (Bloomington, IN: Indiana University Press, 1997) 131-54.

[5] Werner E. Lemke, "The Way of Obedience: 1 Kings 13 and the Structure of the Deuteronomistic History," in *Magnalia Dei. The Mighty Acts of God: Essays on the Bible and Archeology in Memory of G. Ernest Wright* (ed. Frank M. Cross et al.; New York: Doubleday, 1976) 307-17; Knoppers, *Two Nations*, 2. 45-71; Bertram Herr, "Der wahre Prophet bezeugt seine Botschaft mit dem Tod: Ein Verrsuch zu I Kön 13," *BZ* 41 (1997) 75-76; Ernst Würthwein, "Die Erzählung vom Gottesmann aus Juda in Bethel: Zur Komposition von 1 Kön 13," in *Wort und Geschichte: Festschrift für Karl Elliger zum 70. Beburtstag* (ed. H. Gese and H. P. Rüger; Kevelaer: Butzon & Bercker, 1973) 181-89.

[6] Walter Gross, "Lying Prophet and Disobedient Man of God in 1 Kings 13: Role Analysis as an Instrument of Theological Interpretation of an OT Narrative Text" (trans. Robert Robinson) in *Perspectives on Old Testament Narrative* (ed. Robert C. Culley; Semeia 15; Atlanta: Scholars, 1979) 118-24; Dozeman, "The Way," 392-93; Simon J. De Vries, *1 Kings* (WBC; Waco, TX: Word Books, 1985) 171-74; D. Van Winkle, "1 Kings XIII: True and False Prophecy," *VT* 39 (1989) 37-42; Brevard S. Childs, *Old Testament Theology in a Canonical Context* (Philadelphia: Fortress, 1986) 133-44.

[7] Hobbes, *Leviathan* (ed. Edwin Curley; Indianapolis: Hackett, 1994) 247; chap. 32, parag. 7, originally published in 1651.

that there is no criterion for discerning true prophecy, but his discussion still assumes that the chapter is a didactic story about prophecy.[8] Some think the story emphasizes the inevitability of the fulfillment of Yhwh's word.[9] Although this motif is present in the story, it is also present in many prophetic stories and underlies the prophecy-fulfillment schema (cf. Isa 55:10-11).[10] It does not explain the particular details of the present story. Others understand the story as emphasizing the necessity of obedience to the word of Yhwh.[11] The demand for obedience raises the problem of knowing Yhwh's will in the face of prophetic conflict.

Although scholarship has not generally seen the two prophetic figures as foreshadowing the history of their respective nations, there are textual indications that point in this direction.[12] Perhaps the most significant is the placement of the story. It begins immediately after

[8] James L. Crenshaw, *Prophetic Conflict: Its Effect upon Israelite Religion* (BZAW 124; Berlin: de Gruyter, 1971) 47.
[9] A. Šanda, *Die Bücher der Könige: I. Halbband.: Das Erste Buch der Könige* (EHAT 9/1; Münster: Aschendorffsche Verlagsbuchhandlung, 1911) 360; Jacques Briend, "Du message au messager: Remarques sur 1 Rois XIII," in *Congress Volume: Paris 1992* (ed. J. A. Emerton; VTSup 61; Leiden: Brill, 1995) 13-24; Knoppers, *Two Nations*, 2. 58; Burke O. Long, *1 Kings, with an Introduction to Historical Literature* (FOTL 9; Grand Rapids: Eerdmans, 1984) 148; Simon, "A Prophetic Sign," 150-54; Jerome T. Walsh, *1 Kings* (Berit Olam; Collegeville, MN: Liturgical Press, 1996) 191; Mordechai Cogan, *1 Kings* (AB 10; New York: Doubleday, 2001) 374.
[10] On this schema, see Gerhard von Rad, "The Deuteronomic Theology of History in I and II Kings," in *The Problem of the Hexateuch and Other Essays* (New York: McGraw Hill, 1966) 208-214; Ernst Würthwein, "Prophetische Wort und Geschichte in den Königsbüchern: Zu einer These Gerhard von Rads," in *Altes Testament und christliche Verkündigung: Festschrift für Antonius H. J. Gunneweg zum 65. Geburtstag* (eds. Manfred Oeming and Axel Graupner; Stuttgart: Kohlhammer, 1987) 399-411, reprinted in Würthwein, *Studien zum Deuteronomistischen Geschichtswerk* (BZAW 227; Berlin, de Gruyter, 1994); Helga Weippert, "'Histories' and 'History': Promise and Fulfillment in the Deuteronomic Historical Work" (originally published in 1991; trans. Peter T. Daniels), in *Reconsidering Israel and Judah: Recent Studies on the Deuteronomistic History* (ed. Gary N. Knoppers and J. Gordon McConville; SBTS 8; Winona Lake, Ind.: Eisenbrauns, 2000) 46-61.
[11] This theme overlaps with the discernment of true prophecy noted above.
[12] The first and most significant scholar to discern the connection between the prophetic figures and their respective nations was the theologian Karl Barth, "Exegese von 1. Könige 13," *Biblische Studien* 10 (1955) 39-40; trans. I. Wilson in *Church Dogmatics* II/2 (Edinburgh: T & T Clark) 403. Similarly, Childs, *Old Testament Theology*, 142; Jerome T. Walsh, "The Contexts of 1 Kings XIII," *VT* 39 (1989) 359; Peter Leithart, *1 & 2 Kings* (Grand Rapids, Mich.: Brazos, 2006) 101-2. See Bosworth, "Revisiting," 370.

the division of the kingdom and Jeroboam's construction of the Bethel cult. Karl Barth noted:

> One observes, even superficially, the very momentous position that the story of 1 Kings 13 is assigned in the whole of the Old Testament narrative: how it, following immediately after the account of the division of the kingdom, in some sense explains it and at the same time forms a kind of superscription to everything that follows under Rehoboam and Jeroboam—the history of both separate kingdoms of Israel—how everything that follows is here already announced and prefigured![13]

The follow-up on the story in 2 Kgs 23:15-20 further emphasizes the connection between the prophetic story and the political history.[14] The significant placement of the story points to its role in the History of the Divided Kingdom.

The passage includes political and prophetic motifs that connect it to its wider context. The royal sanctuary at Bethel is a major motif in the History of the Divided Kingdom. Almost every king of Israel is condemned by the narrative for imitating the sin of Jeroboam.[15] Jeroboam establishes cults in Bethel and Dan (1 Kgs 12:28-30) because he fears that his dynasty will not be as "firm" as Yhwh promised in 1 Kgs 11:38 if the people continue to worship in the temple in Jerusalem (1 Kgs 12:26-27). The biblical text presents Jeroboam's cult as idolatrous. The golden calves he makes for his twin sanctuaries recall the golden calf episode of Exodus 32.[16] Jeroboam introduces his idols with nearly the

[13] Barth, "Exegese," 39-40. See also Childs, *Old Testament Theology*, 142; Bosworth, "Revisiting," 370.

[14] Martin Noth (*1 Könige* [BKAT IX/1; Neukirchen-Vluyn: Neukirchener Verlag, 1968] 306-307) evaluated Barth's reading negatively, and Noth's verdict has largely shaped subsequent scholarship (see Bosworth, "Revisting," 373-75). However, Leithart (*1 & 2 Kings*) notes that the two prophetic figures represent their respective kingdoms and that "the whole history of Israel and Judah is somehow foreshadowed in this chapter" (p. 99). His articulation of the foreshadowing is sparse; he notes only that "Judah remains for centuries as a prophetic witness against the northern kingdom, but at some time, Israel seduces Judah as the old prophet seduces the man of God" (p. 101).

[15] The exceptions are Shallum (2 Kgs 15:13), who reigned only one month, and Hoshea (2 Kgs 17:2), the last king.

[16] Stuart Lasine, "Reading Jeroboam's Intentions: Intertextuality, Rhetoric, and History in 1 Kings 12," in *Reading Between Texts: Intertextuality and the Hebrew*

same words with which the people welcome Aaron's calf: "Behold your gods (הנה אלהיך), O Israel, who brought you up from the land of Egypt" (1 Kgs 12:28; cf. Exod 32:4, 8). Some modern translations treat this exclamation as referring to a single god.[17] Usually, אלהים refers to Yhwh and does not take a plural adjective, although it sometimes takes a plural adjective or verb even when referring to Yhwh.[18] Here, however, the plural verb seems to portray Jeroboam's cult as polytheistic. The characterization of Yhwh as "the one who brought you up from (or: out of) the land of Egypt" always uses a singular form of the verb עלה or יצא.[19] The exceptional plural here and at Exod 32:4, 8 indicate that אלהים in these verses should be construed as plural (as with LXX).[20] Furthermore, Ahijah upbraids Jeroboam for making "other gods and molten images" (1 Kgs 14:9). Ahijah's denunciation portrays Jeroboam's cult as both idolatrous and polytheistic.[21] It thereby vio-

---

Bible (ed. D. N. Fewell; Louisville, KY: Westminster, 1992) 133-52. The similarities between the stories have led scholars to conclude "that one or the other of the writers has deliberately described the event in terms drawn from the other account" and that Kings is the earlier source (Walter Houston, "Exodus," in *The Oxford Bible Commentary* [eds. John Barton and John Muddiman; Oxford: Oxford University Press, 2001] 88). The Exodus narrative was apparently written as a criticism of Jeroboam's cult. See also Brevard S. Childs, *The Book of Exodus: A Critical, Theological Commentary* (OTL; Louisville, KY: Westminster, 1974) 559-561.

[17] "Behold your God...," *NJPSV, NAB, NJB; KJV* translates "gods" in 1 Kgs 12:28 and "god" in Exod 32:4, 8.

[18] Bruce K. Waltke and Michael O'Connor, *An Introduction to Biblical Hebrew Syntax* (Winona Lake, IN: Eisenbrauns, 1990) 122-23. For אלהים with plural adjectives referring to Yhwh, see Deut 5:23; Josh 24:19; 1 Sam 17:26, 36; Jer 10:10; 23:26. For plural verbs, see Gen 20:13; 31:53; 35:7.

[19] The verb is עלה in Judg 13:6; 1 Sam 12:6; 2 Kgs 17:36; Jer 16:14; 23:7 and יצא in Exod 16:6; Deut 1:27; 6:12, 23; 7:8, 19; 1 Kgs 19:9. See H. Donner, "'Hier sind deine Götter Israel'," in *Wort und Geschichte: Festschrift für Karl Elliger zum 70. Geburtstag* (ed. Hartmut Gese and Hans Peter Rüger; Butzon & Berker, 1973) 47; J. Wijngaards, "*hwṣ y* and *hʿlh*: A Twofold Approach to the Exodus," *VT* 14 (1964) 91-101.

[20] Paul Joüon and Takamitsu Muraoka (*A Grammar of Biblical Hebrew* [Subsidia Biblica 27; Rome: Editrice Pontificio Instituto Biblico, 2006] §150f) note that the plural of majesty normally takes a singular verb (אדניו יתן in Exod 21:1; בעליו יומת in Exod 21:29), but there are exceptions (הלכו־אלהים in 2 Sam 7:23). He regards 1 Kgs 12:28 as one of these exceptions. I prefer to read 1 Kgs 12:28 in the context of the narrative (mis) representation of Jeroboam's cult as polytheistic (cf. 1 Kgs 14:9).

[21] The presentation of Jeroboam's cult is normally understood as Judahite polemic. Jeroboam's cult was Yahwistic and the calves may represent the throne of the invisible deity. See H. Th. Obbink, "Jahwebilder," *ZAW* 47 (1929) 264-74; followed by W. F. Albright, *From the Stone Age to Christianity: Monotheism and the Historical Process* (2d ed.; Garden City, NY: Doubleday Anchor Books, 1957) 299-301 and Noth, *1 Könige*,

lates the Decalogue (Deut 5:7-8) in addition to the cultic centrality of Jerusalem.[22] Jeroboam also appoints priests who are not Levites and introduces innovations in the calendar.[23] The Bethel cult is central to the History of the Divided Kingdom. The cult is the basis for consistently negative evaluations of kings of the North and its ultimate destruction by Josiah creates the conditions under which a restoration of Davidic-Solomonic kingdom is possible. The placement of the story of the two prophetic figures appears therefore to be significant. The prophetic conflict mirrors the political division.

The focus on Bethel in 1 Kings 13 and the larger narrative both place particular emphasis on the altar. The oracle of the man of God is addressed to the altar: "He called out against the altar (ויקרא על־המזבח) by the word of Yhwh and said, 'Altar, altar (מזבח מזבח), thus says Yhwh" (13:2). The man of God addresses the altar in the second person. The prophetic speech is unusual for being addressed to an inanimate object. The double vocative normally seeks to capture the attention of a human listener (Gen 22:11; 46:2; Exod 3:4; 1 Sam 3:4, 10). The altar becomes again the specific focus of the fulfillment in 2 Kgs 23:15-20 and is mentioned four times (23:15, 16 bis, 17).[24] The altar thereby stands at the center of this example of the prophecy-fulfillment schema in the

---

283. See also Rainer Albertz (*A History of the Israelite Religion in the Old Testament Period* (2 vols.; trans. John Bowden; OTL; Louisville, KY: Westminster John Knox, 1994) 1. 143-46; Gomes, *The Sanctuary of Bethel*, 25-28.

[22] The tenfold division (Exod 34:28; Deut 4:13; 10:4) of the Decalogue (Exod 20:1-17; Deut 5:10-21) is a complicated problem. The Jewish, Catholic and Lutheran traditions identify idolatry and polytheism as a single crime, but the Orthodox and Reformed traditions separate them. See Eduard Nielsen, *The Ten Commandments in New Perspective* (SBT 27; Naperville, IL: Allenson, 1968) 10-13; Mordechai Breuer, "Dividing the Decalogue into Verses and Commandments," in *The Ten Commandments in History and Tradition* (ed. Ben-Zion Segal and Gershon Levi; Jerusalem: Magnes, 1990) 291-330; Moshe Greenberg, "The Decalogue Tradition Critically Examined," in *The Ten Commandments in History and Tradition*, 83-119.

[23] For a fuller discussion of Jeroboam's cult in recent scholarship, see Gomes, *The Sanctuary*; E. Theodore Mullen, Jr., "The Sins of Jeroboam: A Redactional Assessment," *CBQ* 49 (1987) 212-32; Wesley I. Toews, *Monarchy and Religious Institution in Israel under Jeroboam I* (SBLMS 47; Atlanta: Scholars, 1993); Henrik Pfeiffer, *Das Heiligtum von Bethel im Spiegel des Hoseabuches* (FRLANT 183; Göttingen: Vandenhoek & Ruprecht, 1999) 26-64.

[24] The term occurs also in v. 20, but does not appear to refer specifically to the altar at Bethel. In v. 17, the expression "against the altar at Bethel" seems superfluous and therefore particularly singles out Josiah's action against the altar above all his other activities in Bethel.

Deuteronomistic History. The altar at Bethel is likewise important to the wider historical narrative. Since the narrative of Jeroboam's creation of the cult center and its denunciation focuses on the altar, the altar seems especially implicated in the frequently cited "sin of Jerobam," which emerges as the decisive error of the Northern Kingdom (2 Kgs 17:21-23).[25] The focus on the altar contributes to the Deuteronomistic concern for cultic matters. The narrative evaluates the kings of Israel and Judah largely on the basis of their cultic policy. The altar at Bethel contrasts with the altar in Jerusalem. This difference mirrors the disparity between the two nations and the two prophetic figures in 1 Kings 13.

The narrative maintains the prophetic divergence between the two anonymous prophetic figures. The narrator differentiates them by the titles: man of God (איש אלהים) and prophet (נביא).[26] Scholars have sought to determine the precise meanings of these words and differences between them, but the evidence does not support any firm conclusions.[27] Scholars have mistakenly attempted to understand the term נביא from its etymology.[28] The title man of God may be partially

---

[25] Marvin A. Sweeney, *King Josiah of Judah: The Lost Messiah of Israel* (Oxford: Oxford University Press, 2001) 78-79.

[26] In 1 Kgs 13:23, the ל in לנביא indicates possession and therefore refers to the old prophet, not to the man of God. Thus DeVries (*1 Kings*, 165) contra John Gray, *I & II Kings: A Commentary* (2d ed.; OTL; Philadelphia: Westminster, 1964) 238), Leithart, *1 & 2 Kings*, 101; *RSV, NJPSV* (cf. LXX).

[27] See W. F. Albright, *The Biblical Period from Abraham to Ezra* (2d ed.; New York: Harper, 1963) 231-32; Alfred Jepsen, "Gottesmann und Prophet," in *Probleme biblischer Theologie: Gerhard von Rad zum 70. Geburtstag* (ed. H. W. Wolff; Munich: Chr. Kaiser Verlag, 1971) 179-81; Raphael Hallevy, "Man of God," *JNES* 17 (1958) 237-44; J. Jeremias, "*nābî*" and J. Kühlewein, "*ʾîš*," both in *Theologisches Handwörterbuch zum Alten Testament* (ed. E Jenni and C. Westermann; 2 vols.; Munich: Chr. Kaiser, 1976) 2. 7-26 and 1. 130-38, respectively; Manfred Görg, "Weiteres zur Etymologie von *nābî*," *BN* 22 (1983) 9-11; Görg, "Randbemerkungen zum jüngsten Lexikonartikel zu *nābî*," *BN* 26 (1985) 7-16; Görg, "Addenda zur Diskussion um *nābî*," *BN* 31 (1986) 25-26; N. P. Bratsiotis, "*ʾîš*," in *TDOT*, 1. 222-35; Hans-Peter Müller, "Zur Herleitung von *nābî*," *BN* 29 (1985) 22-27, Robert R. Wilson, *Prophecy and Society in Ancient Israel* (Philadelphia: Fortress, 1980) 136-38, 140.

[28] Joseph Blenkinsopp (*A History of Prophecy in Israel* [rev. and enlarged ed.; Philadelphia: Westminster John Knox, 1996] 28) notes the fallacy of such argument: "Etymologies do not carry over into usage in a straightforward way. The decisive factor will always be context." The etymology of the term has been disputed. John Huehnergard ("On the Etymology and Meaning of the Hebrew *nābî*," *ErIsr* 26[1999] 88*-93*) argues that nouns pattern is passive, not active, (i.e., "one who is called"),

understood by analogy with other construct phrases such as "servant of God." The term refers to people regarded as messengers of Yhwh (e.g., Moses in Deut 33:1; Elijah in 1 Kgs 17:18). The difference (if any) between the two titles remains obscure. Robert R. Wilson concludes that "it is possible that the characteristics of the man of God were originally different from those of the prophet, and the two titles may have been used in different geographical areas, but it is now impossible to separate the two figures."[29] From the evidence of 1 Kgs 12:22 and 1 Kings 13, the term "man of God" would seem to refer to prophetic figures in Judah and "prophet" to those in Israel. However, both terms are much more frequently applied to northern figures in Kings, and both titles refer to Elijah (1 Kgs 17:18; 18:22) and Elisha (1 Kgs 4:7; 9:1). Furthermore, the Judean Isaiah is called a prophet (2 Kgs 19:2; 20:1, 11, 14), and both kingdoms are warned by prophets (2 Kgs 17:13). Consequently, the biblical evidence does not support a geographical distinction between these two terms. Unfortunately, we cannot determine the force of the Bethel prophet's statement, "I am a prophet like you" (גַם־אָנִי נָבִיא כָּמוֹךְ, 1 Kgs 13:18). He establishes an equivalence that the narrative denies by always maintaining a terminological distinction between the two figures.

The anonymity of the prophetic figures facilitates the connection between the individuals and the kingdoms they represent. The man of God, like Josiah (2 Kgs 23:15), condemns the northern apostasy and the old prophet, like Jeroboam (1 Kgs 13:7), strives to undermine the man of God's message by inviting him to enjoy a meal in Bethel. The text aligns the old prophet and the man of God with Jeroboam and Josiah respectively. The episode prior to 1 Kgs 13:11-32 focuses especially on the altar in Bethel constructed by Jeroboam. The man of God predicts the desecration of this altar by Josiah in 1 Kgs 13:2. The prophecy is unique within the prophecy-fulfillment schema because the person who fulfills the prediction is identified by name. In all other cases, the person who fulfills a prediction is named in the fulfillment notice, if at all. The story of the two prophetic figures unfolds in Bethel and 2 Kgs 23:15-20 notes the fulfillment of the man of God's prophecy and recalls

---

contra Daniel E. Fleming, "The Etymological Origins of the Hebrew *nābî*ʾ: The One Who Invokes God," *CBQ* 55 (1993) 217-24.

[29] Robert R. Wilson, *Prophecy and Society in Ancient Israel* (Philadelphia: Fortress, 1980) 140.

and completes the story of the two prophetic figures buried together in Bethel.

The presence of the prophetic figures places 1 Kings 13 within the context of prophetic stories in Kings. The prophetic stories are often intimately intertwined with the political history. Although some scholars believe that the Elijah-Elisha "cycle" was incorporated into the Deuteronomistic History at a relatively late stage, Nadav Na'aman argues that the stories were among Dtr's sources. "The close correspondence between the prophetic stories and the Dtr value judgments on Jehoshaphat and the Omrides indicates that the historian based his statements on these stories."[30] Specifically, the judgment that Ahab was worse than all other Israelite kings derives from 1 Kings 17-19 and 2 Kings 9-10. The evaluation of Ahaziah depends on 2 Kgs 1:2-17 and the presumed continuity between father and son. The conclusion that Joram was not as bad as the other Omrides (2 Kgs 3:2) derives from his willingness to consult Elisha in 2 Kgs 3:10-19 even after Elisha's refusal (3:13), and the respect he shows Elisha in 2 Kgs 6:8-10, 21-22; 8:4-6. Similarly, the positive evaluation of Jehoshaphat derives from 1 Kgs 22:1-38 and 2 Kgs 3:4-27. Na'aman's arguments articulate a relationship between the prophetic stories and the political history that has eluded many commentators. He also notes that the evaluations of the kings are not made merely on the basis of their cultic policies, but also on the related matter of their receptiveness to the prophetic

---

[30] Na'aman, "Prophetic Stories as Sources for the Histories of Jehoshaphat and the Omrides," *Bib* 78 (1997) 162. Similarly, Patrick D. Miller, "The Prophetic Critique of Kings," in Miller, *Israelite Religion and Biblical Theology: Collected Essays* (JSOT-Sup 267; Sheffield: Sheffield Academic Press, 2000) 527; originally published 1986. By contrast, most recent commentators think the prophetic stories were interpolated at a late date. Noth (*Überlieferungsgeschichtliche Studien*, 68) thought the stories were included by Dtr without significant redaction, but G. Fohrer (*Elia* [2d ed.; ATANT 31; Zurich: Theologischer Verlag, 1968] 33-50) argues for Dtr redaction of 1 Kings 17–19. However, several of those who follow the double redaction hypothesis tend to agree with Steven L. McKenzie, (*The Trouble with Kings: The Composition of the Book of Kings in the Deuteronomistic History* [TSup 42; Leiden: Brill, 1991] 85-87) that much of the prophetic material was interpolated during the exile or after. Those who follow the Smend school think the prophetic stories were added to DtrG by DtrP. For further discussion of scholarship, see Susanne Otto, *Jehu, Elia und Elisa: Die Erzählung von der Jehu-Revolution und die Komposition der Elia-Elisa-Erzählungen* (BWANT 152; Berlin: Kohlhammer, 2001) 11-25; see also English summary, Otto, "The Composition of the Elijah-Elisha Stories and the Deuteronomistic History," *JSOT* 27 (2003) 487-508.

word.[31] His diachronic argument supports synchronic attempts to read the prophetic and political narratives together.[32]

In 1 Kings 13, the two prophets are closely aligned with two kings and their respective nations. The old prophet repeats Jeroboam's invitation to the man of God and the man of God identifies himself with Josiah, who appears by name in his message. The relationship between the prophets mirrors the relationship between their nations. The prophetic story, therefore, seems especially connected to the prophetic stories that involve both kingdoms (most involve only one, and most of those only the North). This criterion points to the importance of 1 Kings 22 and 2 Kings 3. In both texts, the kings of Judah and Israel appear together before a prophet. These narratives in which prophetic figures intersect with the histories of both nations parallel 1 Kings 13 and contribute to the articulation of the *mise-en-abyme*. The story of prophetic conflict in 1 Kings 13, therefore, should be read in its political context rather than as a didactic tale about prophecy.

The distribution of the prophetic stories within the History of the Divided Kingdom follows a pattern. During the divided monarchy, the majority of prophetic stories concern northern figures. The only Judean prophets mentioned are Isaiah (2 Kings 19–20), Hulda (2 Kgs 22:14-20), and the anonymous man of God (1 Kings 13). By contrast, the history of Israel includes several anonymous figures (1 Kings 13; 20) as well as Jehu (1 Kgs 16:1-4), Micaiah (1 Kgs 22:9-28), Elijah (1 Kings 17–2 Kings 2), Elisha (1 Kgs 19:19–2 Kgs 13:21), and Jonah (2 Kgs 14:25). Since prophets frequently admonish wayward kings and people (2 Kgs 17:13), this difference between Judah and Israel suggests that Israel is less faithful to Yhwh. The distribution of prophetic stories also tends to uphold Solomon's reign as ideal. No prophets are mentioned in Solomon's time; instead Yhwh speaks to Solomon directly (1 Kgs 3:4-15; 9:1-9; 11:11-13). Similarly, the high concentration of prophetic stories during Omri's dynasty indicates the particularly serious sins of this royal house. Under Ahab and the influence of his

[31] Knoppers (*Two Nations*) overemphasizes the cult as the sole criterion of evaluation. He is reacting in part to the emphasis scholarship has placed on 1 Samuel 8–12 to determine Dtr's attitude to the monarchy (*Two Nations*, 2. 250 n. 29).

[32] Na'aman, "Prophetic Stories," 171-72: "Narratives that are included in the Book of Kings should be studied in conjunction with the passages composed by Dtr, since on many occasions the former formed the source-material for the latter."

wife Jezebel, Israel worships Baal. The series of stories concerning Elijah and Elisha shows these prophets resisting Omride influence and calling the people back to Yhwh (esp. 1 Kings 18). The narrative tempo slows during the Omride dynasty due to the inclusion of the Elijah-Elisha stories. The forty-eight years of Omride rule occupy over fifteen chapters (1 Kgs 16:23–2 Kgs 9:26) compared, for example, to the forty-two years covered in just over two chapters from Menachem to Hoshea (2 Kgs 15:8–17:6). The distribution of prophetic stories varies greatly between Judah and Israel. The preponderance of stories concerning prophets in Israel indicates that Israel is the less faithful nation that stands in greater need of prophets.

The story of the anonymous prophet and man of God in 1 Kings 13 also contributes to the prophecy-fulfillment schema in the Deuteronomistic History. The schema occurs with particular frequency during the History of the Divided Kingdom, when prophets are more common. Prophets announce Yhwh's judgment and state what Yhwh will do. Since Yhwh's word never fails, the predicted events come to pass. The narrative of the fulfillment typically uses terms that recall the prediction (e.g., 1 Kgs 22:17 and 22:36). Sometimes the narrative specifically recalls the past prophecy and notes its fulfillment (e.g., 1 Kgs 16:1-4, 12-13). The motif of prophecy-fulfillment can connect texts at considerable distance from one another (e.g., 1 Sam 2:27-35 and 1 Kgs 2:26-27; Josh 6:26 and 1 Kgs 16:34; 1 Kgs 13:11-32 and 2 Kgs 23:15-20). The pattern suggests that history unfolds according to divine will. This motif is present in 1 Kings 13, where the expression "by the word of Yhwh" occurs seven times (בדבר יהוה, 1 Kgs 13:1, 2, 5, 9, 17, 18, 32), but is otherwise rare in Kings. The story in 1 Kgs 13:11-32 and 2 Kgs 23:15-20 is unique in that it delimits a major textual unit, the History of the Divided Kingdom.[33] Its placement and the beginning and end of the history may indicate that it has functions beyond contributing to the portrait of Yhwh's control of history. Its placement may be a clue to its role as a prophetic story that parallels the political history.

---

[33] The prophecies against the Israelite dynasties similarly delimit shorter textual units concerning these dynasties (1 Kgs 14:10-11 and 1 Kgs 15:29 on Jeroboam's house; 1 Kgs 16:1-3 and 1 Kgs 16:12 on Baasha's house; 1 Kgs 21:21-22 and 2 Kgs 10:8-11 on Ahab's house).

The story of the prophetic figures in 1 Kgs 13:11-32 and 2 Kgs 23:15-20 contributes to several motifs in Kings, including the concern with cultic policy and the sin of Jeroboam, prophetic stories (including prophetic-royal conflict), and the prophecy-fulfillment schema. Furthermore, the placement of the story at the beginning and end of the History of the Divided Kingdom points to its role as a prophetic analogue to the political history. The association between the two prophetic figures and their respective nations furthers the expectation of a parallel with the political history.

1 Kings 13 as *Mise-en-abyme*

As its strategic placement suggests, the story of the prophetic figures in 1 Kgs 13:11-32 and 2 Kgs 23:15-20 is a *mise-en-abyme* in the History of the Divided Kingdom because the relationship between the two individuals duplicates the relationship between their respective kingdoms. These parallel relationships unfold in four major stages. First, the relationship is hostile and the man of God (Judah) has the better claim to fidelity to Yhwh because the old prophet (Israel) acts to gain tolerance for an idolatrous cult. Second, the man of God (Judah) and the old prophet (Israel) enjoy a friendship (alliance) based on a tolerance for idolatry which Yhwh has prohibited. Third, in a reversal of their previous roles, the old prophet (Israel) serves Yhwh and condemns the man of God (Judah) for his disobedience. Fourth, the man of God (Judah) saves the remains of the old prophet (Israel) in a final act of friendship.

At first, the introduction of Jeroboam's cult (1 Kgs 12:25-33) and its condemnation by the man of God in 13:1–13:10 seem a separate story from the tale of the old prophet and the man of God in 13:11-32, which therefore, many commentators have taken as a separate story.[34]

---

[34] Otto Thenius, *Die Bücher der Könige erklärt* (2d ed.; Leipzig: S. Hirzel, 1873) 188-89; Noth, *1 Könige*, 291; Würthwein, "Die Erzählung," 181-82; Ernst Würthwein, *Die Bücher der Könige* (2 vols.; ATD 11/1-2; Göttingen: Vandenhoeck & Ruprecht, 1977-1984) 1. 168; Gray, *I & II Kings*, 325; Lemke, "Way of Obedience," 304; Gross, "Lying Prophet," 107; Knoppers, *Two Nations*, 2. 55-64; Briend, "Du message," 13-15; Herr, "Der wahre Prophet," 71; Erhard Blum, "Die Lüge des Propheten (I Reg 13)," in *Mincha: Festgabe für Rolf Rendtorff zum 75. Geburtstag* (ed. Erhard Blum; Neukirchen-Vluyn; Neukirchener, 2000) 28-29.

These commentators respond to the isolatability of the story. Others, however, have noted the connections between these two parts and argued for a more unitary interpretation.[35] Jeroboam and the old prophet invite the man of God to a meal with almost identical words (באה־אתי הביתה וסעדה, 13:7 and לך אתי הביתה ואכל לחם, 13:15). The man of God refuses both times with nearly identical words (לא אבא עמך ולא־אכל לחם ולא אשתה־מים במקום הזה, 13:8 and לחם ולא־אשתה אתך מים במקום הזה, 13:16). On both occasions, the man of God cites the divine prohibition against eating in Bethel as reason for his refusal (13:9, 17). This repetition associates the old prophet with Jeroboam.[36] Both men attempt to undermine the man of God's message by inducing him to remain in Bethel for a meal. The turning point of the story occurs in 13:19, when the man of God accepts the invitation.[37] The outcome of the story is revealed when the prophecy is fulfilled in 2 Kgs 23:15-20. Josiah's reform is connected to 1 Kings 13 by the fulfillment notice and by Josiah's treatment of the bones of the man of God and the old prophet.[38] The story of the two prophetic figures can be isolated from its context, but it is also connected to 1 Kgs 12:25-13:10. As an isolatable story, it satisfies a criterion of the *mise-en-abyme*. However, its connection to the prior narrative indi-

---

[35] Van Winkle, "True and False Prophecy," 102-4; Dozeman, "The Way," 385-87; Richard D. Nelson, *First and Second Kings* (IBC; Atlanta: John Knox, 1987) 85; Walsh, "Contexts," 359; James K. Mead, "Kings and Prophets, Donkeys and Lions: Dramatic Shape and Deuteronomistic Rhetoric in 1 Kings XIII," VT 49 (1999) 193-97.

[36] Many scholars dismiss this connection as a late redactional effort to connect two unrelated stories.

[37] Mead, "Kings and Prophets," 194-96; followed by Jerome T. Walsh, *Style and Structure in Biblical Hebrew Narrative* (Collegeville, MN: Liturgical Press, 2001) 179-80.

[38] Some scholars suggest that 1 Kings 13 and 2 Kgs 23:15-23 were originally part of a single document. Jepsen, "Gottesmann und Prophet," 179-81; Martin A. Klopfenstein, "1. Könige 13," in *Parrhesia: Karl Barth zum achtzigsten Geburtstag am 10. Mai 1966* (Zurich: EVZ-Verlag Zürich, 1966) 648-52; Šanda, *Die Bücher,* 359-60; Simon, "1 Kings 13," 99-100; Simon, "A Prophetic Sign," 131-32. Similarly, A. H. J. Gunneweg, "Die Prophetenlegende 1 Reg 13—Mißdeutung, Umdeutung, Bedeutung," in *Prophet und Prophetenbuch: Festschrift für Otto Kaiser zum 65. Geburtstag* (ed. Volkmar Fritz, Karl-Friedrich Pohlmann, and Hans-Christoph Schmitt; BZAW 185; Berlin: de Gruyter, 1989) 74; John Van Seters, "On Reading the Story of the Man of God from Judah in 1 Kings 13," in *The Labor of Reading: Desire, Alienation, and Biblical Interpretation* (SBLSS 36; ed. Fiona C. Black et al.; Atlanta: SBL, 1999) 226; J. Van Seters, "The Deuteronomistic History: Can It Avoid Death by Redaction?" in *The Future of the Deuteronomistic History* (BETL 147; ed. T. Römer; Leuven: Leuven University Press, 2000) 221.

cates its role as a prophetic story that parallels the political history of the divided monarchy. The present study will treat 1 Kgs 13:11-32 and 2 Kgs 23:15-20 as a unitary text that functions as an alternately distributed *mise-en-abyme* within the History of the Divided Kingdom. I will sometimes refer to the text as 1 Kgs 13:11-32 + 2 Kgs 23:15-20.

The following chart will facilitate comparison between the relationship of the man of God and the old prophet in 1 Kgs 13:11-32 + 2 Kgs 23:15-20 and the relationship of Judah and Israel over the course of the History of the Divided Kingdom (1 Kings 11–2 Kings 23). It illustrates the parallel relationships between the prophetic figures and the nations that they represent. Both the personal and political relationships begin with *mutual hostility* that melts into *friendship* which ends with a dramatic *role-reversal* and *resumption of hostility*. It ends in a shared tomb in which the *southern partner saves the northern one*.

	Man of God and Prophet	**Judah and Israel**
Mutual hostility	1 Kgs 13:11-18 The prophet seeks to undermine the judgment of the man of God (from 1 Kgs 13:1-2) by inviting the prophet to share a meal in Bethel and lying about a divine revelation.	1 Kings 11–21 Judah and Israel are mutually hostile and fight several border skirmishes
Friendship	1 Kgs 13:19 The two prophetic figures share a meal together against God's command (vv. 16-17)	1 Kings 22–2 Kings 8 Judah (under Jehoshaphat) makes an alliance with Israel (under the Omride dynasty) which is evaluated negatively
Role-Reversal	1 Kgs 13:20-23 The prophet announces the judgment of God on the man of God	2 Kings 9–11 Jehu's coup initiates a reversal by which Baal worship is eliminated in Israel, but introduced in Judah (under Athaliah).

	Man of God and Prophet	Judah and Israel
Resumption of hostility	1 Kgs 13:24-34 The figures part company with the understanding that their shared meal was unfaithful to God and based on a lie. The old prophet buries the man of God in his own tomb, in fulfillment of the divine judgment	2 Kings 12-17 Judah and Israel return to their mutual hostility, with their wars going beyond border skirmishing.
Southern Partner Saves Northern One	2 Kgs 23:15-20 Josiah does not disturb the bones of the old prophets because they share a tomb with the man of God who predicted Josiah's reform of Bethel.	2 Kings 22–23 Josiah's reforms eliminate the causes of the division of Israel after Solomon death and create the conditions for a possible renewal of the United Monarchy.

The chart indicates how the prophetic story parallels the political history. As a *mise-en-abyme*, the prophetic story duplicates salient aspects of the larger whole. For example, the period between the destruction of Israel and the reform of Josiah (2 Kings 18-21) does not advance the relationship between the two nations because Judah then stands alone, without reaching north as Josiah will do. Similarly, 2 Kings 24–25 does not advance this relationship, since it narrates a history involving Judah only. The above parallel also indicates that the relationship between Israel and Judah is a major concern of the history (in contrast to Chronicles). The events on which this relationship hinges receive particular attention, especially the alliance between Judah and Israel during the Omride dynasty and the striking role-reversal of the contemporaneous coups of Jehu and Athaliah. Below, I will discuss each parallel element indicated in the chart in detail.

Mutual Hostility

The prophetic figures enter into a conflict marked by the fact that they both claim to speak for the same Yhwh. Similarly, the nations from which they come also engage in warfare following their political separation. In both cases, the parties involved restrain their quarrel. The prophetic conflict does not erupt into violence as it does when Zedekiah slaps Micaiah (1 Kgs 22:24) or Hananiah breaks Jeremiah's yoke and is punished with death (Jer 26:10-17). Rather, the two prophets maintain polite relations. Similarly, the kingdoms refrain from offensive operations and limit their military conflict to border skirmishes.

A man of God comes from Judah to condemn Jeroboam's unlawful cult. He says that a Davidic king named Josiah will come from Jerusalem to destroy the altar and burn human bones on it. As a sign that his prophecy is genuine, he declares that the altar will collapse, which it does (1 Kgs 13:3, 5).[39] After failing to arrest the man of God, Jeroboam invites him to dine with him and receive a gift. If the man of God accepts the invitation, then he would seem to approve of Jeroboam and his cult, thereby undoing (or at least undermining) the force of the message he just delivered. The man of God emphatically refuses the invitation, citing Yhwh's prohibition that he should not eat or drink in Bethel nor return to Bethel.

Yhwh's command to the man of God is central to the story.[40] The prohibition occurs several times (1 Kgs 13:9, 17, 22), and the man of God dies for disobeying it. The prohibition against eating or drinking forbids the man of God to participate in any form of communion with the condemned cult and its supporters. Eating and drinking together indicate friendship.[41] Yhwh's command stresses the severity of the divine

---

[39] Several scholars have claimed the scene absurdly depicts Jeroboam standing on top of the altar undisturbed as it collapses. For example, Würthwein, *Bücher der Könige*, 169; Dozeman, "The Way," 383; Simon, "1 Kings 13," 88 n. 22; W. Boyd Barrick, *The King and the Cemeteries: Toward a New Understanding of Josiah's Reform* (VTSup 88; Leiden: Brill, 2002) 56; Cogan, *1 Kings*, 368. The alleged absurdity has been used to reinforce the argument that a confused redactor mistakenly inserted the collapse of the altar as a sign of the man of God's mission when it should have been part of the prophecy itself (cf. 2 Kgs 23:15). This argument has merit without the alleged absurdity. The preposition על can simply mean that Jeroboam was standing beside the collapsing altar (e.g., Gen 18:2; 24:30; 28:13; 1 Sam 4:20; 1 Kgs 22:19, and with reference to altars in Num 23:3; Amos 9:1; cf. BDB 752-58, esp. 756).

[40] For Roland Boer ("National Allegory in the Hebrew Bible," *JSOT* 74 [1997] 95-116), "it is precisely this prohibition...that that provides the means of identifying the workings of political allegory in this text" (p. 108).

[41] Gerald A. Klingbeil ("'Momentaufnahmen' of Israelite Religion: The Importance of Communal Meals in Narrative Texts in I/II Regnum and Their Ritual Dimension," *ZAW* 118 [2006] 40) points out that the meal likely has "some cultic/ritual

judgment against Bethel. Yhwh enjoins the man of God to reinforce the content of his message by this symbolic rejection of communion with the North (cf. Jer 15:17; 16:1-5). Eating and drinking in Bethel would seem to undermine the content of the man of God's message.

The second part of Yhwh's prohibition is widely misunderstood. Uriel Simon articulates the usual interpretation that the man of God must not return to Judah on the same road by which he came to Bethel because to retrace one's steps is to cancel one's journey. However, the texts cited by Simon do not clearly support his claim.[42] David Marcus offers a better argument for a different interpretation.[43] Yhwh prohibits the man of God from returning to Bethel after he delivers his message.[44] This understanding is preferable for three reasons. First, the demand not to go back to Bethel reinforces the judgment against the Bethel cult. The only business for a Judean man of God in Bethel is to deliver Yhwh's oracle against it. He should have no further contact with it. Second, this understanding indicates the connection between the crime and punishment of the man of God. Since he disobeys the command not to return to Bethel, he will never be permitted to leave, even to be buried with his ancestors. Third, the old prophet is repeatedly referred to as the one "who brought him back" (הֲשִׁיבוֹ, 13:20, 23, 26). This expression identifies the old prophet as the one who caused the man of God to violate Yhwh's prohibition against "turning" (לֹא־תָשׁוּב, 13:9, 17, cf. 22). This prohibition does not refer to the particular road by which the man of God returns to Judah, but rather, the fact that he turned back to Bethel at all. Like the prohibition against eating

---

overtones" given its location at Bethel and the fact that both participants are religious personnel.

[42] Simon, "Prophetic Sign," 140-41. He translates the prohibition, "nor shall you go back [to Judah] by the road by which you came." He cites 1 Sam 25:12 and 2 Kgs 19:33 // Isa 37:34. The second example indicates a military defeat manifested by retreat, and armies commonly retreat along their previously established lines of communication. Sennacherib could not have achieved a moral victory by taking another route. The example of David's young men returning empty-handed from Nabal is similar: no matter what path they take, they bring no provisions.

[43] Marcus, *From Balaam to Jonah: Anti-prophetic Satire in the Hebrew Bible* (BJS 301; Atlanta: Scholars, 1995) 78-82.

[44] Therefore the prohibition (לֹא־תָשׁוּב לָלֶכֶת בַּדֶּרֶךְ אֲשֶׁר־הָלַכְתָּ בָּהּ) may be translated, "You shall not return in the direction from which you came [i.e., you shall not return to Bethel]." The significance of the prohibition lies in the returning, not the particularities of the path. The man of God should not return to Bethel by any road. The sense of דֶּרֶךְ here is broadly "direction" (cf. 1 Kgs 8:44, 48; 18:43).

or drinking, the demand that the man of God stay away from Bethel underscores the force of Yhwh's condemnation of Jeroboam's cult.

Once the man of God's interaction with Jeroboam is complete, the story turns to the parallel interchange with the old prophet. The old prophet learns from his sons about Jeroboam's invitation and the reasons the man of God gave for his refusal. Nevertheless, the prophet sets out to accomplish what Jeroboam could not: make the man of God eat and drink in Bethel. The prophet finds the man of God and extends the same invitation, but the man of God repeats Yhwh's prohibition and declines the prophet's invitation as he declined the offer of the king (13:16-17).[45]

The hostility of the man of God toward Israel and its cult are evident in the content of his message and his obedience to the divine prohibitions. This animosity is reciprocated in the efforts of Jeroboam and the old prophet to lead him into disobedience and communion with the North. The enmity between the man of God and the old prophet is mitigated by the fact that they worship the same God. The man of God's mission to Bethel assumes that Israel and Judah belong together and that Israel should return to the cult in Jerusalem. Judean men of God do not show a similar interest in the cults of other kingdoms because no other nation belongs with Judah the way Israel does.

This prophetic enmity within unity finds political expression in the constant low-level warfare between Israel and Judah. Yhwh checks the initial desire of the South to chastise and correct the North by military force. Rehoboam wants to make war on the North and reestablish the rule of the house of David over the northern tribes. Shemaiah speaks by the word of Yhwh (1 Kgs 12:22) to prevent this fratricidal war (12:24). Rehoboam obediently disbands his "180,000 chosen troops" (12:21).

---

[45] Pamela T. Reis ("Vindicating God: Another Look at 1 Kings XIII," *VT* [1994] 376-86; reprinted in *Reading the Lines: A Fresh Look at the Hebrew Bible* [Peabody, MA: Hendrickson, 2002] 197-209) notes several differences between the man of God's statement to Jeroboam and to the old prophet. Most significantly, he tells Jeroboam, "I will not go with you," but says to the prophet, "I am not able to go with you." He tells Jeroboam that Yhwh "commanded" him, but says to the prophet that Yhwh "said" to him. Reis concludes that "the old prophet is made aware of the man of God's intense longing to join him" (p. 382). However, her claim that the man of God refused invitations in the hope of a larger reward is unfounded. The man of God is genuinely sympathetic to the old prophet's plea for kinship and community. Similarly, Nathan Klaus (*Pivot Patterns in the Former Prophets* [JSOTSup 247; Sheffield: Sheffield Academic Press, 1997] 55-56) notes that the three-fold repetition of the prohibition moves from emphatic to weakened to disobeyed.

Nevertheless, the two kingdoms are repeatedly in a state of war until the reign of Jehoshaphat (1 Kgs 14:30; 15:6, 16). These wars, however, are mere border skirmishes.[46] Neither kingdom makes an effort at extensive conquest. The bloodless war between Baasha of Israel and Asa of Judah well exemplifies how the kings of Judah and Israel refrain from major battles because of the kinship of the two kingdoms. David Elgavish comments:

> Baasha's military action had limited aims; he was not tempted to extend his occupation of Judean territory. Nor did Asa use the opportunity of Baasha's defeat by Aram to inflict a crushing defeat on him. The restraint in determining war aims shows that the spirit of brotherhood between the two Hebrew kingdoms was recognizable in days of war as in days of peace.[47]

This skirmishing conforms to the limited hostility between the prophetic figures in 1 Kgs 13:11-18.

Friendship and Alliance

The hostility between the man of God and the old prophet melts in the friendly communion of a shared meal. This communion is false, however, because it is grounded in a lie and violates Yhwh's command prohibiting such a meal. The false communion between these indi-

---

[46] John Bright (*A History of Israel* [4th ed.; Philadelphia: Westminster, 2000] 233) says, "Such fighting as occurred was sporadic and concerned with the rectification of the mutual frontier on the soil of Benjamin." The fortifications along the frontier suggest a stable but not peaceful border. See John S. Holladay, "The Kingdoms of Israel and Judah: Political and Economic Centralization in the Iron Age IIA-B (ca. 1000-750 BCE)," in *The Archeology of Society in the Holy Land* (ed. Thomas E. Levy; New York: Facts On File, 1995) 373. J. Maxwell Miller and John H. Hayes (*A History of Ancient Judah and Israel* [Philadelphia: Westminster, 2006] 280) agree that "one should think in terms of a general state of hostilities with occasional frontier skirmishes." Cogan (*1 Kings*, 391) understands the skirmishes "as being mostly concerned with the defense of Judah's capital; they all took place within Benjamin, at times as close as 5 km to Jerusalem."

[47] Elgavish, "Objective of Baasha's War against Asa," in *Studies in Historical Geography and Biblical Historiography Presented to Zecharia Kallai* (eds. Gershon Galil and Moshe Weinfeld; VTSup 81; Leiden: Brill, 2000) 141-49. Similarly, Cogan, *1 Kings*, 399-403. Cogan thinks the war receives detailed attention because of the narrator's "interest in the payment to Ben-Hadad that was commandeered from the temple and the palace" (p. 403).

viduals reflects the failed alliance that develops between the houses of David and Ahab (1 Kgs 22:44).

After the man of God refuses the invitations of Jeroboam and the old prophet, the old prophet employs a means of compelling the man of God that was unavailable to Jeroboam. First, the prophet identifies himself as a prophet and claims a prophetic kinship with the man of God (13:18). With the words "I am a prophet like you" (נביא כמוך גם־אני), the old prophet attempts to obfuscate the distinction between the two prophetic figures that the narrator strictly maintains. The prophet's opening statement indicates that he understands that the man of God must be obedient to Yhwh's revelation. He then continues by presenting the man of God with a revelation that demands obedience. He claims that an angel spoke to him by the word of Yhwh, telling him to bring the man of God home to eat and drink.[48] The narrator immediately relates that this claim is false: "he lied to him" (כחש לו, 13:18).[49]

The prophet's goal in pursuing the man of God and lying to him is to bring him back to Bethel for a meal. He repeats Jeroboam's invitation to dine (1 Kgs 13:7, 15) and thereby assumes as his own the goal of Jeroboam. Like Jeroboam, the old prophet understands that Yhwh's rejection of the northern cult is made absolute and inflexible by the man of God's refusal to eat, drink, or return to Bethel. By his message and his obedience to Yhwh's prohibitions, the man of God rejects the northern tribes as co-religionists. Jeroboam and the prophet hope to change the man of God's attitude toward the Northern Kingdom and leave open the possibility of a "greater Israel" encompassing both

---

[48] Alexander Rofé (*The Prophetical Stories: The Narratives about the Prophets in the Hebrew Bible: Their Literary Types and History* [trans. D. Levy; Jerusalem: Magnes, 1988] 170-82) interprets the story as a polemic against angels. Subsequent commentators have rightly rejected this proposal, but the angel remains a curious detail. Cogan (*1 Kings*, 370) says that the old prophet's reference to the angel "was not a signal, missed by the man of God, that he was lying, for it would not have been considered unusual for an angel to do YHWH's bidding, even when a man of God was the recipient of the act or message (e.g., 1 Kgs 19:5-7)."

[49] Several commentators, following Šanda (*Könige*, 354), reject this notice as a later gloss and thereby read a story dramatically different from the one in the manuscript tradition. The conjunction is missing from 1 Kgs 13:18b MT but is supplied by LXX[MSS] and Syr[MSS]. Cogan (*1 Kings*, 370) notes other asyndetic circumstantial clauses (Gen 21:14; 1 Kgs 7:51; 18:6). Crenshaw (*Prophetic Conflict*, 44) mistakenly reports that the notice is missing from some LXX manuscripts.

kingdoms. The man of God believes the old prophet's lie and returns home with the prophet and dines with him.

The history of the two kingdoms mirrors the story of the prophetic figures through a similar shift from hostility to alliance. The state of low-level war between Judah and Israel is interrupted by the period of alliance between the two nations. King Jehoshaphat of Judah initiates the alliance with Ahab (1 Kgs 22:41, 44), who is the most notorious king of Israel because of his marriage to the Sidonian Jezebel, which leads to the worship of Baal in Israel. Jehoshaphat's alliance eventuates in the marriage of Ahab's daughter Athaliah to his son Jehoram, which causes the house of David to walk in the ways of the house of Ahab (2 Kgs 8:18, 27).[50]

Through this alliance with the North, Jehoshaphat seems to strive after Solomonic greatness and unity. He is the first king since Solomon to attempt an expedition to Ophir (1 Kgs 22:49-50; cf. 1 Kgs 9:26-28).[51] His desire for unity overwhelms his judgment about what peace with Ahab may mean for Judah. Since Israel is the more powerful kingdom, it assumes the position of leadership in the alliance. Instead of drawing Israel away from the worship of Baal, the alliance leads Judah into it. Jehoshaphat's desire for unity is not necessarily wrong, but Judah can have no real friendship with Israel while Israel follows the sin of Jeroboam and also worships Baal. A precondition of real unity is the cultic centrality of Jerusalem and the political leadership of the house

---

[50] The genealogy of Athaliah is a problem. She is identified as the daughter of Ahab in 2 Kgs 8:18 and 2 Chr 21:6, but as the daughter of Omri in 2 Kgs 8:26 and 2 Chr 22:2. Most translators resolve this contradiction by rendering the latter references as "granddaughter of Omri" (but Lucianic MSS read Ahab instead of Omri). These are the only texts in which *bat* is translated as "granddaughter." Most commentators accept this solution, but some argue that Omri was the father of Athaliah. For arguments in favor of Ahab's paternity, see Mordechai Cogan and Hayim Tadmor, *II Kings* (AB 11; Garden City: Doubleday, 1988) 98-99; Sarah Japhet, *I & II Chronicles* (OTL; Louisville, KY: Westminster John Knox, 1993) 809; Hannelis Schulte, "The End of the Omride Dynasty: Social-Ethical Observations on the Subject of Power and Violence," in *Ethics and Politics in the Hebrew Bible* (ed. Douglas Knight and Carol Meyers; Semeia 66; Atlanta: Scholars, 1994) 135-36. For arguments favoring Omri's paternity, see H. J. Katzenstein, "Who Were the Parents of Athaliah?" *IEJ* 5 (1955) 194-97; Donald V. Etz, "The Genealogical Relationships of Jehoram and Ahaziah, and of Ahaz and Hezekiah, Kings of Judah," *JSOT* 71 (1996) 39-53.

[51] On the various problems with this passage and its parallel in 2 Chr 20:35-37, see David A. Glatt, *Chronological Displacement in Biblical and Related Literatures* (SBLDS 139; Atlanta: Scholars, 1993) 64-67; Japhet, *I & II Chronicles*, 801-3; Cogan, *1 Kings*, 500.

of David. The alliance, like the fellowship between the old prophet and the man of God, is based on a lie and cannot stand.[52]

Judah and Israel participate together in two joint military expeditions (1 Kings 22; 2 Kings 3). These two demonstrations of unity and alliance are undermined by the involvement of prophets in the two narratives. The prophets show the difference between the kingdoms and thereby criticize the alliance as founded on a lie. The kingdoms are not so similar as the kings would like to pretend.

In 1 Kings 22, Ahab is referred to as "the king of Israel" (seventeen times) or "the king" (twelve times). Only Yhwh refers to him by name (22:20). Only in 1 Kings 20; 22 and 2 Kings 3 is the title "king (of Israel)" used frequently without an accompanying personal name. All three chapters concern Israel's wars and prophetic opposition to the house of Ahab.[53] That Jehoshaphat rather than Ahab suggests prophetic consultation before the attack of Ramoth-gilead illustrates the difference between the kings and their kingdoms. Jehoshaphat and Judah are basically faithful to Yhwh, while Ahab and Israel follow in the sin of Jeroboam and even worship Baal. The kings and their kingdoms are not the same, despite Jehoshaphat's claim, "I am as you are,

---

[52] The Chronicler makes the negative evaluation of the alliance more explicit through the condemnation by the prophet Jehu son of Hanani (2 Chr 19:2). The Chronicler views any Judahite alliance with any foreign power (including Israel) as a violation of the exclusive loyalty owed to Yhwh. See Gary N. Knoppers, "'Yhwh is not with Israel': Alliances as a Topos in Chronicles," CBQ 58 (1996) 601-626; Steven L. McKenzie, "The Trouble with Jehoshaphat," in Reflection and Refraction: Studies in Biblical Historiography in Honor of A. Graeme Auld (ed. Robert Rezetko et al.; VTSup 113; Leiden: Brill, 2007) 299-314. McKenzie states that "Kings describes Jehoshaphat's cooperation with Ahab and his peace with Israel without condemning them" (p. 313). However, as noted above (and by McKenzie), Jehoshaphat's alliance ultimately brings Baal worship to Judah and Hanani condemns it. Evidently, Kings includes an implicit critique of the alliance furthered by analogy with 1 Kings 13 and the role of prophets in 1 Kings 22 and 2 Kings 3 (see below). The Chronicler discerns this implicit evaluation and makes it explicit.

[53] For source-critical conclusions from these data, see the survey of scholarship in Benjamin Uffenheimer, Early Prophecy in Israel (trans. David Louvish; Jerusalem: Magnes, 1999) 315-35, 414-29. All three chapters may have been part of a single historiographical work distinct from the Elijah-Elisha source. The almost total lack of personal names has lead to speculation concerning the identity of the king of Israel. Furthermore, 1 Kings 20 and 22 are more closely associated in LXX[B], as chaps. 20 and 21 are transposed.

my army as your army, my horses as your horses" (כמוני כמוך כעמי כעמך‎
כסוסי כסוסיך‎, 1 Kgs 22:4).[54]

Several aspects of the prophetic conflict in this story contribute to the contrast between the two kingdoms. Jehoshaphat, unlike Ahab, is not satisfied with the assurances of the prophets and insists on consulting another prophet.[55] Ahab does not want to consult Micaiah because Micaiah will say something unpleasant that may spoil his plans to take Ramoth-gilead. Micaiah's vision of Yhwh seated on his throne (22:29) contrasts with the presentation of the two kings seated on their thrones (22:10). The two kings attempt to heal the division by alliance, but their separateness emerges in the division between the prophets. The content of Micaiah's vision also contrasts with the assurance of the other prophets. He says that Ahab will die in battle, and that the other prophets' assurance comes from a "spirit of deceit" (רוח שקר‎, 1 Kgs 22:22, 23).

Like 1 Kgs 13:11-32, the prophetic conflict in 1 Kings 22 has elicited discussion of true and false prophecy. The narrative, however, does not separate the prophetic conflict from the political problem. The four hundred prophets who prophesy favorably are not "false prophets" in the sense of people who claim divine authority for their own words.

---

[54] Some commentators understand this statement to mean that Judah is a vassal of Israel; e.g., Walsh, *1 Kings*, 344. However, the Hebrew construction suggests alliance, unity, and equality, not subservience. On the כ...כ‎ construction, see Waltke and O'Connor, *Introduction*, 202-5; Gen 18:25; 44:18; Lev 24:22; BDB 454a; Cogan and Tadmor, *II Kings*, 44, and the interpretation of the present verse in 2 Chr 18:3. A subservient expression would use ל‎ rather than כ‎, as in 1 Kgs 20:1-10, contra Knoppers ("'Yhwh is not with Israel,'" 613 and n. 46) who does not note the difference between כ‎ and ל‎. Furthermore, the statement that "Jehoshaphat made peace with the king of Israel" (וישלם יהושפט עם־מלך ישראל‎, 1 Kgs 22:45) suggests parity rather than subservience (cf. שלם‎ in 2 Sam 8:2, 6; 2 Kgs 17:3; Akkadian *šalāmu*, "to make peace," *CAD* 16. 89-91). The Hiphil of שלם‎ ("to be at peace," denominative of שלום‎, to be distinguished from the Hiphil of שלם‎ "to be complete") occurs with את‎ (Josh 10:1, 4; 2 Sam 10:19) or עם‎ (Deut 20:12) to suggest parity, and with אל‎ (Josh 11:19) to indicate submission. Mark S. Smith ("'Your People Shall be My People': Family and Covenant in Ruth 1:16-17," *CBQ* 69 [2007] 242-58) notes that the expression here and in 2 Kgs 3:7 reflects treaty language, which in turn is grounded in familial relations. In this case, the alliance between Jehoshaphat and Ahab was cemented in the marriage of Omride Athaliah to Jehoshaphat's son Jehoram (2 Kgs 8:18, 27). Furthermore, Jehoshaphat may not have been able to refuse to bring Ahab's servants on the expedition to Ophir if he were Ahab's vassal (1 Kgs 22:49).

[55] The Leningrad Codex (*BHS*) reads אדני‎ rather than the tetragrammaton in the prophets' statement (22:6), but many medieval Hebrew MSS read the tetragrammaton.

Rather, Yhwh sends a spirit of deceit to confound their prophecy and lead Ahab to his death. Furthermore, Micaiah's initial favorable prophecy is not true, but it does not make him a "false prophet."[56] His vision of the divine council does not include any commission by which he is sent to announce Yhwh's plan to anyone. Only the spirit of deceit is so commissioned. Therefore, Micaiah's initial prophecy is in keeping with Yhwh's plan, and he divulges the truth only when Ahab demands it in the name of Yhwh. As with 1 Kings 13, the prophetic conflict serves to illuminate the problem of the divided monarchy, not the problem of false prophecy.

The kings go to war despite Micaiah's warning, and Ahab dies. Israel and its deceived prophets retain the leadership of the alliance. The two prophets Micaiah and Zedekiah act out the animosity that should persist between the kings. Micaiah speaks the truth about the Northern Kingdom that Jehoshaphat prefers to ignore: the North is inspired by a spirit of deceit.

Jehoshaphat agrees to another joint expedition with his northern neighbor that also ends in failure (2 Kings 3). This time, the enemy is Moab and Ahab's son Jehoram is king of Israel. After Ahab's death, the king of Moab had rebelled against the king of Israel. Jehoram mobilizes his army and asks Jehoshaphat to join him. Jehoshaphat responds with the same answer he had given to Ahab before the war with Aram: "I am as you are, my army as your army, my horses as your horses" (כמוני כמוך כעמי כעמך כסוסי כסוסיך, 2 Kgs 3:7; 1 Kgs 22:4). The involvement of a prophet in the expedition serves to draw a distinction between the kingdoms, which Jehoshaphat's expression of unity ignores. When the expedition runs out of water in the desert, the kings consult Elisha. The prophet heaps contempt upon the king of Israel. He tells Jehoram to go to the prophets of his father Ahab and his mother Jezebel (3:13). He even says, "Were it not that I show favor to Jehoshaphat king of Judah, I would not look at you or see you" (לולי פני יהושפט מלך־יהודה אני נשא אם־אביט אליך ואם־אראך 3:14). Elisha sharply differentiates the two kingdoms and their kings so that Judah looks far better than Israel. Even with Elisha's help, this expedition ends in failure like the first.[57]

---

[56] Contra Walsh, *1 Kings*, 352.

[57] The defeat of the allies is clear, however one understands the several interpretive problems in the chapter. See Gray, *I & II Kings*, 482-91; Stefan Timm, *Die Dynastie*

The alliance between Israel and Judah does not enjoy the blessing of military success. Despite the attempt of the allies to recreate the glory of the United Monarchy and the Davidic Empire, they prove unable to achieve a single military victory. Instead, Moab and Edom, which David had conquered (2 Sam 8:2, 13-14), gain their independence (2 Kgs 3:26-27; 8:20-22), and the alliance cannot gain a victory over the Arameans, whom David had subdued (2 Sam 8:6; cf. 1 Kgs 11:24). By its lack of achievement, the alliance may be judged an overall failure. Furthermore, the unity desired by the allies is undermined by the prophetic conflict of 1 Kings 22 and Elisha's distinction between them in 2 Kings 3.

Reversal

The communal meal which the old prophet and the man of God share is interrupted by a reversal. The old prophet, who had lied, suddenly speaks the word of Yhwh. The alliance between the two kingdoms experiences a similar reversal. Jehu's rebellion ends the alliance and purifies Israel of Baal worship, while leaving a daughter of Ahab on the throne in Jerusalem, who further encourages the worship of Baal in Judah. The man of God, like Judah, appears to be the more faithful follower of Yhwh until this reversal. After the reversal, the North becomes more faithful to Yhwh and executes Yhwh's judgment on the now disobedient South.

During the meal, the prophet tells the man of God that he will be punished for his disobedience: his corpse will not rest with his ancestors. On his way home, a lion kills the man of God. This punishment relates to the prohibition in 1 Kgs 13:9, 17. The lion prevents the man of God from returning safely home after he has dined in Israel. If he had returned to Judah, then his message against the altar would have been undermined by his communion with the North. The old prophet had

---

Omri: Quellen und Untersuchungen zur Geschichte Israels im 9. Jahrhundert vor Christus (FLRANT 124; Göttingen: Vandenhoeck & Ruprecht, 1982) 171-80; Baruch Margalit, "Why King Mesha of Moab Sacrificed his Oldest Son," *BARev* 12 (Nov-Dec 1986) 62-63; Cogan and Tadmor, *II Kings*, 40-52; Philip D. Stern, "Of Kings and Moabites: History and Theology in 2 Kings 3 and the Mesha Inscription," *HUCA* 64 (1993) 1-14; Christopher T. Begg, "Filling in the Blanks: Josephus' Version of the Campaign of the Three Kings, 1 Kings 3," *HUCA* 64 (1993) 89-109.

hoped for precisely this result. The death of the man of God in fulfillment of the word of Yhwh frustrates the prophet's plan to mitigate the
man of God's message.

Similarly, Jehu's Elisha-inspired coup (2 Kings 9–10) ends the dubious alliance between Israel and Judah and establishes Israel as the
more faithful kingdom in comparison with a now apostate Judah. Jehu
fulfills Yhwh's promise to exterminate the house of Ahab, but he also
executes a judgment on the house of David for following the way of
the house of Ahab (2 Kgs 8:18, 27). The North, like the old prophet,
suddenly speaks the word of Yhwh, and Judah, like the man of God,
suffers for disobedience.

The Judean royal family suffers almost as much as the house of Ahab
as a consequence of Jehu's coup. In addition to killing King Ahaziah
king of Judah (2 Kgs 9:27-29), Jehu also captures and executes forty-
two relatives of Ahaziah who, in the spirit of the North-South alliance,
were on their way to Samaria to visit the sons of Jezebel (10:12-14). Jehu
is like the lion that executes Yhwh's judgment concerning the man of
God.[58] As with the Levites (Exod 32:25-29) and Phineas (Num 25:6-13),
Yhwh rewards Jehu for his violent zeal (2 Kgs 10:16, 30).[59] The error of

[58] Marvin A. Sweeney (*I & II Kings: A Commentary* [OTL; Louisville, Ky: Westminster John Knox, 2007] 181) notes the association of the Judean royal house with
lions (Gen 49:8; 1 Sam 17:16; Ariel in Isaiah 29). He thinks the lion in 1 Kings 13 reinforces the image of Judah as the faithful nation that will punish the North for its
infidelity. He also notes the connection with the lions that trouble the settlers in Assyr-
ian-occupied Israel in 2 Kgs 17:24-41 (Sweeney, *King Josiah*, 90). This observation may
have merit, but Sweeney flattens the story of the two prophetic figures into an etiology
for the tomb mentioned in 2 Kgs 23:15-20 and argues that the story focuses on the old
prophet as a liar. He neglects that the lying prophet also speaks a true word of God
and that the man of God violates the divine command. The episode does not easily fit
into a strictly pro-Judean or pro-Josiah agenda.
[59] E. Theodore Mullen ("The Royal Dynastic Grant to Jehu and the Structure of
the Books of Kings," *JBL* 107 [1988] 193-206) notes the similarities between the dynastic grants to Jehu and David. The violence of Jehu's coup has troubled interpreters.
Uffenheimer (*Early Prophecy*, 456-58, 476-76, 503) suggests that Jehu's violence caused
Israelite prophecy to shift from the militancy of Elijah and Elisha to the educational
prophecy of the classical prophets. Roger Tomes ("Come and See My Zeal for the
Lord: Reading the Jehu Story," in *Narrativity in Biblical and Related Texts* [eds. G.
J. Brooke and J.-D. Kaestli; BETL 149; Leuven: Leuven University Press, 2000] 53-67)
notes that recent scholarship tends to identify textual elements that indicate a religious
motive for the coup as later interpolations. Tomes suggests that the interpolations are
an ancient (deuteronomistic) "reading" of the story (i.e., the interpolations do not contradict their context, but represent a possible interpretation of the prior narrative).

Judah's ways, which it learned from Israel, are ultimately corrected by the intervention of a zealous Israelite king.

Jehu's coup leaves Judah without a king. After the king and his forty-two relatives die at Jehu's hands, Athaliah takes murderous measures to gain the throne of Judah. This daughter of Ahab perverts the worship of Judah, just as Jezebel had perverted the religion of Israel. The narrative suggests the violence of Athaliah's rule by noting that the land was at peace after her execution (2 Kgs 11:20; cf. Judg 3:11, 30; 5:31; 8:28; Josh 11:23; 14:15). The destruction of the temple of Baal and execution of Baal's priest (2 Kgs 11:18) indicate that Athaliah had introduced or expended the worship of Baal in Judah.[60]

The roles of the two kingdoms are reversed in Jehu's coup. Judah becomes the apostate while the North wipes out the worship of Baal. Jehu does not, however, abolish the cult of Jeroboam. He only returns Israel to the lesser level of apostasy that it displayed prior to the rise of Ahab and his marriage to Jezebel. In Judah, meanwhile, Athaliah's rule resembles Jezebel's in Israel. This role reversal corresponds to the reversal in 1 Kings 13 in which the prophet declares Yhwh's judgment to the man of God who strayed from the path of obedience to have communion with the North.

Resumption of Hostility

The reversal that follows the friendship and alliance does not last long. The apostasy of Judah lasts only as long as Athaliah's seven-year reign. Following Jehoiada's coup, Judah returns to its prior tarnished state of obedience to Yhwh (2 Kgs 12:4). Israel, meanwhile, returns to its pre-Omride sin; Baal worship is extirpated, but the sin of Jeroboam remains (2 Kgs 10:29). The two kingdoms appear to return to the state of mutual hostility that prevailed before Jehoshaphat's alliance with Ahab. The relationship between the two prophetic figures in 1 Kings 13 is less explicit. The old prophet announces Yhwh's judgment against the man of God, which suggests the end of communion and a return

---

[60] The narrative makes several historical claims that have been questioned. Some scholars do not accept that there ever was a temple of Baal in Jerusalem. Cogan and Tadmor (*II Kings*, 134) remark, "Due to the lack of evidence other than 1 Kgs 11, any number of scenarios can be written."

to animosity. However, the man of God finishes his meal and the old prophet supplies him with a donkey for his journey, which indicates lingering friendship.

This phase of the relationship as described in the History of the Divided Kingdom does not clearly correspond to anything in 1 Kgs 13 + 2 Kgs 23:15-20. This stretch of historiography (2 Kings 12–21) may lack a correspondence in 1 Kings 13 because it is not pertinent to the issue of the relationship between Israel and Judah. Similarly, a significant portion of the Story of Jacob's Line (Genesis 39–41) has no correspondence in Genesis 38 because Joseph's rise is merely preliminary to his deception and part of the Story of David and the House of Saul lacks relevance to 1 Samuel 25 because David and Saul are not in contact during most of David's wilderness period and his sojourn with the Philistines. This part of the History of the Divided Kingdom is extraneous in a different way. The two kingdoms are in relationship, but the relationship has become unusually violent. Since the dealings between the nations are anomalous during this time, 2 Kings 12–21 is not relevant to the motif of the connection between Judah and Israel.

Between the restoration of Joash and the reforms of Josiah, the relationship between Israel and Judah is aberrant. During this period, Judah and Israel fight two fratricidal wars. The first originates in the pride of a Judean king. After he defeats the Edomites, Amaziah of Judah challenges Jehoash of Israel to battle (2 Kgs 14:8). Jehoash responds with a parable in which Judah is the small thistle or thornbush seeking to be the equal of the mighty cedar. Amaziah ignores Jehoash's warning and marches out to war to be defeated as Jehoash predicted. Jehoash tears down a section of the walls of Jerusalem, takes the treasures of the temple and the king's palace and returns to Samaria with his booty and hostages. Perhaps as a result of this foolish war, Amaziah becomes one of the few Judean kings to be assassinated in a conspiracy (2 Kgs 14:19).[61]

The second war between Israel and Judah is the Syro-Ephraimite war. Israel allies with Aram to wage war on Judah (2 Kgs 15:37; 16:5-9). Ahaz of Judah remains under siege in Jerusalem and sends the treasures of his palace and the temple to the Assyrians with an appeal for help. By this means, Ahaz saves the city, but commits himself and his

---

[61] Miller and Hayes, *History*, 307.

successors to subservience to Assyria. The results of his subservience are seen in his modifications to the temple (2 Kgs 16:10-18).[62]

Both of these wars are unjust. They constitute the kind of fratricidal bloodshed that Yhwh warned Rehoboam against (1 Kgs 12:21-24). These anomalous wars have no parallel in the story of the prophets in 1 Kings 13. The *mise-en-abyme* duplicates pertinent aspects of the whole, and these wars seem not to be relevant to the presentation of the relation between the kingdoms because of their anomaly. The Chronicler emphasizes this judgment of the wars by presenting the first as retribution for Amaziah's infidelity (2 Chr 25:14-28) and the second as retribution for Ahaz' apostasy (2 Chronicles 28). The speech of the prophet Oded (2 Chr 28:9-11) draws particular attention to the fratricidal nature of the war.

Southern Partner Saves Northern One

The story of 1 Kgs 13:11-32 ends with the burial of the man of God and the old prophet in the same tomb. The significance of this arrangement becomes apparent in the resumption of their story in 2 Kgs 23:15-20: Josiah refrains from burning the bones of the old prophet out of respect for the man of God.[63] The story of the two prophetic figures continues to mirror the history of the two kingdoms. This reflection may be seen in two different ways. First, just as the man of God saves the old prophet's bones from desecration, so the king of Judah saves the remnant of the North from the sin of Jeroboam. This incident shows that Israel can hope for salvation only through Judah. Second, the two prophetic figures sharing a common tomb may be likened to the two nations sharing a common exile in Mesopotamia.[64] However, the deaths of the two individuals should not primarily be understood as foreshadowing the destruction of their respective nations. As individuals, their lifespans are much shorter than the histories of nations. The content of

[62] For historical evaluation of this passage, see M. Cogan, *Imperialism and Religion: Assyria, Judah and Israel in the Eighth and Seventh Centuries B.C.E.* (SBLMS 19; Missoula, MT.: SBL and Scholars, 1974) 73-77.

[63] According to LXX[B MSS], the old prophet wanted to be buried with the man of God precisely "so that my bones will be saved with his bones" (1 Kgs 13:31).

[64] Barth ("Exegese," 55) and Leithart (*1 & 2 Kings*, 102) articulate this interpretation.

2 Kgs 23:15-20 indicates a more optimistic interpretation of the common grave. The emphasis falls not on the fact that both are dead (how could they not be?), but on the fact that they share a common grave together and that the southern figure is able to save his northern neighbor. In addition to mirroring the history of the kingdoms, the story also functions to legitimate Josiah's reforms. He emerges as a prophetically predicted savior who addresses the root cause of Israel's destruction and piously spares the grave of a true prophet. As the story continues and Judah suffers a fate nearly identical to Israel, the fact that both individuals are buried in the same grave may take on a more ominous meaning (although this burial is not recalled after 2 Kgs 23:15-20).

The man of God's posthumous act on behalf of the prophet is similar to Josiah's activity in the North. Josiah reforms the cult of both the South and North and thereby lays a firm foundation for reestablishing the United Monarchy.[65] Josiah's reforms are more complete than those of prior kings. For example, Hezekiah had destroyed the high places (2 Kgs 18:4), but he did not disturb the high places for Chemosh and Milcom that Solomon established (1 Kgs 11:7). Josiah destroys these places of worship and thereby "removes the cause of the division of the kingdom" (2 Kgs 23:13).[66]

After reforming Judah, Josiah turns his attention to the North. According to the account, he goes to Bethel and carries out the reforms that the man of God had prophesied. The account of his activity in Bethel recalls Jeroboam's establishment of the Bethel cult and the man of God's prophecy against it. As predicted, Josiah burns human bones on the altar (2 Kgs 23:16, 20; 1 Kgs 13:2), slaughters the priests of the high places (2 Kgs 23:10; 1 Kgs 13:2), and destroys the high places of Samaria (2 Kgs 23:20; 1 Kgs 13:32). His actions are "according to the word of

---

[65] Josiah's intentions are not explicit in the narrative, but interpreters recognize that he has no business in Bethel unless, like David (cf. 1 Kgs 22:2), he has ambitions beyond Judah. For discussion of the extensive scholarship on Josiah's reform, see Norbert Lohfink, "Recent Discussion on 2 Kings 22–23: The State of the Question" (originally published as "Zur neuren Diskussion über 2 Kön 22–23," in *Das Deuteronomium: Entstehung, Gestalt und Botschaft* [ed. Norbert Lohfink; BETL; Leuvain: Louvain University Press, 1985] 24-48), in *A Song of Power and the Power of Song: Essays on the Book of Deuteronomy* (trans. Linda M. Maloney; Sources for Biblical and Theological Study 3; ed. Duane L. Christensen; Winona Lake: Eisenbrauns, 1993) 36-61; Knoppers, *Two Nations*, 2. 171-228; Sweeney, *King Josiah*, 33-92.

[66] Gary N. Knoppers, "'There Was None Like Him:' Incomparability in the Books of Kings," *CBQ* 54 (1992) 428.

Yhwh that the man of God proclaimed when Jeroboam was standing by the altar at the feast" (2 Kgs 23:16).[67] Josiah notices the grave of the man of God and orders that his bones not be disturbed because he prophesied the demise of the altar.[68] No one seems to remember that the bones of "the prophet who came from Samaria" (2 Kgs 23:18) are also in the grave.[69] The prophet's bones are spared because they are with those of the man of God. Josiah's activity on behalf of the North mirrors the man of God's posthumous act on behalf of the old prophet. The salvation and rehabilitation of the North depend on the efforts of the South.

Mise-en-abyme: Pattern of Repetition

Unlike the Story of Jacob's Line and the Story of David and the House of Saul, the narrative of the History of the Divided Kingdom lacks doublets and no originally parallel sources are recognized in Kings.[70] The only apparent doublets involve parallel stories of Elijah and Elisha (1 Kgs 17:1-16, 17-24; 2 Kgs 4:1-7, 8-37). Such parallels are normally explained as a development of one tradition from the other, not two originally separate sources.[71] The primary forms of repetition

---

[67] Reading LXX[B MSS], which continues, "he turned and raised his eyes to the grave of the man of God" and then agrees with MT "who called out these words." MT has lost the words by homoioteleuton of איש האלהים. See *BHS* apparatus.

[68] Possibly, the grave is indicated by a marker. Such inscriptions have been found in 8th-early 6th century contexts in Judah. The tomb inscriptions outside Jerusalem follow the Phoenician custom of pronouncing a curse on anyone who would disturb the tomb. One broken inscription has been tentatively associated with Shebna (cf. Isa 22:15-19). See Klaas A. D. Smelik, *Writings from Ancient Israel: A Handbook of Historical and Religious Documents* (trans. G. I. Davies; Louisville, KY: Westminster John Knox, 1991) 72-75.

[69] Many commentators note the anachronous reference to Samaria, which did not exist at the time of the story in 1 Kings 13. The reference strengthens the connection between the old prophet and the royal house(s) of Israel by indicating the he came from the royal capital presumably to prophesy at the royal sanctuary in Bethel. Cogan and Tadmor (*II Kings*, 290) think it "betrays the usage of the seventh century when Samaria was a regional territory, juxtaposed to Judah." Similarly, Gomes, *Sanctuary*, 39, who thinks the language reflects the situation after 720 (cf. 2 Kgs 17:24, 26; 23:19).

[70] Isolated attempts to discern J and E in Kings have been abandoned; see Otto Eissfeldt, *The Old Testament: An Introduction* (trans. Peter R. Ackroyd; Oxford: Basil Blackwell, 1974) 297-300.

[71] Most often, the Elijah stories are regarded as secondary to the Elisha stories. Hermann Gunkel, *Elias, Jahve und Baal* (Tübingen: Mohr, 1906) 38-39; Rofé, *Pro-*

in Kings concern the regnal notices and prophecy-fulfillment schema. These repetitions establish motifs and create analogies within the narrative.

The regnal notices repeat a narrative interest in religious and cultic policy (among other things).[72] Kings in both kingdoms are described as good or bad depending largely on their cultic practice, although their responses to prophets also matter.[73] Almost all the kings of Israel are said to imitate Jeroboam by continuing his cult, which is represented as idolatrous and polytheistic. The kings of Judah, meanwhile, are compared unfavorably to David. These evaluations establish several sets of analogies. The text explicitly compares kings to the two founders of Judah and Israel, respectively. By extension, all the kings of Israel stand in comparison to one another, as do the kings of Judah. Furthermore, the kings of Judah and Israel may be compared to one another. In addition to the general analogies encouraged by the regnal notices, the paratactic arrangement of the reigns of kings sometimes reveals or prompts specific analogies, explicit or implicit. For example, the coups of Jehu and Jehoiada occur in immediate proximity (2 Kings 9–10 and 11, respectively). The extreme violence of Jehu's coup contrasts with the nearly bloodless coup of Jehoiada. Within these stories, the queens

---

phetical Stories; H. Chr. Schmitt, *Elisa* (Gütersloh: Gütersloher Verlagshaus/Gerd Mohn, 1972) 454-55; H.-J. Stipp, *Elischa—Propheten—Gottesmänner* (ATSAT 24; St. Ottilien: EOS, 1987) 451-58; McKenzie, *The Trouble with Kings*, 82. Other scholars are reluctant to draw conclusions concerning priority: Long, *1 Kings*, 184; T. R. Hobbs, *2 Kings* (WBC 13; Waco, TX: Word Books, 1985) 46.

[72] The regnal formulas have been the subject of extensive study, normally undertaken with a view to discerning the redactional development of the Deuteronomistic History. See C. F. Burney, *Notes on the Hebrew Text of the Books of Kings* (Oxford: Clarendon, 1903) ix-xii; Alfred Jepsen, *Die Quellen des Königsbuches* (Halle: Max Niemeyer, 1956) 7-11; Shoshana R. Bin-Nun, "Formulas from Royal Records of Israel and of Judah," *VT* 18 (1968) 414-32; Helga Weippert, "Die 'deuteronomischen' Beurteilungen der Könige von Israel und Juda und das Problem der Redaktion der Königsbücher," *Bib* 53 (1972) 301-39; Hans-Detlef Hoffmann, *Reform und Reformen: Untersuchungen zu einem Grundthema der deuteronomischen Geschichtsschreibung* (ATANT 66; Zurich: Theologischer Verlag, 1980) 33-38; Richard D. Nelson, *The Double Redaction of the Deuteronomistic History* (JSOTSup 18; Sheffield: JSOT, 1981) 29-42; Timm, *Die Dynastie Omri*, 28-40; Long, *1 Kings*, 22; Antony F. Campbell, *Of Prophets and Kings: A Late Ninth-Century Document (1 Samuel 1–2 Kings 10)* (CBQMS 17; Washington, D.C.: Catholic Biblical Association of America, 1984) 139-202; André Lemaire, "Vers l'histoire de la rédaction des livres des rois," *ZAW* 98 (1986) 221-36; Baruch Halpern and David S. Vanderhooft, "The Editions of Kings in the 7th-6th Centuries B.C.E.," *HUCA* 62 (1991) 179-244.

[73] Na'aman, "Prophetic Stories," 153-73.

Jezebel and Athaliah both exercise political power to the detriment of Israel and Judah, respectively. The explicit comparison of Israelite kings to Jeroboam establishes a similarity of all of them. The praise accorded to Joash, Hezekiah, and Josiah brings these three reformers into an analogous relationship with one another.

Richard D. Nelson notes: "Analogy provides inner unity to the otherwise loose paratactic structure of Kings. It bridges the divisions caused by the chronological structure of the reigns. It provides rich harmonies and overtones to the individual narratives when they are read with a sense of the whole."[74] Within this network of analogies, 1 Kgs 13:11-32 + 2 Kgs 23:15-20 is a *mise-en-abyme* standing within and for the History of the Divided Kingdom.

Conclusion

The story of the two prophetic figures in 1 Kgs 13:11-32 + 2 Kgs 23:15-20 is a *mise-en-abyme* within the History of the Divided Kingdom. The relationship between the man of God and the old prophet parallels the relationship that unfolds between Judah and Israel. This relationship moves through four stages. First, the man of God and the old prophet, like their respective kingdoms, are hostile to one another, yet mindful of their kinship. Second, the man of God, like Judah, is deceived by his northern counterpart into infidelity to Yhwh. Third, the friendship between the man of God and the old prophet ends, like the alliance between the kingdoms, with a reversal in which the North becomes the faithful executor of Yhwh's will. Fourth, the old prophet and the man of God share a common grave and the man of God protects the old prophet's bones. Similarly, Judah acts for the North through Josiah's elimination of Jeroboam's cult.

The fulfillment of the man of God's prophecy from 1 Kings 13:1-2 in 2 Kgs 23:15-20 indicates the scope within which the story of the prophetic figures functions as a *mise-en-abyme*. Knoppers recognizes that the History of the Divided Kingdom is a definable segment in the his-

---

[74] Nelson, *First and Second Kings*, 11. Long (*1 Kings*, 19-21) compares this feature of the biblical narrative with Herodotus' *Histories*. See also John Van Seters, *In Search of History: Historiography in the Ancient World and the Origins of Biblical History* (New Haven: Yale University Press, 1983) 31-40.

tory of the monarchy as told in Kings. It is bracketed by 1 Kings 11–14 and 2 Kings 22–23. However, Knoppers does not include the bulk of 1 Kings 13 in his list of passages that comment on major events in Israelite history during the divided monarchy.[75] The recognition of 1 Kings 13 as a *mise-en-abyme* may not alter this assessment. Some of the textual comments noted by Knoppers are expository texts (2 Kgs 17:7-41) and others are speeches that reflect on the narratives in which they occur (1 Kgs 14:7-16; 2 Kgs 19:15-19). The story of the two prophetic figures, however, does not provide the kind of commentary afforded by such expository passages. Rather, as a *mise-en-abyme*, it duplicates the whole in which it occurs and provides a parallel story to the larger narrative. As a *mise-en-abyme*, the story does not comment directly on the history, but creates an analogy with it. The analogy invites comparison between the two narratives such that the *mise-en-abyme* elucidates aspects of the larger history.

The recognition that 1 Kgs 13:11-32 + 2 Kgs 23:15-20 is a *mise-en-abyme* within the History of the Divided Kingdom has several implications for future research. The parallel between the story of the two prophetic figures and the larger history concerns the relationship between the two kingdoms. The *mise-en-abyme* therefore indicates the importance of this relationship in the history. The narrative develops its theme in a variety of ways. The parallel history of both kingdoms, connected by synchronistic chronological notices, indicates the narrator's interest in "all Israel," not only Judah (as in Chronicles). Furthermore, some of the stories involving prophets comment directly on the relationship between the two kingdoms (1 Kings 22; 2 Kings 3). Although scholars agree that the history reflects a Judean perspective, Judah is not represented as blameless: the negative evaluation of the alliance and the consequent reversal following Jehu's coup indicates a criticism of Judah and parallel praise of Israel. The considerable interest that Kings shows in the relationship between the two kingdoms is not adequately reflected in scholarship on the historiography.[76]

---

[75] Knoppers (*Two Kingdoms*, 2. 231) isolates 1 Kgs 13:1-3, 31-34, along with 1 Kings 11; 14:7-16; 2 Kgs 17:7-41; 19:15-19; 20:2-3; and 2 Kings 22–23 as passages that comment on major events.

[76] Like many commentators, Sweeney (*I & II Kings*, 11-13) sees the narrative as decidedly pro-Judahite. However, Sweeney also recognizes the often overlooked significance of the alliance between the houses of David and Omri. He sees in this alliance, with the intermarriage between the houses, the root cause of the fall of David's

The synchronic analysis of 1 Kings 13 within the History of the Divided Kingdom may contribute to diachronic discussions about the composition of Kings. As noted above, the common grave shared by the two prophetic figures indicates that Judah can save Israel. The focus on the common grave of the two prophetic figures involves the bones of the old prophet being saved by the presence of those of the man of God. It does not primarily point toward the common exile in Mesopotamia of the two kingdoms. This consideration may imply that 1 Kgs 13:11-32 + 2 Kgs 23:15-20 fits best within a narrative framework that does not include 2 Kings 24–25. The placement of the two passages may indicate their original context. The story begins when the kingdoms divide. The political division quickly leads to cultic separation and prophetic conflict. The History of the Divided Kingdom would seem to end with the destruction of Israel in 2 Kings 17. However, the reforms of Josiah indicate a Judean interest in the North, and his reform of the Bethel altar attacks the root causes of Israel's defeat and exile. By addressing the fundamental causes, the narrative offers hope that Josiah may be a new King David who will unify "all Israel." The placement of 2 Kgs 23:25-20, therefore, shows the true limits of the History of the Divided Kingdom. The division does not end until Josiah ends it. Within this Josianic context, 1 Kgs 13:11-34 + 2 Kgs 23:15-20 mirrors the history of Judahite-Israelite relations and adds a final chapter that hopes for a new beginning without separation. The deaths of the two individuals should not primarily be understood as foreshadowing the destruction of their respective nations. In short, the story of the two prophetic figures functions as a *mise-en-abyme* within 1 Kings 11–2 Kings 23, which may indicate that the tale was part of a Josianic edition of the Deuteronomistic History.

The division between Judah and Israel is also of interest in other biblical books. Chronicles offers noteworthy interpretations of the relationship between the two kingdoms (2 Chr 13:3-12; 18:1-3; 19:1-3; 20:35-37; 21:12-15; 22:3-15; 28:5-15). The division is also a significant motif in some of the writing prophets (e.g., Isa 7:17; Jer 3:6-18; 23:13-14; Ezek 16:46-52;

dynasty. The mention of the Omride Ahab in 2 Kgs 21:3 concerning the apostasy of Manasseh indicates that the curse of the house of Omri (1 Kgs 21:17-29) affects the house of David as a result of the intermarriage between the houses. Sweeney is right to highlight the importance of this connection, although he still misses the ways in which the pro-Judahite narrative of 1–2 Kings shows that Judah can fail and Israel succeed as occurred in the role reversal of Jehu's coup.

23:1-49; 37:15-28). Amos may be of particular interest in this regard. Like the man of God, Amos is a Judean called to prophesy in Bethel (1 Kgs 13:1; Amos 1:1; 7:12-15). Both men focus their judgment against the altar at Bethel (1 Kgs 13:2-3; Amos 3:14) and encounter resistance from Jeroboam (I and II, respectively) or his representative (1 Kgs 13:4-7, 15-18; Amos 7:10-13). Amos rejects the title prophet, which is never applied to the man of God (Amos 7:14). These parallels between the man of God of 1 Kings 13 and Amos have led several scholars to identify the anonymous man of God as Amos, or suggest that the story of the man of God is derived from traditions regarding Amos.[77]

These speculations tend to detract attention from the political and religious problems involved in the division of the kingdom as reflected in the biblical literature. Furthermore, the identification of Amos and the man of God is unlikely. The historical argument minimizes the fact that the man of God and Amos operated in different centuries and that the Bible nowhere else confuses Jeroboam I and Jeroboam II. It also neglects other connections between the Former Prophets and the Latter Prophets. When a single prophetic figure occurs in both sections of the Bible, the relationship is explicit (Jonah and Isaiah). In the cases in which material from a writing prophet occurs in the historical books, it is nearly identical rather than used in the free manner imagined by some scholars for Amos and 1 Kings 13. Indeed, the Deuteronomist may have deliberately not mentioned Amos in the historical narrative precisely because of his opposition to Jeroboam II. The Deuteronomistic presentation of his reign, and of the whole dynasty of Jehu, is generally positive despite the continuation of the cult of Jeroboam I. The involvement of prophets in this dynasty is uncharacteristically positive (e.g., 2 Kgs 10:30; 13:4-5, 14-19; 14:25-27). These observations suggest that Dtr may have omitted Amos from the narrative because Amos contradicted the portrait Dtr wished to paint of the dynasty of Jehu generally and of the reign Jerobaom II in particular.[78]

---

[77] Julius Wellhausen, *Die Composition des Hexateuchs und der historischen Bücher des Alten Testaments* (2nd ed.; Berlin: George Reimer, 1889) 280; Crenshaw, *Prophetic Conflict*, 41-42; Lemke, "The Way," 315-16; Baruch Halpern, *The First Historians: The Hebrew Bible and History* (New York: Harper & Row, 1988 [reprint Pennsylvania University Press, 1996]) 248-54; Halpern, *David's Secret Demons*, 255; Barrick, *The King*, 217-21.

[78] Christopher T. Begg, "The Non-mention of Amos, Hosea and Micah in the Deuteronomistic History," *BN* 32 (1986) 48-50.

The above discussion of 1 Kgs 13:11-32 + 2 Kgs 23:15-20 and similar prophetic stories (1 Kings 22; 2 Kings 3) suggest that the prophetic and political strands of the biblical historiography are not as separate as scholarship has sometimes assumed. Patrick D. Miller, speaking primarily about the writing prophets, notes that "the prophetic critique of kings and their administration of the kingdom is not confined to those texts that speak to or about kings."[79] Similarly, the prophetic stories directly involving kings (e.g., 1 Kings 21; 22; 2 Kings 1; 3) are not the only means by which the prophetic stories concern the political history. The distribution of prophetic stories indicates a difference between Israel and Judah. Prophets are more common in the North than the South (and especially during the Omride dynasty) because prophets are needed most when the kings are disobedient to God. Furthermore, some of the stories indicate the unjust conditions under the monarchy (2 Kgs 4:1), divine punishment for injustice and infidelity (1 Kgs 17:1; 2 Kgs 8:1; cf. Deut 11:13-17), and the authority of the prophets who denounce the kings (1 Kgs 17:24). Furthermore, in addition to cultic concerns, royal reaction to prophetic figures also influences the evaluations of the kings. These considerations suggest that, as in the books of Samuel, the prophetic stories in Kings have a significant relationship to the political history.

Finally, the strange story of 1 Kgs 13:11-32 makes sense as a *mise-en-abyme* in the History of the Divided Kingdom. The problem interpreters have long had with the narrative is the difficulty that the man of God is punished for his gullibility while the prophet who deceived him goes unpunished. Scholars have struggled to locate a didactic lesson in the seemingly unedifying story. Such efforts have not succeeded because the story has been read apart from its immediate context concerning the division of the kingdom and its larger context of the History of the Divided Kingdom. Those scholars who have interpreted the story within its political context have had less difficulty with the strangeness of the story.[80] The narrative foreshadows Judah's temptation to betray its fidelity to Yhwh in the hope of communion with Israel. It also indicates that Israel will become the instrument by which

---

[79] Miller, "Prophetic Critique," 532.

[80] Barth, "Exegese"; Lemke, "The Way," 317; Walsh, "Contexts," 367-68; D. Van Winkle, "1 Kings XII 25–XIII 34: Jeroboam's Cultic Innovations and the Man of God from Judah," VT 46 (1996) 112-13; Gunneweg, "Die Prophetenlegende," 81.

Judah will return to Yhwh. Commentators have not discovered a criterion by which true prophecy can be discerned because the story of the prophetic figures, like the history of the two kingdoms, blurs the distinction. Judah has no monopoly on true prophecy, and Israel is not entirely lost. This complex attitude to the schism in Israel contrasts with the more one-sided narrative of Chronicles. Although written from a Judahite perspective, the history narrated in 1 and 2 Kings acknowledges Judean errors and Israelite virtues. The historiography is not as simple as Judean or Josianic "propaganda."

Although the overall function of the *mise-en-abyme* depends on similarity, differences may also be exegetically interesting. Perhaps the most striking difference concerns the communal meal shared by the prophetic figures and the alliance between the nations. In 1 Kings 13, the old prophet initiates the meal by appealing to a fictitious revelation. Readers puzzle over the harsh punishment of the deceived man of God because the sin seems more the fault of the old prophet. In the subsequent history, however, the Judahite king Jehoshaphat initiates the alliance with the North (1 Kgs 22:24). If communion with the North represents participation in Israelite apostasy, the blame for this crime falls squarely on Judah. Jehoshaphat can not claim that Ahab tempted him with a revelation.

Unlike the prior examples of the *mise-en-abmye*, the present instance does not involve parallel personal relationships. Rather, the relationship between the prophetic figures mirrors the relationship between their respective nations. Although this feature distinguishes this example of the *mise-en-abyme* from the others, biblical literature elsewhere uses individuals as representatives of their social or political groups. Scholars have long recognized that Jacob/Israel and his twelve sons represent Israel and its twelve tribes. Other eponymous ancestors function similarly (Ishmael, Esau, Moab, Ben-ammi) and kings commonly represent the nations they rule (cf. Isa 7:8-9). In 1 Kings 13, the old prophet and man of God identify with Jeroboam and Josiah, respectively. Thus, the personal relations between the prophetic figures may represent the diplomatic relations between their nations.

To return to the original question: what is 1 Kgs 13:11-32 + 2 Kgs 23:15-20 doing within the History of the Divided Kingdom? This prophetic story acts as a *mise-en-abyme* that emphasizes the central theme of the relationship between Judah and Israel. The role-reversal complicates any simple characterization of this relationship. Israel is not simply dismissed as apostate and Judah briefly falls into serious apostasy during the reign of Athaliah. Furthermore, the role of the prophetic story as a *mise-en-abyme* articulates its connection to the political history. Without this connection, the strangeness of the story becomes inexplicable. The recognition of the *mise-en-abyme* demystifies the peculiar story and accounts for both its isolatability and its role in the larger History of the Divided Kingdom.

CHAPTER FIVE

Conclusion

The brief stories in Genesis 38, 1 Samuel 25, and 1 Kings 13 are *mises-en-abyme*; they duplicate pertinent aspects of the larger contexts in which they occur. All of the examples involve parallel relationships, so that each may be expressed as an analogy. The deception practiced by Tamar parallels that of Joseph; both characters practice deception on those who wronged them in order to restore the family (Tamar : Judah :: Joseph : Judah and his brothers). David's conflict with Nabal recapitulates his conflict with Saul; in both cases, David receives evil for good, but refrains from exacting vengeance for himself (David : Nabal :: David : Saul). The relationship between the prophetic figures in 1 Kgs 13 + 2 Kgs 23:15-20 mirrors the relationship that unfolds between their respective kingdoms during the history of the Divided Monarchy (man of God : prophet :: Judah : Israel).

Below, I will connect the biblical examples to the theory of the *mise-en-abyme* described in Chapter One. Specifically, I will note how the biblical examples compare to the broader set of *mises-en-abyme* according to the typology outlined by Lucien Dällenbach. I will also note how the biblical examples satisfy several of the criteria for recognizing a *mise-en-abyme* that Dällenbach and Moshe Ron discuss.

The Biblical *Mises-en-abyme*

Typology

Of the three types of *mise-en-abyme*, all three biblical examples are simple. They do not show the infinite dimension of André Gide's *Les faux-monnayeurs* or the paradoxical aspect of *Don Quixote*. Like most examples of the device, they duplicate pertinent aspects of the larger whole within which they occur.

Two biblical examples of the *mise-en-abyme* occur en bloc. Genesis 38 and 1 Samuel 25 do not alternate with the larger narrative or repeat periodically. However, 1 Kgs 13:11-32 + 2 Kgs 23:15-20 appears in two different places in the larger narrative and is therefore an example of the alternating method of incorporation.

Prospective and retrospective *mises-en-abyme* are rare. In this respect, the biblical examples again conform to the most common pattern for the *mise-en-abyme*: they are retro-prospective. In other words, they duplicate aspects of the larger narrative that both precede and follow the device itself. Genesis 38, 1 Samuel 25, and 1 Kgs 13:11-32 + 2 Kgs 23:15-20 all conform to the most common pattern of the *mise-en-abyme*. Although all are retro-prospective, their precise location within their contexts is noteworthy. Dällenbach regards a *mise-en-abyme* as retro-prospective if it duplicates aspects both preceding and following its placement. However, according to this definition, the "middle" of the narrative may be anywhere between the first and last sentence. One of the biblical examples (Genesis 38) is placed near the beginning of the whole in which it occurs (Genesis 37–50), and one is closer to the middle (1 Samuel 25 within 1 Sam 13:1–2 Sam 5:3). In Dällenbach's terms, both are retro-prospective because they duplicate material both before and after their occurrence. The case of 1 Kgs 13:11-23 + 2 Kgs 23:15-20 occurs near the beginning and end of the narrative that it duplicates (1 Kings 11–2 Kings 23). Dällenbach still calls this retro-prospective even though 1 Kgs 13:11-32 has reflects little material before its placement (only the fact of the division of the kingdom and Jeroboam's cult) and 2 Kgs 23:15-20 reflects little material after its placement (only Josiah's concurrent reform of Bethel, and his Passover celebration).

The placement of each biblical *mise-en-abyme* may be related to larger narrative issues. In the case of Genesis 38, the chronology of the Story of Jacob's Line may be a consideration. Contrary to the arguments of some scholarship, the story of Judah and Tamar can fit into the chronology, which may influence its placement in Genesis 37–50. The chronology assumes that no more than twenty-two years may pass for the events of Genesis 38. Since most of this time is consumed by Judah's sons coming of age, the story may be located immediately after the sale of Joseph in order to better fit into the chronology of the larger narrative.

The story of the prophetic figures in 1 Kgs 13:11-32 similarly occurs near the beginning of the History of the Divided Monarchy, but unlike the other examples, it resumes later in 2 Kgs 23:15-20. This arrangement may serve to connect the prophetic story to its larger political context and indicate the scope within which the story operates as a *mise-en-abyme*. The narrative of 1 Kings 11–14 closely analyzes the causes and consequences of the division of the kingdom, much as 1 Samuel 8–12 examines the monarchy itself. By including the narrative of the Judean man of God's encounter with the Israelite prophet immediately after the condemnation of Jeroboam's cult and the man of God's prediction of Josiah's reform, the narrator draws the larger issues of the national history into the story of two individuals. The significant context of the story invites consideration of its parallelism to the larger narrative. Such parallelism might recede into invisibility were the episode located elsewhere.

Unlike Genesis 38 and 1 Kings 13, 1 Samuel 25 does not occur near the beginning of the larger narrative. The plot of the Story of David and the House of Saul may motivate its placement in two respects. First, 1 Samuel 25 presupposes that David is a fugitive from Saul. Therefore, it needs to be located in David's "wilderness period." Second, the parallel between Nabal and Saul would not be evident except in this wilderness period. If David still appeared to enjoy favor in Saul's court, or if David were established in Hebron, then Nabal's inhospitality would be inexplicable. If David were in Ziklag as a Philistine vassal, then Nabal's inhospitality would be understandable, but David's request would not. Within the wilderness period, 1 Samuel 25 is bracketed by two episodes in which David spares Saul's life. This immediate context suggests the parallel between Saul and Nabal and emphasizes the motif of justice in David's relationships.

Criteria

Dällenbach identifies five criteria that may indicate the presence of a *mise-en-abyme*. These criteria do not necessarily define the device, nor does the presence of one or more of them guarantee the existence of a *mise-en-abyme*. Dällenbach's third criterion is similarity or identity of title. Since biblical stories do not include titles, this criterion does not apply. Although the Story of Jacob's Line does have a title of sorts (תלדות יעקב, Gen 37:2), Genesis 38 has no comparable superscription (like תלדות יהודה). The criteria are useful guidelines for judging whether a given biblical text duplicates pertinent aspects of the whole within which it occurs. Genesis 38 and 1 Samuel 25 meet three of the remaining four criteria, and 1 Kings 13 meets two of the four.

The first criterion is the presence of words that posit an analogy between the *mise-en-abyme* and its context. Such an explicit signal of the device occurs in Hamlet's statement that the play he is about to produce will duplicate his uncle's murder of his father. Biblical story telling makes extensive use of narrative analogy, but these analogies are rarely explicit. Jezebel makes an explicit comparison between Jehu and Zimri, but most analogies are suggested by more subtle means.[1] The only explicit analogy in any of the biblical examples occurs in 1 Samuel 25, but it is too vague to have much diagnostic value by itself. The narrative states that Nabal hosts a feast "like the feast of a king." However, this explicit similarity is confined to Nabal's banquet and does not specifically name Saul. Similarly, Abigail hopes that anyone who pursues David to take his life may be like Nabal. This remark more clearly connects Saul and Nabal, but the connection is not fully explicit and does not by itself posit 1 Samuel 25 as a *mise-en-abyme*. Therefore, none of the biblical examples posit an explicit analogy between the *mise-en-abyme* and the larger narrative.

The second criterion is similarity of character name or character identity. Dällenbach only notes the first of these, apparently because he does not know examples of the second. Also, character identity can only occur in a *mise-en-abyme* that is itself on the same narrative level as the rest of the story. Most *mises-en-abyme* occur as embedded narrative, but the biblical examples are episodes within a larger story (and not embedded separate stories). Two of the three biblical examples employ character identity. Judah is a character in both Genesis 38 and the larger Story of Jacob's Line. Similarly, David occurs in 1 Samuel 25 and the larger Story of David and the House of Saul. Character identity alone is not significant (David and Judah appear in many

---

[1] Jezebel likens Jehu to another murderous usurper who was himself quickly murdered by Omri. See S. B. Parker, "Jezebel's Reception of Jehu," *Maarav* 1 (1978) 67-78.

episodes), but their roles in each pericope duplicate their roles in the larger context. Judah is deceived by someone he wronged and admits his error. David refrains from taking vengeance against someone who has returned his favors with harm. The character identity corresponds to similar character roles. These parallel roles fit the larger duplication of the whole in one of its parts.

As noted above, Dällenbach's third criterion concerning similar titles does not apply, but the fourth criterion is repetition of character combination and setting. By "setting," Dällenbach seems to mean not the physical place in which the story occurs, but the circumstances of the narrative. This criterion applies to all three biblical examples, but in different ways. In Genesis 38 and 1 Samuel 25, Judah and David find themselves in circumstances similar to those of the larger narrative. Judah wrongs and is deceived by Tamar and Joseph, and David suffers injustice from both Nabal and Saul. The example of 1 Kgs 13:11-32 + 2 Kgs 23:15-20 is different because the prophetic figures do not occur in the larger narrative. The relationship between these two characters, however, parallels the relationship between their respective kingdoms. This parallel constitutes similar circumstances. The peculiarity of 1 Kgs 13:11-32 + 2 Kgs 23:15-20 is that the similar "characters" are prophetic figures in the *mise-en-abyme*, but kingdoms in the larger narrative. Although this feature differentiates this story from the other examples, individuals in the Bible do represent larger social or political groups. For example, scholars have long regarded the sons of Jacob as representatives of the Israelite tribes. Genesis 49 seems to encourage this interpretive trend, although few would reduce the Genesis narratives to mere tribal allegory.

The fifth criterion is repetition of textual elements. In the case of Genesis 38, I noted the recurrence of the roots נכר ("to recognize") and ערב ("to go surety") and the motif of deception. These textual links point to the connection between the chapter and its context. In 1 Samuel 25, I noted several connections between Nabal and Saul, most importantly the motif of receiving evil (רע) for good (טוב), and the root ריב ("[legal] dispute"). The text also uses the terms נפש, שׁ בקש, רדף, אב/בן, איב, and דמים/דם. These elements suggest the similarity between Saul and Nabal and their relationship to David. The textual links between 1 Kgs 13 + 2 Kgs 23:15-20 and its context involve the proper names Jeroboam, Josiah, and Bethel (with particular concern for the altar) in addition to נביא and איש האלהים. The anonymity of the two prophetic figures may invite consideration that they each represent their respective kingdoms, like the kings with whom they are associated.

In addition to the five criteria indicated by Dällenbach, Moshe Ron discusses several points that may guide the judgment of critics in discerning a *mise-en-abyme*. Below, I will discuss the biblical examples with reference to Ron's notions of totality, isolatability, orientation, extent, general function, and motivation.

Ron notes that totality is the most important element of the *mise-en-abyme*. By definition, the device must duplicate pertinent aspects of the whole within which it occurs. I have argued that all three biblical examples meet this definition. In each case, the plot of the *mise-en-abyme* parallels the plot of the larger narrative and duplicates significant motifs.

The clearest examples of the *mise-en-abyme* are isolated from their contexts. The *Gonzago* play within *Hamlet* is separable from its context because the actors in *Hamlet* become the spectators of *Gonzago*. Furthermore, the poetry of *Gonzago* is more regular and ornamental than that of *Hamlet*. Although a *mise-en-abyme* must be isolatable, the limits of its separability are a matter of subjective judgment. All of the biblical examples are isolatable. Genesis 38 and 1 Samuel 25 both involve a change in the set of characters and geographical setting. Only one common character connects these chapters to their contexts (Tamar and Abigail are peripheral figures outside the chapters). Similarly, the change of focus from royal to prophetic characters from 1 Kgs 13:1-10 to 11-32 isolates the second story from its context. All three biblical narratives have been identified by some historical critics as additions to the narrative from some other source. These historical critics respond to the isolatability of the stories.

Ron's feature of orientation is related to isolatability. A *mise-en-abyme* must occur at the same or lower narrative level as compared to its context. For example, *Hamlet* cannot be a *mise-en-abyme* within *Gonzago* because *Gonzago* occurs within *Hamlet* and subordinated to its plot. Several examples of the device occur as narratives embedded within a context to which they are subordinate. The biblical examples occur at the same narrative level as their contexts. It seems noteworthy that biblical narrative does not include entirely separate and subordinate narratives of the kind sometimes found in novels. Parables and fables are relatively rare in Genesis–Kings, and the few examples are too implicated in their contexts to be isolated as *mises-en-abyme*. Unlike the old woman comforting Charite in *The Golden Ass*, biblical characters do not tell stories that are as isolatable as the story of Cupid and Psyche. Rather, their tales have immediate and explicit application that implicates them in their contexts.

Extent concerns the length of a *mise-en-abyme* as compared to the whole within which it occurs. A long *mise-en-abyme* may become a subplot. All three biblical examples are relatively short compared to their context. Measured by chapters, Genesis 38 is approximately one fourteenth of the Story of Jacob's Line, 1 Samuel 25 is one twenty-third of the Story of David and the House of Saul, and 1 Kgs 13:11-32 + 2 Kgs 23:15-20 is one thirty-fifth of the History of the Divided Kingdom. However, each is relatively long compared to examples of the device in novels or the *Iliad*.

Ron observes a general function for the *mise-en-abyme* in modern literature. He finds that the device tends to unify fragmentary narrative (Robbe-Grillet's *La jalousie*), but fragment unified representational stories (*Hamlet*). This function does not seem to apply in all cases. Similarly, the biblical examples do not disrupt the pattern of biblical narrative representation. Rather, they duplicate pertinent aspects of the whole for the purpose of drawing attention to those aspects. For example, Genesis 38 underscores the motifs of family and deception that concern the Story of Jacob's Line. The story of Nabal and David repeats in miniature the issue of justice in David's relations with Saul's house. The narrative of the two prophetic figures in 1 Kgs 13 + 2 Kgs 23:15-20 highlights the interest that the larger history shows in the relationship between Judah and Israel. In contemporary criticism, the *mise-en-abyme* has stirred interest in (post)modern aesthetic problems concerning representation. This interest may be due in part to André Gide's fascination with these problems and his use of the device in *Les faux-monnayeurs* to explore the issue of mimesis. Within biblical narrative, however, the device does not question or undermine biblical methods of narrative representation. Instead, the biblical examples of the *mise-en-abyme* fit well into the larger biblical patterns of repetition and narrative analogy.

The motivation for including the *mises-en-abyme* will vary in each case. All the biblical examples provide an analogy with the whole that invites the reader to compare stories and consider commonalities and differences. For example, both Tamar and Joseph engage in deceptions that, unlike the many other deceptions in Genesis, are justified by the wrongs they suffer and the reconciliatory aims of their manipulations. However, the two deceivers differ in gender and their power relative to those they deceive. This similarity and difference invite the reader to consider the uses and ethics of deception and to question the common view that deception is an instrument of the weak. Also, the use of the device in general in connection with the frequency of narrative analogy in biblical literature may point to more general motives. This analogous method of composition creates opportunities for the reader to reflect on the stories and their relationship to one another. It also invites the reader to recognize patterns in history and notice that the created order is not chaotic, but events unfold according to discernable patterns. An understanding of these patterns may provide insights into the nature of people, God, and creation that may be useful for decision-making. In this way, the biblical narrative may have educational purposes similar to those expressly stated in many classical histories.

In summary, the biblical examples are all simple, retro-prospective *mises-en-abyme* that occur en bloc near the beginning or middle of the main narrative or alternately near the beginning and the end. The examples lack the clearest means of indicating the device: explicit analogy and similarity of title. However, they each have textual elements common to the *mise-en-abyme* and the main narrative. Each has a plot and character combination parallel to the larger narrative. The analogy between part and whole established by the *mise-en-abyme* opens up the texts to one another and elucidates aspects of the whole.

Bibliography

Abrams, M. H. *A Glossary of Literary Terms*. 7th ed. Fort Worth, TX: Harcourt Brace, 1999.

Ackerman, James S. "Joseph, Judah, and Jacob." In *Genesis*. Edited by Harold Bloom. Modern Critical Interpretations. New York: Chelsea House, 1986. Pp. 87-109. Repr. from *Literary Interpretations of Biblical Narratives: Volume II*. Edited by Kenneth R. R. Gros Louis with James R. Ackerman. Nashville: Abingdon, 1982. Pp. 85-113.

Albertz, Rainer. *A History of the Israelite Religion in the Old Testament Period*. 2 vols. Translated by John Bowden. OTL. Louisville, KY: Westminster John Knox, 1994.

Albright, William Foxwell. *The Biblical Period from Abraham to Ezra*. 2nd ed. New York: Harper, 1963.

———. *From the Stone Age to Christianity: Monotheism and the Historical Process*. 2nd ed. Garden City, NY: Doubleday Anchor Books, 1957.

Alt, Albrecht. "Das Verbot des Diebstahls im Dekalogue." In *Kleine Schriften zur Geschichte des Volkes Israel*. 4 vols. Munich: C. H. Beck, 1953-59. 1. 333-40.

———. "The Formation of the Israelite State in Palestine," in *Essays on Old Testament History and Religion*. Translated by R. A. Wilson. Garden City, NY: Doubleday, 1966. Pp. 223-309.

Alter, Robert. *The Art of Biblical Narrative*. New York: Harper Collins, 1981.

Amit, Yairah. *Reading Biblical Narratives: Literary Criticism and the Hebrew Bible*. Translated by Yael Lotan. Minneapolis: Fortress, 2001.

Anderson, A. A. *2 Samuel*. WBC 11. Dallas: Word Books, 1989.

Avishur, Y. "The Second Amulet Incantation from Arslan-Tash." *UF* 10 (1978) 29-36.

Bach, Alice. "The Pleasure of Her Text." *USQR* 43 (1989) 41-58. Repr. in *The Pleasure of Her Text: Feminist Readings of Biblical and His-*

torical Texts. Edited by Alice Bach. Philadelphia: Trinity, 1990. Pp. 25-44.

Bal, Mieke. *Femmes imaginairies: L'ancien testament au risqué d'une narratologie critique.* Paris: Nizet, 1986.

———. "Mise en Abyme et iconicité." *Littérature* 29 (1978) 116-28.

———. *Narratology: Introduction to the Theory of Narrative.* 2nd ed. Toronto: University of Toronto Press, 1997.

———. "Response." In *Reasoning with the Foxes: Female Wit in a World of Male Power.* Edited by J. Cheryl Exum and Johanna W. H. Bos. Semeia 42. Atlanta: Scholars, 1988. Pp. 133-55.

Baldick, Chris. *Concise Oxford Dictionary of Literary Critical Terms.* Oxford: Oxford University Press, 1990.

Barr, James. "The Symbolism of Names in the Old Testament." *BJRL* 52 (1969) 11-29.

Barrick, W. Boyd. *The King and the Cemeteries: Toward a New Understanding of Josiah's Reform.* VTSup 88. Leiden: Brill, 2002.

Barth, Karl. *Church Dogmatics.* Vol. II/2. Translated by G. W. Bromily et al. Edinburgh: T & T Clark, 1957.

———. "Exegese von 1. Könige 13." *Biblische Studien* 10 (1955) 12-56. Trans I. Wilson in *Church Dogmatics* II/2. Edinburgh: T & T Clark. Pp. 393-409.

Barthélemy, Dominique et al., eds. *The Story of David and Goliath: Textual and Literary Criticism, Papers of a Joint Research Venture.* OBO 73. Göttingen: Vandenhoeck & Ruprecht, 1986.

Begg, Christopher T. "The Abigail Story (1 Samuel 25) according to Josephus." *EstBib* 54 (1996) 5-34.

———. "Filling in the Blanks: Josephus' Version of the Campaign of the Three Kings, 2 Kings 3." *HUCA* 64 (1993) 89-109.

———. "The Non-mention of Amos, Hosea and Micah in the Deuteronomistic History." *BN* 32 (1986) 41-53.

Berlin, Adele. *Poetics and Interpretation of Biblical Narrative.* Bible and Literature Series 9. Sheffield: Almond, 1983. Repr. Winona Lake, IN: Eisenbrauns, 1994.

Benz, Frank L. *Personal Names in the Phoenician and Punic Inscriptions: A Catalog, Grammatical Study and Glossary of Elements.* Studia Pohl 8. Rome: Biblical Institute Press, 1972.

Berman, Joshua A. *Narrative Analogy in the Hebrew Bible: Battle Stories and Their Equivalent Non-battle Narratives.* VTSup 103. Leiden: Brill, 2004.

Bevington, David, ed. *Twentieth Century Interpretations of Hamlet: A*

Collection of Critical Essays. Englewood Cliffs, NJ: Prentice-Hall, 1968.

Biddle, Mark E. "Ancestral Motifs in 1 Samuel 25: Intertextuality and Characterization." *JBL* 121 (2002) 617-38.

Bin-Nun, Shoshana R. "Formulas from Royal Records of Israel and Judah." *VT* 18 (1968) 414-32.

Bird, Phyllis A. *Missing Persons and Mistaken Identities: Women and Gender in Ancient Israel.* OBT. Minneapolis: Fortress, 1997.

Bivens, Forrest L. "Exegetical Brief: Genesis 38:8-10—the Sin of Onan." *Wisconsin Lutheran Quarterly* 98 (2001) 210-14.

Blenkinsopp, Joseph. *A History of Prophecy in Israel.* Rev. and enlarged ed. Philadelphia: Westminster John Knox, 1996.

Blum, Erhard. "Die Lüge des Propheten (I Reg 13)." In *Mincha: Festgabe für Rolf Rendtorff zum 75. Geburtstag.* Edited by Erhard Blum. Neukirchen-Vluyn; Neukirchener, 2000. Pp. 27-46.

Borgman, Paul. *David, Saul, and God: Recovering an Ancient Story.* Oxford: Oxford University Press, 2008.

Borowski, Oded. *Every Living Thing: Daily Use of Animals in Ancient Israel.* Walnut Creek, CA: AltaMira, 1998.

Boer, Roland. "National Allegory in the Hebrew Bible." *JSOT* 74 (1997) 95-116.

Bos, Johanna W. H. "Out of the Shadows: Genesis 38. Judges 4:17-22. Ruth 3." In *Reasoning with the Foxes: Female Wit in a World of Male Power.* Edited by J. Cheryl Exum and Johanna W. H. Bos. Semeia 42. Atlanta: Scholars, 1988. Pp. 37-67.

Bosworth, David. "Evaluating King David: Old Problems and Recent Scholarship." *CBQ* 68 (2006) 191-210.

———. "Revisiting Karl Barth's Exegesis of 1 Kings 13." *BibInt* 10 (2002) 360-83.

Boyle, Marjorie O'Rourke. "The Law of the Heart: The Death of a Fool (1 Samuel 25)." *JBL* 120 (2001) 401-27.

Bradley, A. C. *Shakespearean Tragedy: Lectures on Hamlet, Othello, King Lear, MacBeth.* 3d ed. New York: St. Martin's Press, 1992. Originally published in 1904.

Bratsiotis, N. P. "ʾîš." In *TDOT* 1. 222-35.

Brawley, Robert. *Text to Text Pours Forth Speech: Voices of Scripture in Luke-Acts.* Bloomington, IN: Indiana University Press, 1995.

Breuer, Mordechai. "Dividing the Decalogue into Verses and Commandments." In *The Ten Commandments in History and Tradition.* Edited by Ben-Zion Segal and Gershon Levi. Jerusalem: Magnes, 1990. Pp. 291-330.

Briend, Jacques. "Du message au messager: Remarques sur 1 Rois XIII." In *Congress Volume: Paris 1992.* Edited by J. A. Emerton. VTSup 61. Leiden: Brill, 1995. Pp. 9-34.

———. "Les figures de David en 1 S 16, 1–2 S 5, 3: Rapports entre literature et histoire." In *Figures de David à travers la Bible: XVIIe congrès de l'ACFEB (Lille, 1er–5 septembre 1997).* Edited by Louis Desrousseaux and Jacques Vermeylen. LD 177. Paris: Cerf, 1999. Pp. 9-34.

Bright, John. *A History of Israel.* 4th ed. Philadelphia: Westminster John Knox, 2000.

Brodie, Thomas L. *Genesis as Dialogue: A Literary, Historical, & Theological Commentary.* Oxford: Oxford University Press, 2001.

Brueggemann, Walter. "The Book of Exodus." *NIB* 1. 677-981.

———. *Genesis.* IBC. Atlanta: John Knox, 1982.

———. *Power, Providence, and Personality: Biblical Insight into Life and Ministry.* Louisville, KY: Westminster John Knox, 1990.

———. *First and Second Samuel.* IBC. Louisville, KY: John Knox, 1990.

Budde, Karl. *Die Bücher Samuel.* Kurzer Handcommentar zum Alten Testament 8. Tübingen: J. C. B. Mohr, 1902.

Burney, C. F. *Notes on the Hebrew Text of the Books of Kings.* Oxford: Clarendon, 1903.

Calvin, John. *Commentaries on the First Book of Moses called Genesis.* 2 vols. Translated by John King. Edinburgh: Calvin Translation Society, 1850.

Campbell, Antony F. *Of Prophets and Kings: A Late Ninth-Century Document (1 Samuel 1–2 Kings 10).* CBQMS 17. Washington, DC: The Catholic Biblical Association of America, 1986.

Carr, David McClain. *Reading the Fractures of Genesis: Historical and Literary Approaches.* Louisville, KY: Westminster John Knox, 1996.

Cassuto, U. "The Story of Tamar and Judah." In *Biblical and Oriental Studies: Volume I: Bible.* Translated by Israel Abrahams. Jerusalem: Magnes, 1973. Pp. 29-40.

Chambers, Ross. *La comédie au chateau: contribution à la poétique du theater.* Paris: José Corti, 1971.

Childs, Brevard S. *Introduction to the Old Testament as Scripture.* Philadelphia: Fortress, 1979.

———. *Old Testament Theology in a Canonical Context.* Philadelphia: Fortress, 1986.

———. *The Book of Exodus: A Critical, Theological Commentary.* OTL. Louisville, KY: Westminster, 1974.

Christie, Agatha. *And Then There Were None.* New York: St. Martin's, 2001. Originally published as *Ten Little Indians* in 1939.

Clifford, R. J. "Genesis 38: Its Contribution to the Jacob Story." *CBQ* 66 (2004) 519-32.

Coats, George W. *From Canaan to Egypt: Structural and Theological Context for the Joseph Story.* CBQMS 4. Washington, DC: The Catholic Biblical Association of America, 1976.

————. *Genesis, with an Introduction to Narrative Literature.* FOTL 1. Grand Rapids, MI: Eerdmans, 1983.

————. "Redactional Unity in Genesis 37-50." *JBL* 93 (1974) 15-21.

————. "Widow's Rights: A Crux in the Structure of Genesis 38." *CBQ* 34 (1972) 461-66.

Cogan, Mordechai. *1 Kings.* AB 10. New York: Doubleday, 2001.

————. *Imperialism and Religion: Assyria, Judah and Israel in the Eighth and Seventh Centuries B.C.E.* SBLMS 19. Missoula, MT: Scholars, 1974.

Cogan, Mordechai, and Hayim Tadmor. *II Kings.* AB 11. Garden City: Doubleday, 1988.

Conklin, Paul Salisbury. *A History of Hamlet Criticism, 1601-1821.* New York: King's Crown, 1947.

Cox, Lee Sheridan. *Figurative Design in Hamlet: The Significance of the Dumb Show.* Columbus: Ohio University Press, 1973.

Crenshaw, James L. *Prophetic Conflict: Its Effect upon Israelite Religion.* BZAW 124. Berlin/New York: de Gruyter, 1971.

Cross, Frank Moore. *Canaanite Myth and Hebrew Epic: Essays in the History of the Religion of Israel.* Cambridge: Harvard University Press, 1973.

————. "Leaves from an Epigrapher's Notebook." *CBQ* 36 (1974) 486-90.

Cruveilhier, P. "Le Lévirat chez les Hébreux et chez les Assyriens." *RB* 34 (1925) 524-46.

Cryer, Frederick H. "David's Rise to Power and the Death of Abner: An Analysis of 1 Samuel 26:14-16 and its Redactional-critical Implications." *VT* 35 (1985) 385-94.

Dällenbach, Lucien. *Le récit spéculaire: essai sur la mise-en-abyme.* Paris: Seuil, 1977. In English as *The Mirror in the Text.* Translated by Jeremy Whiteley with Emma Hughes. Chicago: University of Chicago Press, 1989.

De Vries, Simon J. *1 Kings.* WBC. Waco, TX: Word Books, 1985.

Dietrich, Walter, "Das Biblische Bild der Herrschaft Davids." In *Von David zu den Deuteronomisten: Studien zu den Geschichtsüber-*

lieferungen des Alten Testaments. BWANT 156. Stuttgart: Kohlhammer, 2002. Pp. 9-31.

———. *David: Der Herrscher mit der Harfe.* Biblishe Gestalten 14. Leipzig: Evangelische Verlagsanstalt, 2006.

Dietrich, Walter, and Thomas Naumann. "The David-Saul Narrative." Translated by Peter T. Daniels. In *Reconsidering Israel and Judah: Recent Studies on the Deuteronomistic History.* Edited by Gary N. Knopers and J. Gordon McConville. Sources for Biblical and Theological Study 8. Winona Lake, IN: Eisenbrauns, 2000. Pp. 276-318.

van Dijk-Hemmes, Fokkelein. "Tamar and the Limits of Patriarchy: Between Rape and Seduction (2 Samuel 13 and Genesis 38)." In *Anti-Covenant: Counter-Reading Women's Lives in the Hebrew Bible.* Edited by Mieke Bal. JSOTSup 81. Sheffield: Almond, 1989. Pp. 135-56.

Donner, H. "'Hier sind deine Götter Israel'." In *Wort und Geschichte: Festschrift für Karl Elliger zum 70. Geburtstag.* Edited by Hartmut Gese and Hans Peter Rüger. Butzon & Berker, 1973. Pp. 45-50.

Donner, H. and W. Röllig. *Kanaanaische und aramäische Inschriften.* 3 vols. 2nd edition. Weisbaden: Harrassowitz, 1971-76.

Dozeman, Thomas B. "The Way of the Man of God from Judah: True and False Prophecy in the Pre-Dtr Legend of 1 Kings 13." *CBQ* 44 (1982) 379-93.

Driver, S. R. *Notes on the Hebrew Text and the Topography the Books of Samuel.* 2nd ed. Oxford: Clarendon Press, 1913.

Edelman, Diana Vikander. *King Saul in the Historiography of Judah.* JSOTSup 121. Sheffield: Sheffield Academic Press, 1991.

Edenburg, Cynthia. "How (not) to Murder a King: Variations on a Theme in 1 Sam 24. 26." *SJOT* 12 (1998) 64-83.

Eissfeldt, Otto. *The Old Testament: An Introduction.* Translated by Peter R. Ackroyd. Oxford: Basil Blackwell, 1974.

Elgavish, David. "Objective of Baasha's War against Asa." In *Studies in Honor of Zecharia Kallai.* Edited by Gershon Galil and Moshe Weinfeld. VTSup 81; Leiden: Brill, 2000. Pp. 141-49.

Emerton, J. A. "An Examination of a Recent Structuralist Interpretation of Genesis XXXVIII." *VT* 26 (1976) 79-98.

———. "Judah and Tamar." *VT* 29 (1979) 403-15.

Etz, Donald V. "The Genealogical Relationships of Jehoram and Ahaziah, and of Ahaz and Hezekiah, Kings of Judah." *JSOT* 71 (1996) 39-53.

Exum, J. Cheryl, ed. *Tragedy and Comedy in the Bible.* Semeia 32. Decatur, GA: Scholars, 1984.

———. *Tragedy and Biblical Narrative: Arrows of the Almighty.* Cambridge: Cambridge University Press, 1992.

Fishbane, Michael. "Composition and Structure in the Jacob Cycle (Gen 25:19–35:22)." *JSS* 26 (1975) 15-38.

Flanagan, James W. *David's Social Drama: A Hologram of Israel's Early Iron Age.* JSOTSup 73. Sheffield: Almond, 1988.

Fleming, Daniel E. "The Etymological Origins of the Hebrew *nābîʾ*: The One Who Invokes God." *CBQ* 55 (1993) 217-24.

Fletcher, Angus. *Allegory: The Theory of a Symbolic Mode.* Ithaca, NY: Cornell University Press, 1964.

Fohrer, G. *Elia.* 2nd ed. ATANT 31. Zurich: Theologischer Verlag, 1968.

Fokkelman, J. P. "Genesis 37 and 38 at the Interface of Structural Analysis and Hermeneutics." In *Literary Structure and Rhetorical Strategies in the Hebrew Bible.* Edited by L. J. de Regt et al. Assen: Van Gorcum, 1996. Pp. 152-87.

————. *Narrative Art and Poetry in the Books of Samuel: A Full Interpretation Based on Stylistic and Structural Analysis.* 4 vols. Assen: Van Gorcum, 1981-93.

Forti, Tova L. *Animal Imagery in the Book of Proverbs.* VTSup 118. Leiden: Brill, 2008.

Freedman, David Noel, and M. O'Connor. "*kuttōnet.*" In *TDOT* 7. 383-87.

Fuchs, Esther. "The Literary Characterization of Mothers and Sexual Politics in the Hebrew Bible." In *Women in the Hebrew Bible.* Edited by Alice Bach. New York, Routledge, 1999. Pp. 127-39.

————. "Status and Role of Female Heroines in the Biblical Narrative." In *Women in the Hebrew Bible.* Edited by Alice Bach. New York, Routledge, 1999. Pp. 77-84.

Fung, Yiu-Wing. *Victim and Victimizer: Joseph's Interpretation of his Destiny.* JSOTSup 308. Sheffield: Sheffield Academic Press, 2000.

Furman, Nelly. "His Story Versus Her Story: Male Genealogy and Female Strategy in the Jacob Cycle." In *Women in the Hebrew Bible.* Edited by Alice Bach. New York: Routledge, 1999. Pp. 119-26.

Garsiel, Moshe. "Wit, Words, and a Woman: 1 Samuel 25." In *On Humor and the Comic in the Hebrew Bible.* Edited by Yehuda T. Radday and Athalya Brenner. JSOTSup 92. Sheffield: Almond Press, 1990.

————. *The First Book of Samuel: A Literary Study of Comparative Structures, Analogies and Parallels.* Ramat-Gan, Israel: Revivim, 1985.

Geoghegan, Jeffrey C. "Israelite Sheepshearing and David's Rise to Power." *Bib* 87 (2006) 55-63.

Gibson, John C. L. *Textbook of Syrian Semitic Inscriptions.* 3 vols. Oxford: Clarendon, 1982.

Gide, André. *Journals 1889-1949*. Translated by J. O'Brien. London: Penguin, 1984.

Glatt, David A. *Chronological Displacement in Biblical and Related Literatures*. SBLDS 139. Atlanta: Scholars, 1993.

Gnuse, Robert Karl. *You Shall not Steal: Community and Property in the Biblical Tradition*. Maryknoll, NY: Orbis, 1985.

Golka, Friedemann W. "Genesis 37–50: Joseph Story or *Israel*-Joseph Story?" *Currents in Biblical Research* 2 (2004) 153-77.

Gomes, Jules Francis. *The Sanctuary of Bethel and the Configuration of Israelite Identity*. BZAW 368. Berlin: Walter de Gruyter, 2006.

Gordon, Robert P. "David's Rise and Saul's Demise: Narrative Analogy in 1 Samuel 24-26." *TynBul* 31 (1980) 37-64. Repr. in *Reconsidering Israel and Judah: Recent Studies on the Deuteronomistic History*. o Gary Knoppers and J. Gordon McConville. Sources for Biblical and Theological Study 8. Winona Lake, IN: Eisenbrauns, 2000. Pp. 319-39.

Görg, Manfred. "Addenda zur Diskussion um von *nābî*." *BN* 31 (1986) 25-26.

———. "Randbemerkungen zum jüngsten Lexikonartikel zu *nābî*." *BN* 26 (1985) 7-16.

———. "Weiteres zur Etymologie von *nābî*." *BN* 22 (1983) 9-11.

Gray, John. *I & II Kings: A Commentary*. 2nd ed. OTL. Philadelphia: Westminster, 1964.

Green, Barbara. "Enacting Imaginatively the Unthinkable: 1 Samuel 25 and the Story of Saul." *BibInt* 11 (2003) 1-23.

Greenberg, Moshe. "The Decalogue Tradition Critically Examined." In *The Ten Commandments in History and Tradition*. Edited by Ben-Zion Segal and Gershon Levi. Jerusalem: Magnes, 1990. Pp. 83-119.

Greenspahn, Frederick E. *When Brothers Dwell Together: The Preeminence of the Younger Siblings in the Hebrew Bible*. Oxford: Oxford University Press, 1994.

Greenstein, Edward L. "An Equivocal Reading of the Sale of Joseph." In *Literary Interpretation of Biblical Narratives: Volume II*. Edited by Kenneth R. R. Gros Louis with James S. Ackerman. Nashville, TN: Abingdon, 1982. Pp. 114-25.

Greenstein, Edward L., and David Marcus. "The Akkadian Inscription of Idrimi." *JANES* 8 (1976) 59-96.

Grelot, P. "Le Péché de ʾÔnān" (Gn., XXXVIII,9)." *VT* 49 (1999) 143-55.

Grønbaek, J. H. *Die Geschichte vom Aufstieg Davids (1.Sam. 15–2.Sam. 5): Tradition und Komposition*. Acta Theologica Danika 10. Copenhagen: Munksgaard, 1971.

Gross, Walter. "Lying Prophet and Disobedient Man of God in 1 Kings

13: Role Analysis as an Instrument of Theological Interpretation of an OT Narrative Text." Translated by Robert Robinson. In *Perspectives on Old Testament Narrative*. Edited by Robert C. Culley. Semeia 15. Atlanta: Scholars, 1979. Pp. 97-135.

Gruber, Mayer I. *Aspects of Nonverbal Communication in the Ancient Near East*. 2 vols. Studia Pohl: Dissertationes Scientificae de Rebus Orientis Antiqui 12/1-2. Rome: Pontificio Instituto Biblico, 1980.

Gunkel, Hermann. *Elias, Jahve und Baal*. Tübingen: Mohr, 1906.

———. *Genesis*. Göttingen: Vandenhoeck & Ruprecht, 1964. 6th printing unchanged from 3rd ed. (1910). In English as *Genesis* by Mark Biddle. Macon, Ga.: Mercer University Press, 1997.

Gunn, David M. *The Fate of King Saul: An Interpretation of a Biblical Story*. JSOTSup 14. Sheffield: JSOT, 1980.

Gunneweg, A. H. J. "Die Prophetenlegende 1 Reg 13—Mißdeutung, Umdeutung, Bedeutung." In *Prophet und Prophetenbuch: Festschrift für Otto Kaiser zum 65. Geburtstag*. Edited by Volkmar Fritz, Karl-Friedrich Pohlmann, and Hans-Christoph Schmitt. BZAW 185. Berlin: de Gruyter, 1989. Pp. 73-81.

Hainsworth, Bryan. *The Iliad: A Commentary*. 6 vols. Cambridge: Cambridge University Press, 1993.

Hallevy, Raphael. "Man of God." *JNES* 17 (1958) 237-44.

Halpern, Baruch. *David's Secret Demons: Messiah, Murderer, Traitor, King*. Grand Rapids, MI: Eerdmans, 2001.

———. *The First Historians: The Hebrew Bible and History*. New York: Harper & Row, 1988. Repr., University Park, PA: Pennsylvania State University Press, 1996.

———. *The Constitution of the Monarchy in Israel*. HSM 25. Chico, CA: Scholars, 1981.

Halpern, Baruch, and David S. Vanderhooft. "The Editions of Kings in the 7th-6th Centuries B.C.E." *HUCA* 62 (1991) 179-244.

Hamilton, Victor P. *Handbook on the Historical Books*. Grand Rapids, MI: Baker, 2001.

———. *The Book of Genesis: Chapters 1–17*. NICOT. Grand Rapids, MI: Eerdmans, 1990.

———. *The Book of Genesis: Chapters 18–50*. NICOT. Grand Rapids, MI: Eerdmans, 1995.

Hasel, Gerhard F. "*nāgîd*." In *TDOT* 9. 187-202.

Hayes, C. E. "The Midrashic Career of the Confession of Judah (Genesis XXXVIII 26). Part I: The Extra-Canonical Texts, Targums and Other Versions." *VT* 45 (1995) 62-81.

———. "The Midrashic Career of the Confession of Judah (Genesis XXX-VIII 26). Part II: The Rabbinic Midrashim." *VT* 45 (1995) 174-87.

Herr, Bertram. "Der wahre Prophet bezeugt seine Botschaft mit dem Tod: Ein Versuch zu 1 Kön 13." *BZ* 41 (1997) 69-78.

Ho, Craig Y. S. "The Stories of the Family Troubles of Judah and David: A Study of their Literary Links." *VT* 49 (1999) 514-31.

Hobbes, Thomas. *Leviathan.* Indianapolis: Hackett, 1994. Originally published in 1651.

Hobbs, T. R. *2 Kings.* WBC 13. Waco, TX: Word Books, 1985.

———. "Hospitality in the First Testament and the 'Teleological Fallacy'." *JSOT* 95 (2001) 3-30.

Hoffmann, Hans-Detlef. *Reform und Reformen: Untersuchungen zu einem Grundthema der deuteronomischen Geschichtsschreibung.* ATANT 66. Zurich: Theologischer Verlag, 1980.

Hoffner, Harry A. "A Hittite Analogue to the David and Goliath Contest of Champions?" *CBQ* 30 (1968) 220-25.

Holladay, John S. "The Kingdoms of Israel and Judah: Political and Economic Centralization in the Iron Age IIA-B (ca. 1000-750 BCE)." In *The Archeology of Society in the Holy Land.* Edited by Thomas E. Levy. New York: Facts On File, 1995. Pp. 368-98.

van der Horst, Pieter W. "Tamar in Pseudo-Philo's *Biblical History.*" In *A Feminist Companion to Genesis.* Edited by Athalya Brenner. Sheffield: Sheffield Academic Press, 1993. Pp. 300-4.

Houston, Walter. "Exodus." In *The Oxford Bible Commentary.* Eds. John Barton and John Muddiman. Oxford: Oxford University Press, 2001. Pp. 67-91.

Huddlestun, John R. "Unveiling the Versions: The Tactics of Tamar in Genesis 38:15." *Journal of Hebrew Scriptures* 3 (2001) http://www.purl.org/jhs.

Huehnergard, John. "On the Etymology and Meaning of the Hebrew *nābîʾ.*" *ErIsr* 26 (1999) 88*-93*.

Humphreys, W. Lee. *Joseph and his Family: A Literary Study.* Columbia, SC: University of South Carolina Press, 1988.

———. "The Tragedy of King Saul: A Study of the Structure of 1 Samuel 9–31." *JSOT* 6 (1978) 18-27.

———. "The Rise and Fall of King Saul: A Study of an Ancient Narrative Stratum in 1 Samuel." *JSOT* 18 (1980) 74-90.

Ishida, Tomoo. "The Story of Abner's Murder: A Problem Posed by the Solomonic Apologist." *ErIsr* 24 (1993) 109*-113*.

Isser, Stanley. *The Sword of Goliath: David in Heroic Literature.* Studies in Biblical Literature 6. Atlanta: SBL, 2003.

Jackson, Melissa. "Lot's Daughters and Tamar as Tricksters and the Patriarchal Narratives as Feminist Theology." *JSOT* 98 (2002) 29-46.

Japhet, Sarah. *I & II Chronicles.* OTL. Louisville, KY: Westminster John Knox, 1993.

Jefferson, Anne. "Mise en abyme and the Prophetic Narrative." *Style* 17 (1983) 196-208.

Jenkins, Harold. *Hamlet.* The Arden Shakepseare. London: Methuen, 1982.

Jepsen, Alfred. "Gottesmann und Prophet." In *Probleme biblischer Theologie: Gerhard von Rad zum 70. Geburtstag.* Edited by H. W. Wolff. Munich: Chr. Kaiser Verlag, 1971. Pp. 171-82.

———. *Die Quellen des Königsbuches.* Halle: Max Niemeyer, 1956.

Jeremias, J. "*nābî*." In *Theologische Handwörterbuch zum Alten Testament.* 2 vols. Edited by E. Jenni and C. Westermann. Munich: Chr. Kaiser, 1976. 2. 7-26.

Jarick, John. "The Seven (?) Prophetesses of the Old Testament." *Lutheran Theological Journal* 28 (1994) 116-21.

Jobling, David. *1 Samuel.* Berit Olam. Collegeville, MN: Liturgical Press, 1998.

Kakridis, Johannes Th. *Homeric Researches.* New York: Garland, 1987. Originally published in 1947.

Katzenstein, H. J. "Who Were the Parents of Athalia?" *IEJ* 5 (1955) 194-97.

Kennedy, E. J. "Introduction." In Apuleius, *The Golden Ass, or Metamorphoses.* Translated by E. J. Kennedy. New York: Penguin, 1998.

Kittrie, Nicholas W., and Eldon D. Wedlock, eds. *The Tree of Liberty: A Documentary History of Rebellion and Political Crime in America.* Rev. ed. Baltimore: Johns Hopkins University Press, 1998.

Klaus, Nathan. *Pivot Patterns in the Former Prophets.* JSOTSup 247. Sheffield: Sheffield Academic Press, 1997.

Klein, Johannes. *David versus Saul: Ein Beitrag zum Erzählsystem der Samuelbücher.* BWANT 158. Stuttgart: Kohlhammer, 2002.

Klein, Ralph W. *1 Samuel.* WBC 10. Waco, TX: Word Books, 1983.

Klingbeil, Gerald A. "'Momentaufnahmen' of Israelite Religion: The Importance of Communal Meals in Narrative Texts in I/II Regnum and Their Ritual Dimension." *ZAW* 118 (2006) 22-45.

Klopfenstein, Martin A. "1. Könige 13." In *Parrhesia: Karl Barth zum Achtzigsten Geburtstag am 10. Mai 1966.* Zurich: EVZ-Verlag Zürich, 1966. Pp. 639-72.

Knoll, K. L. *The Faces of David.* JSOTSup 242. Sheffield: Sheffield Academic Press, 1997.

Knoppers, Gary N. "'There Was None like Him': Incomparability in the Books of Kings." *CBQ* 54 (1992) 411-31.

———. *Two Nations Under God: The Deuteronomistic History of Solomon and the Dual Monarchies.* 2 vols. HSM 52 and 53. Atlanta: Scholars, 1993-94.

———. "'Yhwh is not with Israel':" Alliance as a *Topos* in Chronicles." *CBQ* 58 (1996) 601-26.

Kooij, Arie van der. "The Story of David and Goliath: The Early History of Its Text." *ETL* 68 (1992) 118-31.

Krahmalkov, Charles R. *Phoenician-Punic Dictionary.* Orientalia Lovaniensia Analecta 90. Studia Phoenicia 15. Leuven: Peeters, 2000.

Krüger, Thomas. "Genesis 38—ein 'Lehrstück' alttestamentlicher Ethik." In *Kritische Weisheit: Studien zur weisheitlichen Traditionskritik im Alten Testament.* Zurich: Pano, 1997. Pp. 1-22.

Kucová, Lydie. "Obeisance in the Biblical Stories of David." In *Reflection and Refraction: Studies in Biblical Historiography in Honor of A. Graeme Auld.* Edited by Robert Rezetko et al. VTSup 113. Leiden: Brill, 2007. Pp. 241-60.

Kühlewein, J. "*ʾîš.*" In *Theologische Handwörterbuch zum Alten Testament.* 2 vols. Edited by E. Jenni and C. Westermann. Munich: Chr. Kaiser, 1976. 1. 130-38.

Lambe, Anthony J. "Genesis 38: Structure and Literary Design." In *The World of Genesis: Persons, Places, Perspectives.* Edited by Phillip R. Davies and David J. A. Clines. JSOTSup 257. Sheffield: Sheffield Academic Press, 1998. Pp. 102-120.

———. "Judah's Development: The Pattern of Departure—Transition—Return." *JSOT* 83 (1999) 53-68.

Lasine, Stuart. "Reading Jeroboam's Intentions: Intertextuality, Rhetoric, and History in 1 Kings 12." In *Reading Between Texts: Intertextuality and the Hebrew Bible.* Edited by D. N. Fewell. Louisville, KY: Westminster, 1992. Pp. 133-52.

Leithart, Peter. *1 & 2 Kings.* Brazos Theological Commentary on the Bible. Grand Rapids, Mich.: Brazos, 2007.

Lemaire, André. "Vers l'histoire de la redaction des livres des Rois." *ZAW* 98 (1986) 221-36.

Lemke, Werner E. "The Way of Obedience: 1 Kings 13 and the Structure of the Deuteronomistic History." In *Magnalia Dei. The Mighty Acts of God: Essays on the Bible and Archeology in Memory of G. Ernest Wright.* Edited by F. M. Cross, W. E. Lemke, and P. D. Miller. New York: Doubleday, 1976. Pp. 301-26.

Levenson, Jon D. "1 Samuel 25 as Literature and as History." *CBQ* 40 (1978) 11-28.

Levenson, Jon D., and Baruch Halpern. "The Political Import of David's Marriages." *JBL* 99 (1980) 507-18.

Lockwood, Peter F. "Tamar's Place in the Joseph Cycle." *Lutheran Theological Journal* 26 (1992) 35-43.

Lohfink, Norbert. "Recent Discussion on 2 Kings 22–23: The State of the Question." Originally published in 1985. Translated by Linda M. Maloney. In *A Song of Power and the Power of Song: Essays on the Book of Deuteronomy.* Edited by Duane L. Christensen. Sources for Biblical and Theological Study 3. Winona Lake: Eisenbrauns, 1993. Pp. 36-61.

Long, Burke O. *1 Kings, with an Introduction to Historical Literature.* FOTL 9. Grand Rapids: Eerdmans, 1984.

Longacre, R. E. *Joseph: A Story of Divine Providence.* Winona Lake, IN: Eisenbrauns, 1989.

Luther, Bernhard. "The Novella of Judah and Tamar and Other Israelite Novellas." Translated by David E. Orton. In *Narrative and Novella: Studies by Hugo Gressman and Other Scholars 1906-1923.* Edited by David M. Gunn. JSOTSup 116. Sheffield: Almond, 1991. Pp. 89-118.

Lyons, Bridget Gellart. "The Subplot as Simplification in *King Lear.*" In *Some Facets of King Lear: Essays in Prismatic Criticism.* Edited by Rosalie Colie and F. T. Flahiff. Toronto: University of Toronto Press, 1974. Pp. 23-38.

Mann, Thomas W. *The Book of the Torah: The Narrative Integrity of the Pentateuch.* Atlanta: John Knox Press, 1988.

Marcus, David. *From Balaam to Jonah: Anti-prophetic Satire in the Hebrew Bible.* BJS 301. Atlanta: Scholars, 1995.

Margalit, Baruch. "Why King Mesha of Moab Sacrificed His Oldest Son." *BARev* 12 (Nov.-Dec. 1986) 62-3, 76.

Matthews, Victor H. "The Anthropology of Clothing in the Joseph Narrative." *JSOT* 65 (1995) 25-36.

Matthewson, Steven D. "An Exegetical Study of Genesis 38." *BibSac* 146 (1989) 373-92.

McCarter, P. Kyle. *I Samuel.* AB 8. Garden City, NY: Doubleday, 1980.

———. "The Apology of David." *JBL* 99 (1980) 489-504.

McGinnis, Claire Matthews. "Swimming with the Divine Tide: An Ignatian Reading of 1 Samuel." In *Theological Exegesis: Essays in Honor of Brevard S. Childs.* Edited by Christopher Seitz and Katheryn Greene-McCreight. Grand Rapids, MI: Eerdmans, 1999. Pp. 240-70.

McKenzie, Steven L. "The Trouble with King Jehoshaphat." In *Reflection* and Refraction: Studies in Biblical Historiography in Honor of A. Graeme Auld. Edited by Robert Rezko et al. VTSup 113. Leiden: Brill, 2007. Pp. 299-314.

———. King David: A Biography. Oxford: Oxford University Press, 2000.

———. The Trouble with Kings: The Composition of the Book of Kings in the Deuteronomistic History. VTSup 42. Leiden: Brill, 1991.

Mead, James K. "Kings and Prophets, Donkeys and Lions: Dramatic Shape and Deuteronomistic Rhetoric in 1 Kings XIII." VT 49 (1999) 191-205.

Menn, Esther Marie. Judah and Tamar (Genesis 38) in Ancient Jewish Exegesis: Studies in Literary Form and Hermeneutics. JSJSup 51. Leiden: Brill, 1997.

Miller, Geoffrey David. "Attitudes toward Dogs in Ancient Israel: A Reassessment." JSOT 32 (2008) 487-500.

Miller, J. Maxwell, and John H. Hayes. A History of Ancient Judah and Israel. Philadelphia: Westminster, 2006.

Miller, Patrick D. "The Prophetic Critique of Kings." In Israelite Religion and Biblical Theology: Collected Essays. JSOTSup 267. Sheffield: Sheffield Academic Press, 2000. Pp. 526-47.

Mullen, E. Theodore, Jr. "The Royal Dynastic Grant to Jehu and the Structure of the Books of Kings." JBL 107 (1988) 193-206.

———. "The Sins of Jeroboam: A Redactional Assessment." CBQ 49 (1987) 212-32.

Müller, Hans-Peter. "Zur Herleitung von nābîʾ." BN 29 (1985) 22-27.

Naʾaman, Nadav. "Prophetic Stories as Sources for the Histories of Jehoshaphat and the Omrides." Bib 78 (1997) 153-73.

Nagy, Gregory. The Best of the Achaeans: Concepts of the Hero in the Archaic Greek Poetry. Rev. ed. Baltimore: Johns Hopkins University Press, 1998.

Nelson, Richard D. First and Second Kings. IBC. Atlanta: John Knox, 1987.

———. The Double Redaction of the Deuteronomistic History. JSOTSup 18. Sheffield: JSOT, 1981.

Nicholson, Sarah. The Three Faces of Saul: An Intertextual Approach to Biblical Tragedy. JSOTSup 339. Sheffield: Sheffield Academic Press, 2002.

Nielsen, Eduard. The Ten Commandments in New Perspective. SBT 27. Naperville, IL: Allenson, 1968.

Noble, Paul R. "Esau, Tamar, and Joseph: Criteria for Identifying Inner-Biblical Allusions." VT 52 (2002) 219-52.

Noth, Martin. *The History of Israel.* Translated by P. R. Ackroyd. London: Adam & Charles Black, 1950.

———. *Überlieferungsgeschichtliche Studien.* 2nd. ed. Tubingen: Max Niemeyer, 1957. Originally published in 1943. The first section in English as *The Deuteronomistic History.* 2nd ed. Translated by Jane Doull et al. JSOTSup 15. Sheffield: Sheffield Academic Press, 1991.

———. *1 Könige.* BKAT IX/1. Neukirchen-Vluyn: Neukirchener Verlag, 1968.

Nübel, H. U. *Davids Aufstieg in der frühen israelitischer Geschichtsschreibung.* Bonn: Rheinische Friedrich-Wilhelms-Universität, 1959.

Obbink, H. Th. "Jahwebilder." *ZAW* 47 (1929) 264-74.

O'Callaghan, Martin. "The Structure and Meaning of Gen 38—Judah and Tamar." *Proceedings of the Irish Biblical Association* 5 (1981) 72-88.

O'Connor, Michael. "War and Rebel Chants in the Former Prophets." In *Fortunate the Eyes that See: Essays in Honor of David Noel Freedman in Celebration of His Seventieth Birthday.* Eds. Astrid B. Beck et al. Grand Rapids, MI: Eerdmans, 1995. Pp. 322-37.

Otto, Susanne. *Jehu, Elia und Elisa: Die Erzählung von der Jehu-Revolution und die Komposition der Elia-Elisa-Erzählungen.* BWANT 152. Berlin: Kohlhammer, 2001.

Parker, S. B. "Jezebel's Reception of Jehu." *Maarav* 1 (1978) 67-78.

Patton, Michael S. "Masturbation from Judaism to Victorianism." *Journal of Religion and Health* 24 (1985) 133-46.

Perdue, Leo G. "'Is there anyone left of the house of Saul . . .?' Ambiguity and the Characterization of David in the Succession Narrative." *JSOT* 30 (1984) 67-84.

Pfeiffer, Henrik. *Das Heiligtum von Bethel im Spiegel des Hoseabuches.* FRLANT 183. Göttingen: Vandenhoek & Ruprecht, 1999. Pp. 26-64.

Pirson, R. "The Sun, the Moon, and the Eleven Stars: An Interpretation of Joseph's Second Dream." In *Studies in the Book of Genesis: Literature, Redaction and History.* BETL 155. Edited by A. Wénin. Leuven: Leuven University Press, 2001. Pp. 561-68.

Pisano, Stephen. *Additions or Omissions in the Books of Samuel: The Significant Pluses and Minuses in the Massoretic, LXX, and Qumran Texts.* OBO 57. Göttingen: Vandenhoek & Ruprecht, 1984.

Polzin, Robert. *Samuel and the Deuteronomist: A Literary Study of the Deuteronomistic History.* Indianapolis: Indiana University Press, 1989.

Propp, William H. "Hebrew *śāde(h)*, 'Highland'." *VT* 37 (1987) 230-36.

von Rad, Gerhard. "The Deuteronomic Theology of History in I and II

Kings." In *The Problem of the Hexateuch and Other Essays.* New York: McGraw Hill, 1966. Pp. 205-21.

———. *Genesis: A Commentary.* Rev. ed. Translated by John Marks. OTL. Philadelphia: Westminster, 1972.

Redford, Donald B. *A Study of the Biblical Story of Joseph (Genesis 37–50).* VTSup 20. Leiden: Brill, 1970.

Reibetanz, John. "The Gloucester Plot and Its Function." In *Critical Essays on Shakespeare's King Lear.* Edited by John Halio. New York: G. K. Hall, 1996. Pp. 39-57.

Reis, Pamela T. "Vindicating God: Another Look at 1 Kings XIII." *VT* 44 (1994) 376-86. Repr. in Reis, *Reading the Lines: A Fresh Look at the Hebrew Bible.* Peabody, MA: Hendrickson, 2002. Pp. 197-209.

Rendsburg, Gary A. "David and his Circle in Genesis XXXVIII." *VT* 36 (1986) 438-46.

Rendtorf, Rolf. "Beobachtungen zur altisraelischen Geschichtsschreibung anhand der Geschichte vom Aufstiegs David." In *Probleme Biblischer Theologie: Gerhard von Rad zum 70. Geburtstag.* Edited by Hans Walter Wolff. Munich: Kaiser, 1971. Pp. 428-39.

Renz, Johannes. *Handbuch der Althebräischen Epigraphik.* 3 vols. Darmstadt: Wissenschaftlische Buchgesellschaft, 1994.

Richter, Wolfgang. "Die *nāgîd*-Formal." *BN* 9 (1965) 71-84.

Rofé, Alexander. *The Prophetical Stories: The Narratives about the Prophets in the Hebrew Bible: Their Literary Types and History.* Translated by D. Levy. Jerusalem: Magnes, 1988.

Ron, Moshe. "The Restricted Abyss: Nine Problems in the Theory of the *Mise en Abyme.*" *Poetics Today* 8 (1987) 417-38.

Ross, Allen P. *Creation and Blessing: A Guide to the Study and Exposition of the Book of Genesis.* Grand Rapids, MI: Baker Book House, 1988.

Rossier, François. *L'intercession entre les hommes dans la Bible hébraïque: L'intercession entre les hommes aux origines de l'intercession auprès de Dieu.* OBO 152. Göttingen: Vandenhoeck & Ruprecht, 1996.

Rost, Leonard. *The Succession to the Throne of David.* Translated by David Gunn. Historic Texts and Interpreters in Biblical Scholarship 1. Sheffield: Almond, 1982. Originally published in 1926.

Rudman, Dominic. "The Commissioning Stories of Saul and David as Theological Allegory." *VT* 50 (2000) 519-30.

Ruppert, Lothar. *Die Josephserzählung der Genesis: Ein Beitrag zur Theologie der Pentateuchquellen.* SANT 11. Munich: Kösel, 1965.

Salm, Eva. *Juda und Tamar: Eine exegetische Studie zu Gen 38.* FB 76. Würzburg: Echter Verlag, 1996.

Šanda, A. *Die Bücher der Könige: I. Halbband.: Das Erste Buch der Könige.* EHAT 9/1. Münster: Aschendorffsche Verlagsbuchhandlung, 1911.

Sanders, Paul. "So May God Do To Me!" *Bib* 85 (2004) 91-98.

Sanford, John A. *King Saul, the Tragic Hero: A Study in Individuation.* New York: Paulist, 1985.

Sarna, Nahum M. *The JPS Torah Commentary: Genesis.* Philadelphia: Jewish Publication Society, 1989.

Schmitt, H. Chr. *Elisa.* Gütersloh: Gütersloher Verlagshaus/Gerd Mohn, 1972.

Schulte, Hannelis. "The End of the Omride Dynasty: Social-Ethical Observations on the Subject of Power and Violence." In *Ethics and Politics in the Hebrew Bible.* Edited by Douglas Knight and Carol Meyers. Semeia 66. Atlanta: Scholars, 1994. Pp. 133-48.

Schwartz, Joshua. "Dogs, "Water" and Wall." *SJOT* 14 (2000) 100-116.

Sharon, Diane M. "Some Results of a Structural Semiotic Analysis of the Story of Judah and Tamar." *JSOT* 29 (2005) 289-318.

Simon, Uriel. "I Kings 13: A Prophetic Sign—Denial and Persistence." *HUCA* 47 (1976) 81-117. Revised and repr. as "A Prophetic Sign Overcomes Those Who Would Defy It: The King of Israel, the Prophet from Bethel, and the Man of God from Judah." In Simon, *Reading Prophetic Narratives.* Bloomington, IN: Indiana University Press, 1997. Pp. 131-54.

Ska, Jean Louis, S.J. *"Our Fathers Have Told Us:" Introduction to the Analysis of Hebrew Narrative.* Subsidia Biblica 13. Rome: Pontifical Biblical Institute, 1990.

Skinner, John. *A Critical and Exegetical Commentary on Genesis.* 2nd ed. Edinburgh: T & T Clark, 1930.

Smelik, Klaas A. D. *Writings from Ancient Israel: A Handbook of Historical and Religious Documents.* Translated by G. I. Davies. Louisville, KY: Westminster John Knox, 1991.

Smith, Bryan. "The Central Role of Judah in Genesis 37–50." *BSac* 162 (2005) 158-74.

Smith, Mark S. "'Your People Shall be My People': Family and Covenant in Ruth 1:16-17." *CBQ* 69 (2007) 242-58.

Speiser, E. A. *Genesis.* AB 1. New York: Doubleday, 1964.

Spinoza, Benedict. *Theologico-Political Treatise.* 2nd edition. Translated by Samuel Shirley. Indianapolis: Hackett, 2001. Originally published in 1670.

Stern, Philip D. "Of Kings and Moabites: History and Theology in 2 Kings 3 and the Mesha Inscription." *HUCA* 64 (1993) 1-14.

Sternberg, Meir. *The Poetics of Biblical Narrative: Ideological Literature and the Drama of Reading.* Bloomington, IN: Indiana University Press, 1987.

Steussey, Marti J. *David: Biblical Portraits of Power.* Studies on Personalities of the Old Testament. Columbia, SC: University of South Carolina Press, 1999.

Stipp, H.-J. *Elischa—Propheten—Gottesmänner.* ATSAT 24. St. Ottilien: EOS, 1987.

Stoebe, Hans Joachim. *Das erste Buch Samuelis.* KAT VIII/8. Stuttgart: Gütersloher Verlagshaus Gerd Mohn, 1973.

Sweeney, Marvin A. *King Josiah of Judah: The Lost Messiah of Israel.* Oxford: Oxford University Press, 2001.

———. *I & II Kings: A Commentary.* OTL. Louisville, Ky: Westminster John Knox, 2007.

Tengström, Sven. *Die Toledotformel und die literarische Struktur der priesterlichen Erweiterungsschicht im Pentateuch.* ConBOT 17. Lund: Leerup, 1981.

Thenius, Otto. *Die Bücher der Könige erklärt.* 2nd ed. Leipzig: S. Hirzel, 1873.

Thompson, Thomas, and Dorothy Thompson. "Some Legal Problems in the Book of Ruth." *VT* 18 (1968) 79-99.

Tigay, Jeffery H. *The JPS Torah Commentary: Deuteronomy.* Philadelphia: Jewish Publication Society, 1996.

Timm, Stefan. *Die Dynastie Omri: Quellen und Untersuchungen zur Geschichte Israels im 9. Jahrhundert vor Christus.* FRLANT 124. Göttingen: Vandenhoeck & Ruprecht, 1982.

Toews, Wesley I. *Monarchy and Religious Institutions in Israel under Jeroboam I.* SBLMS 47. Atlanta: Scholars, 1993.

Tomes, Roger. "Come and See My Zeal for the Lord: Reading the Jehu Story." In *Narrativity in Biblical and Related Texts.* Eds. G. J. Brooke and J.-D. Kaestli. BETL 149. Leuven: Leuven University Press, 2000. Pp. 53-67.

Tov, Emanuel. "The Composition of 1 Samuel 16-18 in the Light of the Septuagint Version." In *Empirical Models for Biblical Criticism.* Edited by Jeffrey H. Tigay. Philadelphia: University of Pennsylvania Press, 1985. Pp. 97-130.

Tsumura, David Toshio. *First Book of Samuel.* NICOT. Grand Rapids, MI: Eerdmans, 2007.

Uffenheimer, Benjamin. *Early Prophecy in Israel*. Translated by David Louvish. Jerusalem: Magnes, 1999.

VanderKam, James C. "Davidic Complicity in the Deaths of Abner and Eshbaal: A Historical and Redactional Study." *JBL* 99 (1980) 521-39.

Van Seters, John. "The Deuteronomistic History: Can It Avoid Death by Redaction?" In *The Future of the Deuteronomistic History*. BETL 147. Edited by T. Römer. Leuven: Leuven University Press, 2000. Pp. 213-22.

———. *In Search of History: Historiography in the Ancient World and the Origins of Biblical History*. New Haven: Yale University Press, 1983. Repr., Winona Lake, IN: Eisenbrauns, 1997.

———. "On Reading the Story of the Man of God from Judah in 1 Kings 13." In *The Labor of Reading: Desire, Alienation, and Biblical Interpretation*. SBLSS 36. Edited by Fiona C. Black et al. Atlanta: SBL, 1999. Pp. 225-34.

Van Winkle, D. "1 Kings XIII: True and False Prophecy." *VT* 39 (1989) 31-43.

———. "1 Kings XII 25-XIII 34: Jeroboam's Cultic Innovations and the Man of God from Judah." *VT* 46 (1996) 101-14.

de Vaux, Roland. *Ancient Israel*. Translated by John McHugh. Grand Rapids, MI: Eerdmans, 1997. Originally published in 2 vols. in 1958-60.

Vawter, Bruce. *On Genesis: A New Reading*. Garden City, NY: Doubleday, 1977.

Vermeylen, Jacques. *La loi du plus fort: Histoire de la rédaction davidique de 1 Samuel 8 à 1 Rois 2*. Leuven: Leuven University Press, 2000.

———. "La maison de Saül et la maison de David: Un écrit de propagande théologico-politique de 1 S 11 à 2 S 7." In *Figures de David à travers la Bible: XVIIe congrès de l'ACFEB (Lille, 1er–5 septembre 1997)*. Edited by Louis Desrousseaux and Jacques Vermeylen. LD 177. Paris: Cerf, 1999. Pp. 9-34.

Waltke, Bruce K., with Cathi J. Fredericks. *Genesis: A Commentary*. Grand Rapids, MI: Zondervan, 2001.

Walsh, Jerome T. *1 Kings*. Berit Olam. Collegeville, MN: Liturgical Press, 1996.

———. "The Contexts of 1 Kings XIII." *VT* 39 (1989) 355-70.

———. *Style and Structure in Biblical Hebrew Narrative*. Collegeville, MN: Liturgical Press, 2001.

Wassén, Cecilia. "The Story of Judah and Tamar in the Eyes of the Earliest Interpreters." *Literature and Theology* 8 (1994) 354-66.

Weippert, Helga. "'Histories' and 'History': Promise and Fulfillment in the Deuteronomic Historical Work." Originally published in 1991. Translated by Peter T. Daniels. In *Reconsidering Israel and Judah: Recent Studies on the Deuteronomistic History.* Sources for Biblical and Theological Study 8. Edited by Gary N. Knoppers and J. Gordon McConville. Winona Lake, IN: Eisenbrauns, 2000. Pp. 46-61.

———. "Die 'deuteronomischen' Beurteilungen der Könige von Israel und Juda und das Problem der Redaktion der Königsbücher." *Bib* 53 (1972) 301-39.

Weisberg, Dvora E. "The Widow of Our Discontent." *JSOT* 28 (2004) 403-429.

Weiser, Artur. "Die Legitimation des Königs David: Zur Eigenart und Entstehung der sogen. Geschichte von Davids Aufstieg." *VT* 16 (1966) 325-54.

Weiss, Andrea L. *Figurative Language in Biblical Prose Narrative: Metaphor in the Book of Samuel.* VTSup 107. Leiden: Brill, 2006.

Wellhausen, Julius. *Die Composition des Hexateuchs und der historischen Bücher des Alten Testaments.* 2nd ed. Berlin: George Reimer, 1889.

Wenham, Gordon J. *Genesis 1–15.* WBC 1. Waco, TX: Word Books, 1987.

———. *Genesis 16–50.* WBC 2. Waco, TX: Word Books, 1994.

Wénin, André. "L'aventure de Judah en Genèse 38 et l'histoire de Joseph." *RB* 111 (2004) 5-27.

———. "Le temps dans l'histoire de Joseph (Gn 37–50): Repères temporels pour une analysis narrative." *Bib* 83 (2002) 28-53.

———. "David roi, de Goliath à Bathsabée: La figure de David dans la livres de Samuel." In *Figures de David à travers la Bible: XVIIᵉ congrès de l'ACFEB (Lille, 1ᵉʳ-5 septembre 1997).* Edited by Louis Desrousseaux and Jacques Vermeylen. LD 177. Paris: Cerf, 1999. Pp. 75-112

Westbrook, Raymond. "The Law of the Biblical Levirate." In *Property and the Family in Biblical Law.* JSOTSup 113. Sheffield: Sheffield Academic Press, 1991. Pp. 69-89.

———. "International Law in the Amarna Age." In *Amarna Diplomacy: The Beginnings of International Relations.* Edited by Raymond Cohen and Raymond Westbrook. Baltimore: Johns Hopkins University Press, 2000. Pp. 28-41.

Westermann, Claus. *Genesis 1–11: A Commentary.* Translated by John J. Scullion, S.J. Minneapolis: Fortress, 1994.

———. *Genesis 12–36: A Commentary.* Translated by John J. Scullion, S.J. Minneapolis: Fortress, 1995.

———. *Genesis 37–50: A Commentary.* Translated by John Scullion, S.J. Minneapolis: Augsburg, 1986.

Wijngaards, J. "ḥwṣyʾ and ḥʿlh: A Twofold Approach to the Exodus." *VT* 14 (1964) 91-101.

Wildavsky, Aaron. *Assimilation verses Separation: Joseph the Administrator and the Politics of Religion in Biblical Israel.* New Brunswick, NJ: Transaction Publishers, 1993.

———. "Survival Must Not Be Gained through Sin: The Moral of the Joseph Stories Prefigured through Judah and Tamar." *JSOT* 62 (1994) 37-48.

Williams, Michael James. *Deception in Genesis: An Investigation into the Morality of a Unique Biblical Phenomenon.* Studies in Biblical Literature 32. New York: Peter Lang, 2001.

Williamson, Claude C. H., ed. *Readings on the Character of Hamlet, 1661-1947: Compiled from Over Three Hundred Sources.* London: George Allen, 1950.

Wilson, J. Dover. *What Happens in Hamlet.* 3d ed. Cambridge: Cambridge University Press, 1951.

Wilson, Lindsay. *Joseph Wise and Otherwise: The Intersection of Wisdom and Covenant in Genesis 37–50.* Waynesboro, GA: Paternoster, 2004.

Wilson, Robert R. *Prophecy and Society in Ancient Israel.* Philadelphia, Fortress, 1980.

van Wolde, Ellen. "A Leader Led by a Lady: David and Abigail in I Samuel 25." *ZAW* 114 (2002) 355-75.

———. "Texts in Dialogue with Texts: Intertextuality in the Ruth and Tamar Narratives." *BibInt* 5 (1997) 1-28.

Würthwein, Ernst. *Die Bücher der Könige.* 2 vols. ATD 11/1-2. Göttingen: Vandenhoeck & Ruprecht, 1977, 1984.

———. "Die Erzählung vom Gottesmann aus Juda in Bethel: Zur Komposition von 1 Kön 13." In *Wort und Geschichte: Festschrift für Karl Elliger zum 70. Geburtstag.* Edited by H. Gese and H. P. Rüger. Kevelaer: Butzon & Bercker, 1973. Pp. 181-89.

———. "Prophetische Wort und Geschichte in den Königsbüchern: Zu einer These Gerhard von Rads." In *Altes Testament und christliche Verkündigung: Festschrift für Antonius H. J. Gunneweg zum 65. Geburtstag.* Edited by Manfred Oeming and Axel Graupner. Stuttgart: Kohlhammer, 1987. Pp. 399-411. Repr. in Würthwein, *Studien zum deuteronomistischen Geschichtswerk.* BZAW 227. Berlin: de Gruyter, 1994.

Ziegler, Yael. "'As the Lord Lives and as Your Soul Lives': An Oath of Conscious Deference." *VT* 58 (2008) 117-30.

Index of Scripture

Index of Non-Biblical Sources

Index of Modern Authors